J. L. Austin and the Law

J. L. Austin and the Law

Exculpation and the Explication of Responsibility

Daniel Yeager

Lewisburg
Bucknell University Press

New hardcover printing 2016 by Bucknell University Press
Co-published with Rowman & Littlefield
4501 Forbes Boulevard, Suite 200, Lanham, Maryland 20706
www.rowman.com

10 Thornbury Road, Plymouth PL6 7PP, United Kingdom

978-1-61148-233-1 (cloth: alk. paper)

Originally published by Associated University Presses
2010 Eastpark Boulevard
Cranbury, NJ 08512

Library of Congress Cataloging-in-Publication Data
Yeager, Daniel Brian.
J. L. Austin and the law: exculpation and the explication of responsibility / Daniel Yeager.
p. cm.
Includes bibliographical references and index.
ISBN: 0-8387-5621-2 (alk. paper)
1. Austin, J. L. (John Langshaw), 1911–1960. 2. Responsibility 3.Criminal law. 4. Ordinary-language philosophy.
I. Title: John Langshaw Austin and the law. II. Title.
B1618.A84Y42 2005
345'.04—dc22

2005011813

To the memory of my parents

Contents

Preface 9
Acknowledgments 13
Abbreviations 17

Introduction 23
1. Mens Rea 29
2. Inchoate Criminality as Partial Excuse 94
3. Is Criminal Law (Especially) Moral? 110
4. The Ghost in the Machine 124
Conclusion 166

Notes 169
Bibliography 195
Index 206

Preface

AT THE OPENING OF *SENSE AND SENSIBILIA*, J. L. AUSTIN SUMMARIZES his philosophical methods when he sets out there to "try to make clear that our ordinary words are much subtler in their uses, and mark many more distinctions, than philosophers have realized" (*S&S*, 3). So too is his unfinished essay, "Three Ways of Spilling Ink," a sustained comparison of just three "aggravating" adverbs: intentionally, purposely, and deliberately ("INK," 272). To be sure, no one who has read Austin even casually would question whether he makes distinctions and excruciatingly careful comparisons while otherwise betraying an uncommon interest in what he has labeled "loose" or "eccentric" speakers and the various "etiolations" of language.

What many *would* question is what payoff Austin offers us in return for our struggling through his "track[ing] down the detail of our ordinary uses of words" ("TALK," 134), even "hounding down the minutiae" ("EXCUSES," 175). Indeed, the modesty of his assessments of the value of his own projects can be maddening in that it threatens to depict those projects not as the enormous feats they are, but rather as the quibbling exercises for which they can be confused. Examples of his wildly understated claims are not hard to find. For example, the subject of "A Plea for Excuses" is said by Austin to be merely "introduced" and then, at its close, plaintively "commended" to his audience. Austin holds out that his gripping meditation *Other Minds* "at best . . . can hope only to make a contribution to one part of the problem" ("MINDS," 76). He claims that his most widely read book, *How To Do Things With Words*, is at most "true, at least in parts," though "obvious" (*HTDTW*, 1). "The Meaning of a Word" Austin has "divided into three parts, of which the first is the most trite and the second the most muddled: all are too long" ("A WORD," 56). And in "Three Ways of Spilling Ink," he commits himself to "concentrate here on a pretty narrow topic," adding that "since I don't know enough (or even *think* I know enough) about the whole subject: what follows is a sample only of some contributions that might be of use" ("INK," 273).

It is not at all uncommon for Austin's understated, often playful introductory claims to be at complete odds with his intense, even relentless pursuit of a serious matter. For example, a phase in his ongoing debate with P. F. Strawson—"Unfair to Facts"—is introduced as "subject to the law of diminishing fleas" ("FACTS," 154). "Are *cans* constitutionally iffy?" commences a brilliant disquisition on conditionals ("IFS," 205). And in "Pretending," after asking in his final paragraph "[w]hat finally is the importance of all this about pretending?" he dodges (momentarily) that he "is not sure importance is important" ("PRETENDING," 271).[1]

I know I am not the first to be struck by the particular hilarity of some of his examples:[2] to name just three of the more memorable ones, pretending to be a hyena (in one instance at Nero's request) ("PRETENDING," 256 and n.1); how men lesser than Father William would answer the question "What is the point [not 'of doing so-and-so,' but] of doing *anything*?" ("A WORD," 59); or his play on the football spectator's observation that from his poor vantage point the players "look like ants" (*S&S*, 40–41). Each of the three passages to which I too briefly refer above, like so many others in Austin's *oeuvre,* are without fail as full of insight as they are playfulness.

And in other, admittedly much rarer instances, we get glimpses of the sort of social, psychological, even emotional implications of Austin that feed so well into Stanley Cavell's deployment of, or at least stance toward, ordinary-language procedures, or what William Rothman and Marian Keane have called Cavell's "self-consciousness."[3] For example, the skeptic's battle between separateness from and need for others so prevalent in Cavell can be teased out of a brief allusion that Austin makes to the loneliness we all feel when posed with the constant threat of privacy—of blockages caused by deception, misunderstandings, or the difficulties in telling what is accidental from what is intentional ("MINDS," 112).

It is this peculiar combination of brilliance and fun that accounts for the attentiveness with which I have been reading Austin since my friend and colleague Paul Gudel (who was, I seem to recall, taught by one of Cavell's more accomplished students, Ted Cohen) first turned me on to "voluntary means fishy" in 1996 while he was sitting in on my criminal-law-theory seminar. I remember being struck by the good sense behind Austin's mantra "no modification without aberration," and so from there it was only a matter of time before branching out from "Excuses" and "Ink" through the rest of the *Philosophical Papers*, culminating in the at times impenetrable "Other Minds," which of course leads one inexorably, as Gudel's extra copy of *Must We Mean What We Say?* led me, at once both back to Wittgenstein and ahead to Cavell. In that seminar (and others we have shared), Gudel dispensed with a lot of the formality, extravagant politeness, and light shadow fencing that tend to mark public faculty exchanges, leaving me to feel overmatched, I'm afraid, in much the way that Sir Isaiah Berlin reports having felt when he first embarked on coteaching a course on C. I. Lewis's *Mind and the World Order* with Austin at Oxford in the mid-1930s. Berlin recalls Austin having asked him to repeat his thesis on Lewis's *qualia*, after which Austin said: "It seems to me, that what you have just said is complete nonsense."[4]

I don't recall that precise utterance as one of Gudel's responses to my positions taken in front of our students, yet I did get the feeling that this friend of mind was no ordinary academic lawyer; rather, Gudel's immense learning set him apart from even the very best legal minds I have known or read. I am thankful to him for giving me a professional (professorial?) "voice"—a "hobby horse" I think Freud would call it—in the same way that Cavell has credited Austin for the influence that Austin the teacher had on Cavell the student at Harvard in 1955. So too am I thankful, now fourteen years on the same faculty, for what is most likely to be a permanent friendship in which our common interest in *what we should say when* has converted something as public and communal as language into a place where the privacy of our mutual experience has operated, even flourished. If a fraction of the pleasure in hounding down the minutiae that has characterized our mutual testing of the world against the ordinary is evident in my attempt to do the same in this examination of the criminal law, then will it be plain how the pleasures of cooperation that Austin's students so fondly speak of as essential to his methods have, thanks largely to my colleague, teacher, and friend Paul Gudel, happily corrupted my philosophy as well. Ultimately, it is the simultaneous seriousness and playfulness—commitment and distance—that I hope to have taken from my introduction to Austin and brought to a strand of legal philosophy that has assumed a sameness of attitude toward its subject that has left its essence as obscured as (at least according to Austin) aesthetics, which even a half-century ago needed to "forget for a while about the beautiful and get down instead to the dainty and the dumpy." ("EXCUSES," 183). If this book succeeds at all, then, it will take a step toward bringing the language of criminal law—and therefore criminal law itself—through community, "home."

There have been others whose contributions I would be negligent to overlook: the faculty and administration at California Western, particularly Sandra Moreau and Deans Janet Bowermaster and Steve Smith; a handful of generous colleagues, particularly Larry Alexander, Sherry Colb, Don Dripps, Henry Hardy, George Martinez, George Thomas III, and Bucknell's no-longer anonymous referee, Stephen Mulhall; some gifted teachers, particularly Jeffrey Harrison, Stanley Ingber, Toni Massaro, and Walter Weyrauch; and some highly competent assistants: Erin Brooks, Christopher Bush, Marie Hommel, Jennifer McCausland, Tracy Schmidt, and the meticulous Allison Willis. I equally recognize the patient and inquisitive ordinary-language philosophers who one term per academic year spent fourteen weeks reading Austin line by line, never (openly) tiring of hours passed in efforts to separate out, say, "accidentally" from "inadvertently," "spontaneously" from "impulsively," and whether the term "accidentally on purpose" could have point other than ironically. Thanks to those most excellent students, many of whom not only allowed but encouraged me to work these matters out in front of them with no real plan apart from the nontrivial one of operating always with an eye toward the possibility of reaching agreement.

Last, I hope that my appreciation of those dearest to me—Shelly, Madison, Keely, Karen, Stephanie, Bob, and Bully—always shows.

Daniel Yeager
San Diego, California

Acknowledgments

PERMISSION TO REPRINT EXCERPTS FROM THE FOLLOWING SOURCES IS gratefully acknowledged:

Act and Crime: The Philosophy of Action and Its Implications for Criminal Law by Michael S. Moore, copyright © 1993. Reprinted by permission of Oxford University Press.

"The Art of Failure" by Malcolm Gladwell, copyright © 2000. Reprinted by permission of Malcolm Gladwell.

Bad Acts and Guilty Minds: Conundrums of the Criminal Law by Leo Katz, copyright © 1987 by the University of Chicago Press. Reprinted by permission of the University of Chicago Press, Chicago. All rights reserved.

The Best Defense by Alan Dershowitz, copyright © 1982. Reprinted by permission of the author.

"Beyond Causation: The Interpretation of Action and the Mixed Motives Problem in Employment Discrimination Law" by Paul J. Gudel, first appeared in Vol. 70 of the *Texas Law Review*, copyright © 1991 by Texas Law Review. Reprinted by permission of the author and the Texas Law Review Association.

The Blue and Brown Books by Ludwig Wittgenstein, copyright © 1958 by Basil Blackwell, Ltd. Reprinted by permission of Harper Collins Publishers, Inc.

"Choice, Character, and Excuse" by Michael S. Moore, first appeared in *Social Philosophy & Policy*, Vol. 7, No. 2, copyright © 1990. Reprinted by permission of Cambridge University Press.

Cities of Words by Stanley Cavell, p. 356. Cambridge, Mass: Harvard University Press, copyright © 2004 by the President and Fellows of Harvard College. Reprinted by permission of the publisher.

The Claim of Reason: Wittgenstein, Skepticism, Morality and Tragedy by Stanley Cavell, copyright © 1979. Reprinted by permission of Oxford University Press, Inc.

Criminal Attempts by R. A. Duff. Copyright © 1997. Reprinted by permission of Oxford University Press.

Essays on J. L. Austin by Isaiah Berlin, copyright © 1973. Reprinted by permission of Oxford University Press.

Foundations of Ethics: The Gifford Lectures delivered at the University of Aberdeen by W. D. Ross, copyright © 2000. Reprinted by permission of Oxford University Press.

A Grammar of Motives by Kenneth Burke, copyright © 1969. Reprinted by permission of The Regents of the University of California.

How to Do Things with Words by J. L. Austin, edited by J.O. Urmson and M. Sbisa, copyright © 1975. Reprinted by permission of Oxford University Press.

"Ifs and Cans" by J.L. Austin, first appeared in *Philosophical Papers*, 3d ed., edited by J. O. Urmson and G. J. Warnock, copyright © 1979. Reprinted by permission of Oxford University Press.

Intentionality by John Searle, copyright © 1983. Reprinted by permission of Cambridge University Press.

"Justifications and the Criminal Liability of Accessories" by Douglas N. Husak, first appeared in Vol. 80, No. 2 of *The Journal of Criminal Law and Criminology*, copyright © 1989. Reprinted by special permission of the editors of *The Journal of Criminal Law and Criminology* and Northwestern University School of Law.

"Lawyering Up" by Susan Bandes and Jack Beerman, first appeared in *The Green Bag*, 2d ed., copyright © 1998. Reprinted by permission of the editors of *The Green Bag*, 2d ed.

"The Meaning of a Word" by J. L. Austin, first appeared in *Philosophical Papers*, 3d ed., edited by J.O. Urmson and G.J. Warnock, copyright © 1979. Reprinted by permission of Oxford University Press.

Model Penal Code and Commentaries (Official Draft and Revised Comments), copyright © 1985 by The American Law Institute. Reprinted with permission. All rights reserved.

A Modern Treatise on the Law of Criminal Complicity by Keith J. M. Smith, copyright © 1991. Reprinted by permission of Oxford University Press.

Mortal Questions by Thomas Nagel, copyright © 1979. Reprinted by permission of Cambridge University Press.

Must We Mean What We Say?: A Book of Essays by Stanley Cavell, 2d ed., copyright © 2002 by Stanley Cavell. Reprinted by permission of Cambridge University Press.

Overcoming Law by Richard A. Posner. Cambridge, Mass: Harvard

University Press, copyright © 1995 by the President and Fellows of Harvard College. Reprinted by permission of the publisher.

"The Perjurious Client Question: Putting Criminal Defense Lawyers Between a Rock and a Hard Place" by Terrence F. MacCarthy and Kathy Morris, first appeared in Vol. 75, No. 4 of *The Journal of Criminal Law and Criminology*, copyright © 1984. Reprinted by special permission of the editors of *The Journal of Criminal Law and Criminology* and Northwestern University School of Law.

Philosophical Remarks by Ludwig Wittgenstein, edited by Rush Rhees, translated by Raymond Hargreaves and Roger White, copyright © 1975. Reprinted by permission of Blackwell Publishing, Ltd.

A Pitch of Philosophy: Autobiographical Exercises by Stanley Cavell, pp. 87, 91. Cambridge, Mass: Harvard University Press, copyright © 1994 by the President and Fellows of Harvard College. Reprinted by permission of the publisher.

"A Plea for Excuses" by J.L. Austin. Reprinted from *Proceedings of the Aristotelian Society* by courtesy of the Editor of the Aristotelian Society, © 1956–7.

"Pretending" by J. L. Austin. Reprinted from *Proceedings of the Aristotelian Society*, Supplementary Vol. xxxii by courtesy of the Editor of the Aristotelian Society, © 1958.

Punishment and Responsibility by H. L. A. Hart, copyright © 1968. Reprinted by permission of Oxford University Press.

"Reconsidering the Relationship Among Voluntary Acts, Strict Liability, and Negligence in Criminal Law" by Larry Alexander, first appeared in *Social Philosophy & Policy*, Vol. 7, No. 2, copyright © 1990. Reprinted by permission of Cambridge University Press.

"Reconstructing the Criminal Defenses: The Significance of Justification" by Thomas Morawetz, first appeared in Vol. 77, No. 2 of *The Journal of Criminal Law and Criminology*, copyright © 1986. Reprinted by special permission of the editors of *The Journal of Criminal Law and Criminology* and Northwestern University School of Law.

The Republic of Plato, translated by Allan Bloom, copyright © 1968 by Allan Bloom. Reprinted by permission of Basic Books, a member of Perseus Books, L. L. C.

Reversal of Fortune: Inside the von Bulow Case by Alan Dershowitz, copyright © 1986. Reprinted by permission of the author.

Sense and Sensibilia by J. L. Austin, edited by G. J. Warnock, copyright © 1962. Reprinted by permission of Oxford University Press.

Shame and Necessity by Bernard Williams, copyright © 1993. Reprinted by permission of The Regents of the University of California.

Speech Acts: An Essay in the Philosophy of Language by John Searle, copyright © 1969. Reprinted by permission of Cambridge University Press.

Stanley Cavell, edited by Richard Eldridge, excerpts from "The Names of Action" by Timothy Gould, copyright © 2003. Reprinted by permission of Cambridge University Press.

Stanley Cavell: Philosophy's Recounting of the Ordinary by Stephen Mulhall, copyright © 1994. Reprinted by permission of Oxford University Press.

Taking Rights Seriously by Ronald Dworkin. Cambridge, Mass: Harvard University Press, copyright © 1977, 1978 by Ronald Dworkin. Reprinted by permission of the publisher.

"Unfair to Facts" by J. L. Austin, first appeared in *Philosophical Papers*, 3d ed., edited by J.O. Urmson and G.J. Warnock, copyright © 1979. Reprinted by permission of Oxford University Press.

The Words by Jean-Paul Sartre, translated by Bernard Frechtman. Copyright © 1964 by George Braziller, Inc. Originally published in French as *Les Mots*, copyright © 1964 by Editions Gallimard. Reprinted by permission of Georges Borchardt, Inc. for Editions Gallimard.

Abbreviations

The work of J. L. Austin, Stanley Cavell, Paul Gudel, Michael Moore, and Ludwig Wittgenstein that I cite most frequently is referenced throughout the book using the following abbreviations:

HTDTW	Austin, J. L. *How to Do Things with Words.* Ed. J. O. Urmson and Marina Sbisà. 2d ed. Cambridge: Harvard University Press, 1975.
"TALK"	Austin, J. L. "How to Talk—some simple ways." In *Philosophical Papers*, edited by J. O. Urmson and G. J. Warnock. 3d ed. Oxford: Oxford University Press, 1979.
"IFS"	Austin, J. L. "Ifs and Cans." In *Philosophical Papers*, edited by J. O. Urmson and G. J. Warnock. 3d ed. Oxford: Oxford University Press, 1979.
"A WORD"	Austin, J. L. "The Meaning of a Word." In *Philosophical Papers*, edited by J. O. Urmson and G. J. Warnock. 3d ed. Oxford: Oxford University Press, 1979.
"MINDS"	Austin, J. L. "Other Minds." In *Philosophical Papers*, edited by J. O. Urmson and G. J. Warnock. 3d ed. Oxford: Oxford University Press, 1979.
"PERFORMATIVES"	Austin, J. L. "Performative Utterances." In *Philosophical Papers*, edited by J. O. Urmson and G. J. Warnock. 3d ed. Oxford: Oxford University Press, 1979.
"EXCUSES"	Austin, J. L. "A Plea for Excuses." In *Philosophical Papers*, edited by J. O. Urmson and G. J. Warnock. 3d ed. Oxford: Oxford University Press, 1979.
"PRETENDING"	Austin, J. L. "Pretending." In *Philosophi-*

	cal Papers, edited by J. O. Urmson and G. J. Warnock. 3d ed. Oxford: Oxford University Press, 1979.
S&S	Austin, J. L. *Sense and Sensibilia*. London: Oxford University Press, 1962.
"INK"	Austin, J. L. "Three Ways of Spilling Ink." In *Philosophical Papers*, edited by J. O. Urmson and G. J. Warnock. 3d ed. Oxford: Oxford University Press, 1979.
"TRUTH"	Austin, J. L. "Truth." In *Philosophical Papers*, edited by J. O. Urmson and G. J. Warnock. 3d ed. Oxford: Oxford University Press, 1979.
"FACTS"	Austin, J. L. "Unfair to Facts." In *Philosophical Papers*, edited by J. O. Urmson and G. J. Warnock. 3d ed. Oxford: Oxford University Press, 1979.
"AESTHETIC PROBLEMS"	Cavell, Stanley. "Aesthetic Problems of Modern Philosophy." In *Must we mean what we say? A Book of Essays*. Cambridge: Cambridge University Press, 2002.
"CRITICISM"	Cavell, Stanley. "Austin at Criticism." In *Must we mean what we say? A Book of Essays*. Cambridge: Cambridge University Press, 2002.
"LATER WITTGENSTEIN"	Cavell, Stanley. "The Availability of Wittgenstein's Later Philosophy." In *Must we mean what we say? A Book of Essays*. Cambridge: Cambridge University Press, 2002.
"AVOIDANCE"	Cavell, Stanley. "The Avoidance of Love." In *Must we mean what we say? A Book of Essays*. Cambridge: Cambridge University Press, 2002.
CITIES	Cavell, Stanley. *Cities of Words*. Cambridge: Harvard University Press, 2004.
CR	Cavell, Stanley. *The Claim of Reason: Wittgenstein, Skepticism, Morality, and Tragedy*. Oxford: Oxford University Press, 1979.
"K&A"	Cavell, Stanley. "Knowing and Acknowledging." In *Must we mean what we say? A*

	Book of Essays. Cambridge: Cambridge University Press, 2002.
"MEANING IT"	Cavell, Stanley. "A Matter of Meaning It." In *Must we mean what we say? A Book of Essays*. Cambridge: Cambridge University Press, 2002.
"MUSIC"	Cavell, Stanley. "Music Discomposed." In *Must we mean what we say? A Book of Essays*. Cambridge: Cambridge University Press, 2002.
"MWM"	Cavell, Stanley. "Must We Mean What We Say?" In *Must we mean what we say? A Book of Essays*. Cambridge: Cambridge University Press, 2002.
PP	Cavell, Stanley. *Philosophical Passages: Wittgenstein, Emerson, Austin, Derrida*. Cambridge: Blackwell, 1995.
A PITCH	Cavell, Stanley. *A Pitch of Philosophy: Autobiographical Exercises*. Cambridge: Harvard University Press, 1994.
QUEST	Cavell, Stanley. *In Quest of the Ordinary: Lines of Skepticism and Romanticism*. Chicago: University of Chicago Press, 1988.
"BEYOND CAUSATION"	Gudel, Paul J. "Beyond Causation: The Interpretation of Action and the Mixed Motives Problem in Employment Discrimination Law." *Texas Law Review* 70 (1991): 17–107.
M&S	Gudel, Paul J. *Modernism and Skepticism: Terms of Criticism in Clement Greenberg, Michael Fried, and Stanley Carell.*
"CONTRACT THEORY"	Gudel, Paul J. "Relational Contract Theory and the Concept of Exchange." *Buffalo Law Review* 46 (1998): 763–97.
A&C	Moore, Michael S. *Act and Crime: The Philosophy of Action and Its Implications for Criminal Law*. Oxford: Clarendon Press, 1993.
PI	Wittgenstein, Ludwig. *Philosophical Investigations*. Trans. G. E. M. Anscombe. 3d ed. New York: Macmillan, 1958.

J. L. Austin
and the Law

Introduction

Our criminal justice system need not and frequently does not make criminal liability dependent on some showing that the offender deserves moral blame for what he has done. The criminal law does, however, tie legal to moral blame for serious *mala in se* crimes punishable by prolonged confinement or death. To convict the individual of a *mala in se* crime, the state must provide proof of his moral culpability for breaching the law's commands.

Who does the criminal law consider to be morally culpable for engaging in conduct that breaches community moral norms?[1]

The criminal justice system's moral culpability principle reflects one of the major distinctions between the criminal law and other legal methods of constraining people's behavior: criminal convictions for serious nonregulatory offenses convey the message that the offender was morally responsible for his crime and thus deserves moral blame for what he has done. . . . *[W]hy does the criminal law rely on such a "moralized" form of social control?*[2]

WHAT *KINDS* OF QUESTIONS ARE THESE? WHILE I HAVE LIFTED THEM from Peter Arenella's "reassessment of the relationship between legal and moral accountability," the Supreme Court observed a half-century ago that this way of talking about criminal law was even then already "persistent";[3] it is no less so today.[4] As central as it may be to the way we talk about criminal law, still its implications remain opaque. In rehearsing a response to Professor Arenella's questions, I pose and investigate some of my own: If in addition to resembling the rest of the first-year law school courses, criminal law also has its own characteristics, then what are they? What makes criminal law uniquely moral and what difference does it make to us that it is that way? If criminal law really is moral, does this mean that contract and tort are not? Why, exactly? Because "guilt is personal"?[5] Personal as opposed to what? Or is criminal law (especially) moral because it blames the wrongdoer? Blames as opposed to what—holds responsible? What's the difference? Is the difference informed by the half-dozen or so "senses" of responsibility floating around the criminal-law literature?[6] Or is it that blame looks not only for "harm," but also for "wrong?" Don't the two—harm and wrong—go together? Are there "wrongless harms and harmless wrongs,"[7] or does the relation between wrong and harm depend on how swayed you are by "luck"[8] or "causation,"[9] not to be confused with "moral luck"[10] or "moral causation?"[11] Furthermore, if criminals commit "blameworthy," "culpable," "harmful wrongs" through their "volitionally caused bodily movements"[12] animated by the appropriate "mens rea,"[13] does that mean that, say, bad or inattentive drivers commit harms that are innocent? How so? What about someone who breaks a contract? What's so innocent about that? Is it that promising creates an obligation that is legal but not moral?[14] But how could someone who makes a promise *not* be obligated morally?

I am going to try to get at each of the questions I raise above by reflecting on what is meant by "justification," "excuse," and what Austin calls "a miscellany of even less clear terms, such as 'extenuation,' 'palliation,' [and] 'mitigation'" ("EXCUSES," 177);[15] that is, the ways in which someone accused of having done something goes about getting out of it ("EXCUSES," 175–76). This entails an investigation of "the expressions that *aggravate*, such as 'deliberately,' 'on purpose,' and so on" ("EXCUSES," 177)—"words . . . that not only don't get us out of things, but may actually make things worse for us" ("INK," 273). In investigating the relation between accusation and excuse, I hope to uncover something about the criminal law's peculiar way of interpreting human action. Identifying that something, I hope, can get us a little closer to discovery or agreement about just what it is that is staked in criminal law. What is staked in any discussion of criminal law is the meaning and operation of "responsibility," which makes human action, "its consequences, concomitants, upshots, effects, results, and so forth" so open, so vulnerable, so tragic, even "unbearable" (*A PITCH*, 87).

It is my position that the criminal-law vocabulary, or at least its deployment, threatens to freeze up or impede assessments of responsibility. In other words, the prevailing view of criminal law, a view that I trace to skepticism, may at its worst be a real snag in any meaningful attempt to come to grips with who is answerable for what and to what extent. Accordingly, much of what I have to say here cuts against mainstream criminal-law scholarship, cases, and legislation. This is not, however, a book *in* criminal law although it certainly is *on* criminal law. It is an attempt to confront the implicit philosophical theories of criminal law (because that is what they are) with the ordinary moral world in which we deal with wrongs done to us. My purpose is to show that if we were to adopt the criminal-law way of talking about things, the very purpose of ordinary moral language would be undermined.

The first half of this book is divided into two chapters that attempt to show in some detail the ways in which the existing system of criminal law, with its categories and distinctions, not only fails to allow itself to learn from our everyday ways of conceiving of and evaluating responsibility, but in fact prevents us from following through with those ordinary insights. Chapter 1 explores the way that our interpretations of action influence our notion of responsibility, that is, of who is answerable for what. Accordingly, chapter 1 analyzes how skepticism has influenced "mens rea," that crucial criminal-law concept that informs the criteria of "accident" as opposed to "mistake"; "blame" as opposed to "hold responsible" or "be responsible"; "harmful" as opposed to "wrongful"; and "justify" as opposed to "excuse." Each set of terms, I conclude, at least as they are prone to be understood, threatens to produce a too narrow, even superficial, realm both of the responsible (i.e., what we *are* responsible for) and of the excuses (i.e., what we will or will not *be held* responsible for).

This is not to say that I am concerned solely with establishing that the domain of responsibility is broader than conventional criminal-law theory recognizes. If we were to overemphasize the role of intentions in criminal law, we would produce a notion of responsibility that misses that sometimes there are good reasons to let someone at least partially off the hook, even though the untoward action at issue *is* done intentionally. Intentionality is not the be-all/end-all of responsibility. Consequently, chapter 2 focuses on inchoate criminality, that is, the regulation of risk taking through the criminalization of failing (attempting), planning (soliciting, conspiring), and helping (aiding and abetting). In this sphere of criminality, there is some support for the view that failing to commit a crime, or asking, agreeing with, or helping someone else to commit a crime is and should be treated as morally identical to going ahead and (successfully) committing the crime yourself. Despite that support, I maintain that while acts of failure, planning, or helping are both intentional and punishable, intentions are not all that matter in questions of whom to hold responsible and to what extent in this arena. In sum, chapter 2 makes a case for inchoate criminality as partial excuse.

If the first half of this book shows how the existing system of criminal law creates a tremendous linguistic blockage between accuser and accused, the second half of this book, also divided into two chapters, attempts to carefully confront the false picture of action lying at the bottom of it all. The false picture follows from a failure on the part of criminal law (in theory, in practice) to comprehend the relation between accusation and excuse. That is, the false picture of action stems from a misunderstanding of the function of moral discourse generally, of which criminal law is arguably a clear and high example. Moral discourse is *about* intentions, which is to say, *about* the excuses, which in turn are about the possibility of reconciliation. With this in mind, the business of chapter 3 is to locate discussion of criminal law within the context of ordinary moral discourse.

In an attempt to rehabilitate the role of the ordinary in criminal law, my recommendations are entirely methodological. The false picture of action I refer to above depicts accusations and excuses in an odd light under which intentions, their consequences, and action itself are reified "entities." These entities are defined by a complex of causal relations between mind, body, and world, which questions of criminal responsibility are left to somehow decode. This complex of causal relations is presented and endorsed with enthusiasm in an important and representative book by legal philosopher Michael Moore: *Act and Crime: The Philosophy of Action and Its Implications for Criminal Law.*[16] Moore's book expresses the popular, skeptical, and to my mind unfortunate view of human action that accounts for the technical, even extraordinary picture of human action that characterizes the legal doctrines that are the subject of the first half of this book. Chapter 4, accordingly, is a somewhat unsympathetic reading of Moore's *Act and Crime*, a paradigm of the faults of conventional criminal law and theory. In addition, chapter 4 further elaborates the procedures by which ordinary language may be used as a guide for sorting out questions of responsibility, questions that arise in the process of accusation and excuse.

In its most boiled-down form, my aim here is to confront the idea of responsibility by mapping the work of J. L. Austin onto the criminal law. Doing so entails considering closely the extent to which the language of criminal law can be reconciled with ordinary language, a project that entails considering whether the language of criminal law *is* ordinary language. This method of philosophizing—which criminal-law scholarship sometimes alludes to but neither practices nor elaborates[17]—attempts to get a sharpened perception of the world by seeking to understand why we speak as we do in specific speech-situations. Ordinary-language philosophy presupposes, therefore, that to attain knowledge of our language is to attain knowledge of whatever language is about: here, responsibility.

It may, however, be the case that our criminal-law vocabulary might have taken on a technical, "legal" sense that does not or need not conform to our ordinary use of words (like "blame" or "wrong") and it is just a matter of better familiarizing myself with that sense. After all, knowledge could not advance were it not for our willingness to accommodate words like "quark" or "libido," which are true technical terms having no meaning in ordinary language.[18] But it is another thing altogether—tampering (*S&S*, 15)[19]—to take ordinary words and attribute to them an extraordinary meaning in other than extraordinary circumstances.[20] As far as I can tell, the criminal-law terms I take up here are deployed in an illegitimate sense in that they are purported to be used in a technical sense while still trading on what we normally mean by them.[21]

And how is tampering with ordinary language harmful? Tampering with ordinary language inhibits the confrontation between accuser and accused that makes reconciliation *or* blame possible. That is, excuses are the *means* we use to confront the accused. Indeed, it makes absolutely no difference what we *call* misfired actions, be they "mistakes," "accidents," "errors," "slips," or "blunders." What matters is what they *are*. When confronting someone who has done something that is in some way untoward, the accused's response to the accusation can, if competently elaborated, facilitate our coming to grips with the background or history of the episode, how to structure it, understand it. And if an accused's elaboration of an untoward action fails to comport with the criteria for the proffered excuse as used in ordinary speech, then our response may be perverted by our failure to understand both what happened and the accused's stance toward what happened. Consequently, in that long-term project of understanding what it means to do something, be it well, ineptly, inconsiderately, clumsily, or angrily, there must be a place for "so homely, but altogether a central, moral activity as the entering of an excuse" ("CRITICISM," 105), which is crucial to our moral evaluations of what has been done. And even if the criminal law's conventional notion of responsibility turns out to be "useful [and] true" (*A&C*, 109) rather than what Austin would call "Loose (or Divergent or Alternative)" ("EXCUSES," 183), then it is my wish that, as he would say, "the explanation of it can hardly fail to be illuminating" ("EXCUSES," 184).

1

Mens Rea

There is a kind of general disease of thinking which always looks for (and finds) what would be called a mental state from which all our acts spring as from a reservoir.

Wittgenstein, *The Brown Book*[1]

Excusing Accidents

THIS CHAPTER IS AN INVESTIGATION OF THE CONVENTIONAL EXPLANATIONS of "mens rea," that is, explanations of specific excuses that operate in criminal law. This investigation should repay analyzing what we mean by "accident" as opposed to "mistake"; "blame" as opposed to "hold responsible" or "be responsible"; "harmful" as opposed to "wrongful"; and "justify" as opposed to "excuse." After exploring the meaning and operation of this crucial terminology, I take the position that the conventional explanations of "mens rea," explanations that are traceable to skepticism, produce a too-narrow, even superficial, notion of responsibility.

When an accused is asked to elaborate his actions, when he is asked to tell us something about himself, beyond what happened, which extenuating, palliating, or mitigating accounts may we rely on to excuse in whole or in part? "If what a person does was done by accident, then he is not to be blamed—at least not as severely as if he deliberately did it" (*CR*, 262–63). This is a position about which there is much agreement—that accident and blame are incompatible. But just how good an excuse *is* "by accident"? What if the defendant could have exercised greater care? Why exempt harmful actions from criminal liability solely on the ground that they are done by someone who means no harm?

It is hornbook law that infelicitous or poorly performed actions that are done negligently, clumsily, or inadvertently (let's loosely call them "accidents") generally are not the basis of criminal liability. Since accidentally, unlike purposely, knowingly, or recklessly, is not a "mental state"[2] or at least "not a true mental state,"[3] accidents generally are the basis of civil but not criminal liability. The reason is that while accidents do damage, "by themselves they display no moral character flaw" or "wrong in the doer,"[4] since the risks that materialize in such cases are not first considered and then ignored by the doer. Criminal law therefore conditions liability on moral character flaws,[5] which in turn have something to do with mental states.[6]

Another way of expressing the same well-settled notion is that criminals must have some idea of what they are doing, some appreciation of what is likely to go wrong if they do not watch out. Criminals who harm others but don't see the harm coming may deserve some criticism for being *at fault* (i.e., for failing to take cost-justified precautions), in which case they are "tortfeasors," but not criminals.[7] This view is expressed by Larry Alexander:

> Inadvertent negligence and strict liability of all varieties cannot be characterized as wrongs in the doer, because by themselves they display no moral character flaw. Nor can they be characterized as wrongs in the doing in any way that is not far too broad . . . or in many cases where there is no liability—such as a non-negligent auto accident which, of course, involves intentionally taking a risk of injuring; or an intentional battery based upon a reasonable but mistaken belief in the necessity for self-defense—there is wrong in the doing and in the same sense in which inadvertent negligence is wrong in the doing. And if wrong in the doing means merely that we later see a cost-effective way that the harm could have been averted, then wrongs in the doing may include almost everything we do. There is no sense of the objectively wrongful that can be helpful here.[8]

An action performed merely accidentally, or due to what Professor Alexander calls "inadvertent negligence," generally blocks blame for the action on the ground that the agent is not "reckless," that is, he is not aware that what he is doing is excessively risky.[9] Since "guilt is personal,"[10] since it entails a judgment about the defendant and not some fictive, reasonable person, we worry about what the defendant meant to do or the risks he knowingly ran. A defendant who should or could have seen the harm coming but did not may be subject to some criticism, and as such may be judicially coerced into compensating his victim, but failure to appreciate risks is normally not enough to carry the load of what we mean by "guilty."[11]

Criminal law concurs with the significance that Alexander gives the distinction between risks that we take aware of their possible consequences and risks that we take in ignorance of what may happen. Accident is a disfavored if not an altogether bogus basis of criminal liability.[12] The Model Penal Code, which has been adopted in whole or part by most American jurisdictions,[13] haltingly concedes that because it is not "wholly wrong" to presuppose that criminal liability for accidents will deter accidents, accident "should not be wholly rejected as a ground of culpability that may suffice for purposes of penal law."[14] "[W]holly rejected," no: "an exceptional basis of liability,"[15] yes. Why such hesitation? As Alexander puts it, accidents may cause harm, but "by themselves they display no moral character flaw."[16] Moral character flaws are expressed by those who act with "culpable mental states."[17] This must be why we say that "when moral condemnation and social opprobrium attach to the conviction of a crime, the crime should typically reflect a mental state warranting such contempt."[18]

Choosing Crime

THE ROLE OF ALTERNATIVES IN HUMAN ACTION

This implicates the question of which agents can be cut off from responsibility for what they do. In other words, if accidents are less blameworthy than intentional wrongs, then which accidents are we willing to excuse? Professors Alexander and Moore are in good company when they say that an important feature of blame is that the blameless have not "chosen" to commit a crime.[19] Under such a view, playing with the radio, lighting a cigarette, disciplining your children, or cutting corners by inadvertently speeding, running a light, or failing to yield do not involve the sort of behind-the-wheel moves that constitute crime, even though in none of those instances were you nudged by someone else or stung by a bee. For Alexander and Moore, blame depends on actions and outcomes that are chosen rather than (just) performed and brought about.

But when we choose one thing we exclude another, and not just by implication. Wittgenstein captures this when he describes recommencing after having been interrupted in speech:

> When I continue the interrupted sentence and say *this* was how I had been going to continue it, this is like following out a line of thought from brief notes.

> Then don't I *interpret* the notes? Was only one continuation possible under these circumstances? Of course not. But I did not *choose* between interpretations. I *remembered* that I was going to say this (*PI*, 163, para. 634).

Just as you do not interpret a text without confronting other ways of reading it, nor do you choose an action unless you *see* the action as chosen—as one path chosen *over* another:

> *Choose* is an important word in its own right, and needs careful interpretation: "I can if I like" is not the same, although the "can" and the "if" may be the same in both, as "I can if I choose." Choice is always between alternatives, that is between several courses to be weighed in the same scale against each other, the one to be *preferred*. "You can vote whichever way you choose" is different from "You can vote whichever way you like" ("IFS," 213).

Indeed, last night I did not choose oranges over lemons (or any other fruit) at the market because buying lemons (or any other fruit) never occurred to me. I did, however, choose some oranges over other oranges based on my estimation of their ripeness and juiciness after squeezing and examining them.

But even if some, perhaps many, untoward actions really are chosen by our selecting one path over another, does this mean that we choose as well those actions' "consequences, concomitants, upshots, effects, results, and so forth"? (*A PITCH*, 87). If you act "recklessly" when you "consciously disregard a substantial and unjustifiable risk" of harm,[20] then you still have accidentally harmed someone, haven't you? But there your excuse of accident will be rejected if we conclude that you chose your action, having considered the implications of what you were doing—of harms risked—before execution. The same harm *would* be excused were we instead to respond by saying "it was just an accident." But they are *both* accidents, aren't they? So does the former case justify blame because you had a "mental state" of "recklessness?" I take that to mean that, prior to dropping and breaking a vase, you thought about the properties of the vase, considered that dropping it might or might not break it, then dropped it anyway, thereby fulfilling the "conscious disregard" criterion of recklessness.[21] This may well be the law, but how willing a parent is to excuse a child who breaks a vase and pleads "it was an accident" depends on a lot of things, *none* of which is the "accidentalness" of the breakage itself, but instead, whether the child was playing when he should have been eating, whether he has done it before and therefore is expected to have learned better by now, etc. What contributes to whether he is excused is unlikely to be the child's "mental state," be it recklessness or any other description of his having chosen to run a risk by weighing up the likely untoward outcomes and then ignoring them.

If, just like a harm caused by negligent behavior, a harm caused by reckless behavior also is accidental, and if in both cases we can criticize the agent for having taken too little precaution under the circumstances, then why does the excuse "it was an accident"—even if believed—not necessarily require the acquittal of a defendant who is accused of being reckless? Working out a satisfactory response to this question depends on the grammar of the word "accident," which is flexible enough to be both over- and under-inclusive. It is over-inclusive to the extent that "accident" could be said to describe any outcome that is not intentionally, purposely, or deliberately caused. It is under-inclusive to the extent that after the fact, the harm-causer's opportunity to have taken more or better before-the-fact harm-avoidance strategies always looks plausible.

First, the way in which application of the excuse "it was an accident" can be over-inclusive. An example of Austin's should be helpful here:

> I realize that by insisting on payment of due debts I am going to "ruin" my debtor—that is, he will be ruined as a consequence of being compelled to pay. I have absolutely no wish to ruin him, even wish not to: but maybe if I don't get payment both I and others are going to suffer severely; and very likely I think he has been faintly improvident. So I demand payment. He is ruined and, if you like, I ruined him. If this is said—I might resist and resent the imputation a bit—I think it must be admitted that I did ruin him deliberately; not, however, that I ruined him intentionally. At no time did I intend to ruin him; it was never part of my intention. (This, if it be admitted, is an especially interesting case: for plainly I am *not* here responsible for his ruin) ("INK," 278–79).

What Austin means to bring out here, among other things, is the relation of the debtor's ruin to the plan or intention of collecting a just debt. It would be an over-inclusive use of the word "accident" indeed to so characterize the ruin of the debtor. Thus it is critical to our understanding of this example that while the debtor's ruin was never what our creditor intended, this was no unintentional ruining of the debtor, either. That is, the debtor's ruin here was neither intentional (in the creditor's plan) nor unintentional (an unforeseen consequence of the plan): the debtor's ruin was what Austin would call an "incidental." More precisely, Austin would call the debtor's ruin "not intentional" (neither intentional nor unintentional)—a foreseen incidental of the collection of the debt, but an incidental nonetheless.

Incidentals are consequences that were either foreseen (like the debtor's ruin here) or unforeseen (if, say, the creditor unexpectedly falls into a deep depression over having brought about the debtor's ruin by calling in the debt). *Any* consequence that is outside the plan is incidental to the intention. It is just that there are two modes of incidentals: 1) those that you confront or anticipate before acting; and 2) those that you don't. On our facts, we are told that the creditor's plan is to reclaim his money. He wishes things could be otherwise, but if he lets the debtor off the hook, "both [he] and others are going to suffer severely." The creditor has not, therefore, called in the debt *in order* to ruin the debtor. (And if he did, then we could say he ruined the debtor "purposely," but not otherwise). For the creditor, there is no choice. Plus, the debtor has brought it on himself; "very likely . . . he has been faintly improvident" in assuming the debt in the first place, perhaps with no plan or a poor plan for repaying it.

Certainly we can imagine facts where the creditor's plea that the debtor's ruin was incidental to the creditor's intention to reclaim his own money would leave us in deep doubt as to the genuineness of the plea. For example, what if the creditor had more than adequate resources to wait for the debtor to execute a good-faith plan to cover the debt, the default of which was not faintly improvident, but rather, due to a grave, sudden illness? If the creditor in such a case still insists on prompt payment, we would be properly skeptical about a plea that the debtor's ruin was incidental to the plan. There it should strike us that insisting on prompt payment smacks of an intention to ruin the debtor. Otherwise, why demand the debt? There could still be innocent reasons for demanding the debt anyway, some perhaps with sound business justifications, but the point is that those reasons would need to be elaborated to avoid our getting the sense that the plan was to ruin the debtor. In other words, one cannot convert a consequence into an incidental simply by declaring it so, not unless that declaration matches up with what we see in the public observable world.

On the original set of facts posited above by Austin, it is given that the debtor's ruin was incidental to the plan of debt collection. We would not, however, describe the debtor's ruin in that case as accidental. To do so would be to suggest that the debtor's ruin came from out of nowhere, at least from the creditor's perspective. For this creditor to enter a plea of accident would be an awful evasion of responsibility since the creditor "realize[s] that by insisting on payment of due debts I am going to 'ruin' my debtor—that is, he will be ruined as a consequence of being compelled to pay." Once aware of this likely consequence, the creditor will not be heard to say that the debtor's ruin was "just an accident." It wasn't; but it *was* (just) an incidental: "I have absolutely no wish to ruin him, even wish not to"; "At no time did I intend to ruin him; it was never part of my intention."

While it is tempting to say that all consequences that are incidental to one's intentions are accidents, to say so would provide an over-inclusive domain for that plea. The foreseen incidental—what the law calls the "recklessly" caused harm—is, as accidents go, a bogus one. Foreseen incidentals may sometimes be excusable, as they are in cases where "knowledge" (that is, certainty) about a fact is an element of the offense or in cases where the harm in question must be intended. But foreseen incidentals are not accidents, or they are very weak instances of accidents, whose domain is best reserved for the unforeseen incidental. Most (non-bogus) accidents are excusable because the actor did *not* in such a case "consciously disregard a substantial and unjustifiable risk" of harm.

Who acts like *that*? Anyone who does is acting more (though not quite) deliberately than recklessly. I say "not quite" because while choice and deliberation both involve a weighing up, an action over which I deliberate is weighed up against *not* performing it (should I? dare I?) as opposed to performing one action over another (e.g., buying oranges over lemons). Thus we could say that Othello chose to stab (not strangle) Desdemona in her bed after deliberating over whether to kill her (at all). In other words, one can choose anything—a noun, for example, fills in well: I choose *X*; but I do not deliberate *X*. I deliberate *over X*, thus emphasizing a process (should I or not?) which indicates that I am willing to live by what I do or fail to do there.

As Austin puts it: "I act *deliberately* when I have deliberated—which means when I have stopped to ask myself, 'Shall I or shan't I?' and then decided to do *X*, which I did. That is to say, I weighed up, in however rudimentary a fashion, the pros and cons. And it is understood that there must be some cons" ("INK," 286). When we act that way, our actions are neither reckless nor negligent (or spontaneous or impulsive) ("INK," 276–77) and their considered consequences are in no way accidental; our actions and their consequences are in such cases deliberate (though not *necessarily* intentional). Indeed, the very *idea* of recklessness, which is meant to identify accidents that are generally not excused, makes no sense except in instances where the actor chooses between two alternative courses of action—one risky, the other safe—and then executes only after acknowledging the "cons" inherent in the risky course. Or, we could say that the actor weighed up the pros and cons and found the pros heavier when we, sitting *ex post* in judgment of the action, find the cons to be heavier. In either case, I seriously doubt that such a notion can distinguish crime from tort, blame from responsibility, or wrongful from harmful. Such a notion simply does not describe a significant-enough portion of human action to be the basis by which the very large class of criminal-but-not-intentional wrongs (of foreseen incidentals) is distinguished from what must be the equally large class of noncriminal, unintentional wrongs (of unforeseen incidentals).

In fact, much harm in the world expresses the complete absence of weighing up of any kind. Take a well-known criminal case in which the question was whether a drunk driver could be charged with the murder of passengers who rode in a car he smashed into as he sped through an intersection.[22] To a majority of justices on the California Supreme Court, his could be a case of murder because the drunk driver (Watson) was "malicious" for having been aware of a high risk of death when he went to a bar, got drunk, then drove too fast through two stop signs before impact.[23] To the dissent, Watson was no murderer because his having slammed on his brakes just before the crash demonstrated that he took measures to lower, not ignore, the risk of death he posed to others. Accelerating between intersections, the dissent acknowledged, is conscious risk creating, but braking at the intersections, the dissent added, is conscious risk lowering.[24] Thus for both the majority and dissent, Watson's responsibility, or level of responsibility, turned on his "mental state," that is, his calculations, if any, or what he knew, if anything, about whether he could kill anyone that night by driving that way.

But what if Watson, like most people who kill other than intentionally (by accident?), never thought a bit about killing anyone that night? That would preclude a conviction of murder, which requires that he be indifferent to life (by being aware of or "consciously disregarding" the risk of death). One cannot, we are told, be indifferent to life without confronting the possibility that life could be lost.[25] Watson could still be convicted of the less-serious crime of manslaughter, but even that requires *some* awareness or knowledge of an excessive risk, though there the awareness can be "inferred" or "imputed" from the risks he took.[26] This is a rather strange conversation that the law requires at trial, where the defendant is asked to explain what he thought was going to happen as a result of his drunk driving. In the ordinary case, a defendant so situated will have made no such calculations whatsoever: "I just felt like doing it," or "I don't know—it never occurred to me that this could happen," or "I was too drunk to appreciate what was happening" each has more than an air of plausibility to it.

THE SKEPTICISM OF MENS REA

The real problem here is the law's insistence that the defendant's relationship to his own actions be one of knowledge, which jurors infer or impute. Knowing what you were doing *is* an aspect of blaming, but it will only get us so far when the defense is one of accident, where the problem becomes not so much one of coming to grips with what was done, *but with the meaning of "knowing what you are doing."* Watson no doubt knew he was both drunk and driving. Let us assume as well that he knew he was driving over the speed limit and (as the court assumed) that he knew *as a general matter* that drunk driving is dangerous to life.[27] "Certainly one can know a thing without bearing it in mind (fortunately—otherwise there wouldn't be room for much), or having it occur to you at regular intervals" ("MEANING IT," 233). But if knowing what he was doing must include some contemporaneous reflection on his drunk driving's "consequences, concomitants, upshots, effects, results, and so forth" (*A PITCH*, 87), then we are going to have a hard time fairly blaming Watson for "knowing" he would kill someone or "consciously disregarding" that he could kill someone. That is, it is not enough that Watson knew as a general matter that drunk driving is dangerous to life. He must in addition have considered that very possibility much more recently: according to the *Watson* majority, as early as his decision to drive to the bar with the intention of getting drunk; according to the dissent, no earlier than his speeding into the first intersection.

Both sides in *Watson* reflect a pervasive theme in criminal law, which is to treat questions of responsibility not just as questions of action or inaction, but as questions of decision or choice, which in turn are understood as questions of knowledge or belief. The theme is skepticism in its purest form: everything comes down to knowledge, even human action that is performed under conditions that preclude knowledge. The theme is expressed in, among other places, the Model Penal Code's position on the operation of self-defense. To deal with the problem posed by those who defend themselves or others with deadly force when the threat turns out to be not so dangerous after all, the Code responds:

> The solution . . . is that such situations should be taken out of the category of purposeful crime and dealt with as cases of recklessness or negligence. If the belief is recklessly arrived at, i.e., with awareness of the risk that it may be unfounded, then it is appropriate to assess the defendant as one would be assessed who had acted recklessly with respect to the material elements of the offense. . . .
>
> [W]hen the actor's belief in the necessity for using the force that he used was recklessly or negligently formed, or when he was reckless or negligent in acquiring or failing to acquire any knowledge that is otherwise material to the justification for his use of force, the justification is lost in a prosecution for an offense for which recklessness or negligence, as the case may be, suffices for conviction.[28]

But what, exactly, does someone who uses deadly force against another "know" or "believe"? While the Code is consistent in its position that poorly formed (negligent or reckless) beliefs about the need for deadly force are "unreasonable mistakes" subject to partial excuse, none of the pertinent text or commentary contains a single example of such a situation.[29] How in anything except the most limiting circumstances is a belief in the need to use deadly force recklessly or negligently formed or arrived at?

The relation of *some* self-defenders to their actions is one of knowledge or belief; but for many others it is not, since for them to treat their situation as a problem of knowledge or belief will be at odds with other responses to the world, especially when the pressure is on. This very point is suggested by Cavell:

> That couple over there, drinking coffee, talking, laughing. Do I believe they are just passing the time of day, or testing out the field for a flirtation, or something else? In usual cases, not one thing or another; I neither be-

> lieve nor disbelieve. Suppose the man suddenly puts his hands to the throat of the woman. Do I believe or disbelieve that he is going to throttle her? The time for that question, as soon as it comes to the point, is already passed. The question is: What, if anything, do I do? *What I believe hangs on what I do or do not do and on how I react to what I do or do not do* ("AVOIDANCE," 329).[30]

In the italicized closing to this passage, Cavell inverts the way we normally see the relation between thought and action. Normally we say that what we do hangs on what we believe. But here, the belief follows what is done or not done. The belief is about what was done or not done in circumstances where there are consequences for seeing the situation as one in which action hangs on belief, that is, where there are consequences for *conditioning* action on belief. What you do when faced with a claim or demand such as the one you face watching the couple here includes the possibility of treating the problem (as a skeptic would) as one of "what do I know?" "how do I know?" If you do not or cannot know what the man is up to, then the skeptic would let you off the hook for whatever you do or do not do, since the proper response could not be identified without the proper basis—the knowledge—of what it is you are responding to. Still, you *are* responding by asking yourself what you know or believe. Another way of saying this is that there is no position of observer because observing is itself a form of response. And sometimes that response is going to be inadequate to meet your responsibilities. While you are fiddling around (responding by) asking yourself what you believe ("Do I know—am I really sure—what he is doing?")—which is *a* response—the chance to prevent the throttling (if throttling there be) is lost to you. *That* is what makes the burden of action unbearable: there is no avoiding it, not even for the skeptic. If knowing what is happening before you is what you are waiting for, then *that* is what you do, but it is no less a response that you must be prepared to elaborate than any other.

Thus under the Model Penal Code, someone like Bernard Goetz, who "believed" that four unarmed youths on a Bronx subway train were about to "maim" him, would have committed manslaughter had he succeeded in killing the boys, all of whom in actuality he nonfatally shot. Goetz knew that the boys were unarmed; he had not been threatened by them; he had warded off danger successfully in the past by drawing his gun on other aggressors; and he had stalked these youths after he had negated whatever threat he imagined he faced.[31] Accordingly, manslaughter would have been the appropriate charge if he really believed he was going to be maimed, however paranoid that belief might have been. Perhaps such a belief would be what the Code would call a "poorly formed" one; and in that case his poorly formed belief produced a bad decision that would leave Goetz (again, had the boys died) in a middle ground between a justified killing and murder. Decisions that misfire because they are based on faulty and poorly formed beliefs are partially excused under the Code.[32] The residue of the action—that which is not excused—is therefore a criticism of the decision itself. So if Goetz was overreacting to the youths, then he remains partially on the hook because he made a bad decision, which was based on faulty beliefs. But about what? The implications of "give me five dollars"? About whom? African-Americans? *These* African-Americans?

This is all to say that the real issue is only nominally whether we call Watson or Goetz "murderer," "manslaughterer," or neither; and even more tangential is whether either had a "mental state" of "recklessness" by which he "consciously disregarded a substantial risk of death" (Watson) or by which he arrived at the decision to defend with deadly force (Goetz). More important is whether to fully or partially blame them or to let them off the hook altogether. And for that task, their excuses tell us a lot more about what to make of what they did than do various definitions of crime or culpability. Like most killers, Watson's plea is accident. He did not mean to kill anyone, nor would anyone seriously suggest that he did. Like many killers, Goetz's plea is self-defense. He meant to kill, and nowhere suggests that he did not. So it is left for us to separate out those killings (or attempted killings)—be they accidental (as Watson claimed his to be) or overreactions to a perceived threat (as Goetz claimed his to be)—that are fully excusable from those that are partially excusable and inexcusable. This is far from light work, but rarely do we get any nearer to discovery on these distinctions between what is excusable and what is not by reference to Watson's or Goetz's "*mental state*"—to what risks, just before the deadly (or near deadly) actions they took, suspected, knew of, or deliberated over. Most harm-causers who worked out this carefully the "concomitants, upshots, etc." of their actions-in-prospect, I suspect, would not have done what they did had they weighed up *ex ante* what, exactly, could go wrong. And in the unlikely event that this sort of calculation did occur, then "reckless" does an extremely poor job of capturing what they have done.

"Mental States"

If nothing else, "mental state" is a peculiar and misleading term that gets us in trouble from the start. It is peculiar in that it tells us nothing about human action. John Updike uses the term in its ordinary way:

> Q: And your . . . mental state?
> A: If you mean do I still have all my buttons, you'll have to judge that for yourself. Oh, I'm forgetful, but then I always was.[33]

To Updike's character, being asked about your mental state is to be asked if you are okay, functioning, or mentally sound (as opposed to mentally in a state of, say, giddiness, despair, fatigue). George Pitcher recalls Austin's explication of the same notion in the seminar that Austin taught on the excuses, which Pitcher followed at Harvard:

> In distinguishing between a state of mind and a frame of mind, Austin said that if something puts you in a certain state of mind (depressed, bewildered, agitated), it puts your machinery out of gear, whereas if you are in a certain frame of mind, your machinery isn't out of gear—it is rather in a certain special gear. (He supported this point by reminding us that to say of someone that he is "in a state," just like that, is to say that he is distressed, upset, in some way out of order.)[34]

In a similar vein, Wittgenstein says that "[d]epression, excitement, pain are mental states" (*PI*, p. 59 n. a). You feel and express them. But "purpose," "knowledge," "recklessness," and "negligence"? They don't sound like *states* at all. Yet according to the Model Penal Code's drafters, they are "state[s] of awareness"[35] or "mental attitude[s]."[36] These states or attitudes, broken down into "four levels of culpability,"[37] are meant to add "clarity," that is, "to dispel the obscurity with which the culpability requirement is often treated when such concepts as 'general criminal intent,' 'mens rea,' 'presumed intent,' 'malice,' 'wilfulness,' 'scienter' and the like have been employed."[38] Because "of ambiguity in legal usage of the term 'intent,'"[39] the Code's drafters swapped it for "purpose," which is an "attitude" that goes beyond "awareness" of a likely result, instead signifying the actor's "conscious object to perform an action of that nature or to cause such a result."[40] Just how this formulation differs from that of intent is not apparent.[41] Indeed, while the Code insists that its "four levels of culpability" are "a substantial improvement"[42] over past attempts to cope with questions of responsibility, I doubt seriously that swapping purpose for intent can count as an improvement.

When we ask whether an action was done "on purpose," "for a purpose," "with a purpose," or "purposely" (what was your purpose in doing that?), we are more interested in the reasons behind the action than we are in the action itself. Much action that is in no sense accidental—indeed, even much intentional action—is action that is done with no purpose whatsoever:

> A gang of boys decapitates, *seriatim*, every one of the line of young trees newly planted along our street: this is deliberate, wanton damage. But they have, we may say, no interest in killing the trees; very likely they haven't given the matter a thought. Do children pull the wings off flies "on purpose?" Yet see them at it, and it is patent that they do it intentionally, and also deliberately ("INK," 277).

Children who seriatim decapitate a row of trees or pull the wings off flies hardly do it unintentionally, but they may have no reason or motive or purpose, just as you may or may not have any purpose in the act of feeding starving children ("INK," 286 n.1) (or none known to you).[43] It is important to realize that "on purpose" and "purposely" pick out a very specific and relatively small set of actions. When purpose is called into question, we are inquiring into *why* an action is done—"something to be achieved or effected as a result of what I'm doing" ("INK," 285)—where with intention, a term that the Code rejects on grounds of ambiguity, we are inquiring into *what* was done. We say, for example, that "'*A* wounded *B* with the intention of killing him, or of causing him grave bodily injury; or, more formally, with intent to kill him, and so forth.' We do not say, '*A* wounded *B* for the purpose of killing him'" ("INK," 275–76). But why? Because the purpose is not the intention—they cannot be the same. The purpose must be *outside* the intention—the purpose is the payoff of the intention. Take another example of Austin's: a till-dipper who plans to put the money back after he plays the ponies takes the money with the intention of putting it back. But what was his purpose? Clearly he did not take the money for the purpose of putting it back ("INK," 275).

That would be nonsense. The intention *is* the action: "intention is related to our action in a more intimate way than its purpose" ("INK," 280). (Thus the hilarity of the non-response—"to get to the other side"—to "why did the chicken cross the road?" Getting to the other side could never be a *reason* for crossing the road, though the action could certainly have its reasons).

Just how substituting purpose for intention helped anything the Model Penal Code drafters never say. Even worse, they have tampered with the ordinary meaning of "having a purpose in acting." Yet the drafters do not see their deployment of purpose as illegitimate, though their definition of it is trained on only the consequences of the act (e.g., decapitated trees) and not the payoff or reason for the act (e.g., killing time, retaliating against the trees' owner), which would be a purpose. It is likely that the drafters knew that an intentional act need not have a purpose. But then why say "purpose?" Why trade on the customary meaning of purpose and then give it an extraordinary, technical, or special sense? What could be clarified by that?

"Intentional" is as Austin puts it, a much more "intimate" description of an action than "purposefully." To begin with, intend has a positive sense: the action in prospect or future commitment expressed by "I intend *X*." We do not say, however, "I purpose *X*." Like "I promise" or "I'll try," "I intend" *stakes* the speaker, although differently than these other two forms of commitment. A broken promise requires an excuse, no matter why the promise is broken. "I'll try" anticipates a nontrivial possibility of failure *and* success, usually because the matter is outside the control of the agent (as in, "I'll try to strike him out" or "I'll try to convince you"). The only need for excuse with "I'll try" is if too little (or no) effort follows the utterance. "I intend," while still a commitment of sorts (though a weaker commitment than "I promise" or "I'll try"), leaves open the possibility of a change of heart. The withdrawal or modification of an intention is marked by a change of priorities. Still, we *can* criticize the agent after the fact, not just for changing his mind, but, at least when the evidence supports our saying so, for not really having had the commitment in the first place (as in, "you *said* when we graduated high school that you intended to become a doctor, yet you never so much as signed up for a single science course while you were in college"). The failure to lift a finger toward realizing the stated intention makes the claim of having that intention look like a pose.

Still, this is a delicate enterprise: one cannot conclude, merely from the fact that the stated intention was never put into action, that the intention was never present or that the claim of having that intention was for that reason alone unserious:

> I must, of course, have the intention, if I am not to be insincere, at the time of my utterance: but what exactly is the degree or mode of the infelicity if I do not afterwards do it? Or again, in "I bid you welcome," to say which is to welcome, intentions of a kind are presumably vaguely necessary: but what if one then behaves churlishly? Or again, I give you advice and you accept it, but then I round on you: how far is it obligatory on me not to do so? Or am I just "not expected" to do so?: or is part of asking-and-taking advice definitely to make such subsequent conduct out of order? Or similarly, I entreat you to do something, you accede, and then I protest—am I out of order? Probably yes (*HTDTW*, 44).

In the above passage, which I've pinched from his *How To Do Things With Words*, Austin remarks that acting so promptly false to the intention inherent in the utterance is grounds for calling the intention into question. This does not disprove the intention, say, to (really) bid you welcome or give you advice, but the prompt reversal in attitude is, as Austin aptly puts it, "out of order." At a minimum, the prompt reversal calls the genuineness of the stated intention into question.

It is therefore possible to at least take stabs at evaluating—once the evidence is in—the sincerity of these three distinct commitments or actions in prospect: promising, trying, and intending. In this respect these three modes can be distinguished not just from each other, but from purely internal or subjective matters like hoping or wishing. "I hope *X*" or "I wish *X*" are purely subjective matters (like taste). It would be awkward to tell someone what they hope or wish, since their stating their hopes or wishes includes no commitment, no plan, no operation-order the existence or seriousness of which we could then evaluate in the public observable world. While hounding down the differences among these distinct modes of commitment may repay the effort, for now I would like just to reiterate that we do talk about an intention (or a promise, or a trying) as an action in prospect. Hoping and wishing do not point to any future course of action, because they are, again, internal or subjective matters that make no commitment, no claim to action whatsoever. But it is revelatory that, contrary to the actions in prospect of intending, promising, and trying, we do not have a similar way for discussing a purpose in acting: there is no action in prospect "I purpose *X*." The absence of any such verb reveals something about the fact that, contrary to the Model Penal Code's vision of the matter, intentions and purposes are *not* the same.

In addition to the absence of any phrase such as "I purpose," the prepositions deployed with intention and purpose reveal that the two terms are by no means interchangeable:

> We say *on* purpose (to), *for* the purpose of, but *with* the intention of: (possibly also *with* the purpose of). It seems clear that "on" and "for" (compare "on the principle," "on orders," "for the sake of") *dissociate* or *sever* my purpose from my current action in a way that "with" does not do. There are many expressions containing "purpose" ("for the *usual* purposes," "to good purpose," "to some purpose," and so forth) which seem to make purpose as it were *im*personal in a way that is never done with intention ("INK," 282).

One can do something without any purpose at all, that is, do it "purposelessly,"[44] but one cannot do an action with no intention whatsoever ("INK," 280–81). The intention can misfire, as where an unwanted result occurs by way of mistake or accident, but that at least *something* is intended is what makes an action—any action, even the misfired action—an action as opposed to a mere happening or occurrence.[45] Action is thus more intimately (even analytically) related to intention than to purpose.

ACTIONS AND THEIR REASONS: PURPOSES, MOTIVES, PRETEXTS

This distinction between the plan itself (the intention or what is realized) and what the plan is setting up (the purpose or what is achieved) can be made, at least at a high level of generality, by separating out what the actor is doing from why he is doing it. This is a rather generalized distinction because purposes themselves have different modes, which Austin manages just to hint at. Twice in "A Plea for Excuses" he mentions motives—a mode of purpose—but nowhere explores their grammar.[46] And in "Pretending," Austin drops a footnote where he makes a too-brief comparison of "pretence" and "pretext," which are aspects or types of purposes in doing something.[47] Finally, at the end of "Three Ways of Spilling Ink," L. W. Forguson, who on Austin's death prepared the essay from Austin's lecture notes, mentions that those notes invite readers to "not only compare and contrast these three expressions—'intentionally,' 'deliberately,' 'on purpose'—with each other, but each should be compared and contrasted with other expressions as well (e.g., 'motive' with both 'intention' and 'purpose,' 'premeditation' with 'deliberation,' and 'to mean' with 'to intend')" ("INK," 287 n.1). I am going to accept part of Forguson's invitation here, hoping that something about the nature of responsibility will emerge from applying ordinary-language procedures to these two adjuncts to the notion of purpose—motive and pretext—terms commonly deployed in criminal law and in the related body of rules that regulate police practices.[48]

Consider Jean-Paul Sartre's use of the term pretext in the following garden-variety example, which appears in his autobiography:

> By classifying authors in order of merit, he was paying lip-service; this surface hierarchy ill concealed his preferences, which were utilitarian: de Maupassant provided the best translation material for his German pupils; Goethe, beating Gottfried Keller by a nose, could not be equalled for compositions in French. As a humanist, my grandfather held novels in low esteem; as a teacher, he valued them because of their vocabulary. He ended by reading only selected passages, and I saw him, some years later, enjoy an extract from *Madame Bovary* in Mironneau's Readings when the complete Flaubert had been awaiting his pleasure for twenty years. I felt that he lived on the dead, which to some degree complicated my relations with them. *Under the pretext of worshipping them, he kept them in chains and did not refrain from cutting them up in order to carry them more conveniently from one language to another.*[49]

Here, Sartre's grandfather, Charles Schweitzer, is depicted as someone whose action in question is his classifying authors in order of merit. What makes it a pretext is that the reason, if any, one would ordinarily have for doing so would be the authors' imagination, their compassion, their expressiveness, not their tendency to make teaching a foreign language easier. And how do we conclude that Grandfather Schweitzer's rankings were pretextual? The most telling evidence here is the shakiness of his claim to classification by merit in light of the fact that young Sartre observed that his grandfather had a practice of citing canonical works, but never settling down to actually read them.[50] That is to say, Grandfather Schweitzer *used* the great works, but not because they were great works. Instead, his real reasons for the classification by merit might have been to conceal from his grandson his lowbrow tastes, his preference for minor authors, or that what he liked about the great authors was not that they were great authors but that their books were somehow useful to his trade.

It is important to note that Sartre points out that his grandfather's real interest in the great authors was "ill concealed." Ill concealed or not, it *was* concealed, or at least it was meant to be concealed. If Grandfather Schweitzer had admitted that his rankings were not really based on merit, then the claim that the classification by merit was pretextual would be empty, given that a pretext is an action that is characterized by a special sort of underlying reason, a reason at odds with those reasons, if any, that ordinarily provide the grounds for the action. If Grandfather Schweitzer owned up to classifying authors by their vocabulary, then there would be no appearance to penetrate; there would be no special reason at odds with or underlying the action. We would just say: "Grandfather classifies authors by their vocabulary." The action would not be pretextual.

The same would be true of young Sartre, who calls his grandfather's ranking "pretextual." Because Sartre does in fact read the canonical works, we have no occasion to question why *he* would rank the great authors as he does; there would be nothing to suggest that his classification is *not* by merit. When he ranks by merit, there is very likely no motive for the action at all, given that motives exist only when the reasons for the action are at odds with the action in some way. With the ordinary action, there may be no point or answer at all to the question: "Why did you do that?" With pretextual action, oppositely, there is a point and an answer to the question. If there were not, then the term "pretext" would have no specific application to the speech-situation.

So too, if the classification were *not* by merit, then the whole notion of pretext would be inapposite. In other words, "pretext" presupposes here that it really is a classification by merit. If it is a classification by ease of translation or breadth of vocabulary, then it is not a *pretextual* classification by merit; it could not be, because it is not a classification by merit at all. Pretext, properly understood, operates only in settings where the criteria for the action *are* met: it *is* a classification by merit. The best authors are intentionally rated or placed at the top.

In the hope of correcting a common misconception or abuse of the term "pretext," it bears repeating that to say that the action claimed (here, classification by merit) is not the action that occurred (here, classification by vocabulary) is not to describe the action as pretextual, except in a too loose or extravagant sense. With pretexts, the action is not feigned. What is concealed is a special reason, a motive, which, like all motives, cuts against or deviates from the action in a sinister way; what is concealed is something in the world to be achieved or set up by the action, something that normally would not strike us as the upshot of the action.

Soon after the term's first appearance, Sartre uses the term "pretext" again. This time, Sartre imagines himself riding a train without having purchased a ticket. In this reverie, he deflects the ticket collector's demands for a ticket by reversing the situation:

> I therefore revealed that I had to be in Dijon for important and secret reasons, reasons that concerned France and perhaps all mankind. If things were viewed in this new light, it would be apparent that no one in the entire train had as much right as I to occupy a seat. Of course, this involved a higher law which conflicted with the regulations, but if the ticket-collector took it upon himself to interrupt my journey, he would cause grave complications, the consequences of which would be *his* responsibility. *I urged him to think it over: was it reasonable to doom the entire species to disorder under the pretext of maintaining order in a train?*[51]

Here, one would ask this question: If maintaining order on the train by insisting that passengers have tickets is a pretext, then what was the ticket collector really getting at? For pretext to be used in anything but a loose sense, the answer would have to be that the ticket collector was demanding a ticket *in order to* doom the entire species (a motive for collecting the ticket) while *holding himself out* as maintaining order (the ordinary basis of collecting the ticket). But here the evidence is weak. Even if the ticket collector believed Sartre's claim about the fate of mankind, that does not necessarily mean that demanding the ticket anyway demonstrates an intention to doom the species. Even once alerted to what is staked in demanding the ticket, that stake (dooming the species) could still remain incidental to the ticket collector's original plan of maintaining order or enforcing the regulations or doing his job. As long as he demands the ticket despite the fact that it will doom the species, rather than in order to doom the species, then maintaining order or enforcing the regulations or doing his job would not be the motives behind a pretextual action at all. Instead, maintaining order or enforcing the regulations or doing his job would be precisely the point or upshot of demanding the ticket. Talk of pretext in such a case would be inapposite.

A pretext, therefore, is a criticism we make of an action that has a purpose that is, like all purposes, at odds in some way with the action. The normal, conventional reasons for an action are not purposes because they are too intimately related to the action to be cut off from the intention. But among those bases or reasons for actions that are purposes, while they are by definition unconventional bases for the action in question, a purpose in acting is not *necessarily* a negative phenomenon. We say, for example, "to good purposes" or "for good purposes" (just as we say "his intentions were good" or "he did it with the best of intentions"). A motive, contrariwise, is a special type of purpose: not just an unexpected or unconventional basis or payoff for the action, but an underhanded, sinister, or deceptive one at that. We do not say "his motives were good"; "he did it with the best of motives." In fact, not only do we not say that Robin Hood's motive in taking from the rich was "to steal property" (that would be his intention), but neither do we say that Robin Hood's motive was "to give to the poor." It was his purpose (severed, as it were, from the action itself) sure enough, but it would be peculiar in speech to take an act of helping the needy as a "motive" for action.

A pretextual action has a motive that, like all motives, is at odds in some way with the action: the motive for the generous action toward the fragile relative is to inherit under the will. The motive could be greed (because greed is directed at something: here, at the money that the will would make available). If the generous action is just plain generous without such directedness, then it is empty to speak in terms of motive, though there may be reasons for the generosity (for example, feeling good about oneself). But such reasons are not motives if they are psychological or inner,[52] even though we tend to think of motives as inner states rather than as explanations of something to be attained in the world by a certain course of action.[53] While it is common among psychologists to suggest that all actions have motives (or are motivated),[54] in fact we use the word "motive" only infrequently in ordinary speech.[55] We use the word only in reference to actions we feel the need to assess, to make sense of.[56] Among those actions that do have reasons, not all reasons are necessarily directed. Considerateness or punctuality, for example, are reasons for actions, yet they are not motives; they have no aim, no directedness; they are not setting anything up.[57]

Thus, references to motives come up in moral discourse where we need to make sense of an action. If we say, "What was his motive?" it must be because it looks to us as though the action had to be directed at something unusual, even untoward, but we cannot figure out what it was. When we say that Macbeth's motive in killing Duncan was ambition, we are not referring to a feeling or some internal perturbation of Macbeth;[58] instead, the motive of ambition refers to some other actions, some other ends in the world to be attained by the killing, whether or not the actions are known to him.[59] Likewise, "if a man looks pleased when praised for something trivial, or upset when mildly criticized, we can say he is vain, but we cannot say vanity is his motive for being pleased when praised."[60] In other words, vanity may explain certain actions (as in, "he did it *out of* vanity"), but it cannot be considered a motive for them.[61]

"Pretext" is a type of motive: it is a motive that the actor is covering up. While a motive *may* be unknown to the actor, a pretext necessarily involves an act of concealment. Any actor, once put on the spot by being questioned about his motives, will either confirm or dispel our suspicions by going on record and offering a reason for the action or denying having any reason at all. If we accept that the action had no motive, or perhaps had no reason whatsoever (as in "I just did it" or "I just felt like doing it"),[62] then the action cannot be pretextual. Thus "pretext" is the term we apply to an action that we conclude was directed in an unconventional, untoward way that the actor was aware of, regardless of whether he is willing to admit to it when questioned later. Put slightly differently, if after confronting the explanation for the action we cannot accept the action as ordinary or conventional, then we may be inclined to call it a "pretext." For example, we may say: "Your motive in marrying her was greed; you married her for her money." If the accused in such a pinch were to respond: "No, I married for love," to that we may respond: "No, you are incapable of love. The marriage is for you just a pretext for money-making." That is to say, love is the ordinary, conventional reason for marriage, but it is not the reason for this one. Accordingly, in its most boiled down form, "pretext" is a way of criticizing an action that had a motive known to the actor that is incompatible with the ordinary, conventional reason, if any, for the action.

Though various shades of purpose (reasons, pretexts, motives) are implicated by the Model Penal Code's reliance on the term as a basis of responsibility, they play no legal role whatsoever because the drafters, through an act of legislative jujitsu, have declared that "purposely" means "intentionally." Purpose is at the top of the Model Penal Code's hierarchy of culpability. That means that to do something on purpose is the most blameworthy thing that a person can do.[63] Negligence is at the bottom and as such is the least blameworthy thing a person can do and still be punishable. Because negligent acts lack a "mental state," the Code cautions against using them as the basis of punishment.[64] The relation of the four terms—purpose, knowledge, recklessness, and negligence—is one in which one could say (or be tempted to say) that the greater includes the lesser:

> When the law provides that negligence suffices to establish an element of an offense, such element is also established if a person acts purposely, knowingly, or recklessly. When recklessness suffices to establish an element, such element is also established if a person acts purposely or knowingly. When acting knowingly suffices to establish an element, such element also is established if a person acts purposely.[65]

The Code commentary elaborates that "if the crime can be committed recklessly, it is no less committed if the actor acted purposely."[66]

This is not, however, to say that the Code's four terms of culpability necessarily overlap: that purpose somehow "includes," say, recklessness and negligence. To say that an act done purposely is also done recklessly is false to what it would mean to act purposely *or* recklessly. Someone whom you are accusing of being reckless is being criticized in a way that could never be established by proof that they were acting purposely. Inconsiderateness or inattentiveness or doing one thing when you should have been doing another are descriptions (or criticisms) of action that never come up when we think you did it purposely. To show that you acted purposely—that you were setting something up before yourself (if only just the next action)—is a far cry from showing your clumsiness or indifference or inattention. It is not that purposely inflicted harm is not worse than inadvertently inflicted harm—it is—but as terms of criticism, purpose, knowledge, recklessness, and negligence all are getting at something altogether different both in terms of what was done and in terms of revealing something about the doer apart from what was done. Indeed, that an act was done purposely *forecloses* on its recklessness rather than includes it.

Some aggravating terms are overlapping; some are not. For example, "you can't be intending to do a thing if you don't *know* you're doing it, or rather don't know how what you are doing could have that consequence (if you didn't know about the child, you can't have intended to frighten it)" ("MEANING IT," 233). In this way, intention (or what the Code calls "purpose") can be said to include knowledge as a basis of responsibility. Other aggravating terms that are commonly found in criminal laws may be overlapping, but are not necessarily overlapping; whether they overlap depends on the circumstances, not on the terms themselves. Austin demonstrates this by positing an action that could conceivably be done deliberately but not, oddly enough, purposely (or even intentionally):

> I am summoned to quell a riot in India. Speed is imperative. My mind runs on the action to be taken five miles down the road at the Residency. As I set off down the drive, my cookboy's child's new gocart, the apple of her eye, is right across the road. I realize I could stop, get out, and move it, but to hell with that: I must push on. It's too bad, that's all: I drive right over it and am on my way. In this case, a snap decision is taken on what is essentially an *incidental* matter. I did drive over the gocart deliberately, but not intentionally—nor, of course, unintentionally either. It was never part of my intention to drive over the gocart. It was incidental to anything I intended to do, which was simply to get to the scene of the riot in order to quell it ("INK," 278).

I have vivid memories of the difficulties that this passage (a version of the debtor-creditor scenario discussed above) always poses for my students and me. It really does cut sharply across the way lawyers tend to think about intentions. After all, how could someone deliberate over whether to do something, go ahead and do it, and then plead that it was somehow not done intentionally? Here it is important to remember that Austin emphasizes that the destruction of the gocart was not exactly *unintentional* either, since that description of the action has an air that suggests a slip or an accident. This was no accidental gocart-running-over. Austin merely means to establish that the deliberation here, the shall-I-or-shan't-I, must be assessed against its background—against a plan in which the gocart played no, or at most only an incidental, role. What he was doing (getting to the scene of the riot in order to quell it) did not include gocart-running-over, though, unlike the creditor who ruined the debtor, the riot-queller may have a hard time denying responsibility for the damage. (Perhaps he doesn't care to deny responsibility, since his explanation shades most definitely toward justification: the running over the gocart was incidental to a much more *important* project, which is why the question: intentional or unintentional leaves out the most relevant aspect of his story.) Was the cookboy's child "faintly improvident" in leaving the gocart "right across the road"? Austin does not say, though in the debtor-creditor example he shifted blame to the debtor for running up the debt in the first place. Was running over the gocart necessary to the realization of the riot-queller's intentions? Please recall that the creditor had "absolutely no wish to ruin [the debtor]"; but, he went on, "maybe if I don't get payment both I and others are going to suffer severely" ("INK," 278). Here, however, the riot-queller tells us "I realize I could stop, get out, and move it, but to hell with that: I must push on. It's too bad, that's all" ("INK," 278). The coldness of this account suggests that things could have been otherwise: that perhaps the gocart could have been preserved without compromising the mission. If things could not have been otherwise, then there is nothing *to deliberate*. If speed were absolutely essential, then the driver would run the gocart over without hesitation, but not at all deliberately. Even if things could have been otherwise, it is still quite possible that we would accept the plea that running over the gocart was incidental to or outside the plan of getting to the riot to quell it; we can still in such a case see that while he deliberated on the spot over whether to run it over, running it over was never part of the larger scheme of getting to the residency to quell the riot.

But if he could just as easily have realized his plan without running over the gocart, then he runs the risk that we may reject his plea that the running over of the gocart was an incidental. We would reject it if we found ourselves stumped by the question: why not go around the gocart if you just as easily could have without compromising the mission? In this sense, while the riot-quelling is a version of the debtor-creditor example—both illustrate that an action can be done deliberately but not necessarily intentionally—the debtor-creditor example is a clearer one in which the facts are rigged to make our letting the creditor off the hook easier than it may be for us to do in the case of the riot-queller. This distinction between the two examples—which Austin presents side by side in "Spilling Ink"—is not lost on Austin. Indeed, after the debtor-creditor scenario, which appears after the gocart scenario, he adds that the creditor "plainly" is not responsible for the debtor's ruin. No such claim is made of the riot-queller, and I hope I have touched on why we may (but not must) in the end treat these otherwise quite-similar cases differently. Both examples do in any event succeed in establishing that if we "structure" or "bracket" the action around the entire undertaking rather than zero in on one episode within that undertaking ("INK," 285), we may agree that neither the preservation nor destruction of the gocart was ever a part of his intention (of his plan): he had no stance at all toward the gocart in his plan to rush to the residency to quell the riot. Respond to him as you will; a deliberate destroyer of a perfectly good gocart may deserve to be treated identically to someone who did the same thing intentionally. But before determining whether our response to an action is identical regardless of its history (and if it is, that may be revealing about us), we should first know what it is that was done.

The payoff for closely addressing the meaning and operation of these accusatory or aggravating terms, therefore, is not to quibble about the criminal-law vocabulary. Rather, it is to bring out that treating those terms as necessarily overlapping impedes a confrontation with the excuse and thus with the excuse maker, too. That is, not seeing the richness of possible ways in which action can go wrong needlessly limits our ability to understand just what it was that was done—what went wrong—which is of course a precondition of our ever even *having* a response to the accused.

Indeed, I know I am in a small minority of academic lawyers when I say that the Model Penal Code has failed to live up to its intention to "dispel the obscurity with which the culpability requirement is often treated when such concepts as 'general criminal intent,' 'mens rea,' 'presumed intent,' 'malice,' 'wilfulness,' 'scienter' and the like have been employed."[67] Professor Kadish, to name only one of the leading criminal lawyers who thinks the Code is a major coup,[68] recently wrote:

> The Code's mens rea proposals dissipated these clouds of confusion with an astute and perspicuous analysis that has been adopted in many states and has infused thinking about mens rea everywhere. We have been taught to eschew the traditional epithetical and moralistic jurisprudence of mens rea. Instead, we now inquire whether the crime requires that the defendant have acted purposely, knowingly, recklessly, or negligently in doing the action prohibited. Moreover, when necessary, we may also have to ask as to each component of a described action—the action itself, the circumstances of its commission, its result—which of these culpable mental states is required.
>
> That is all old hat now, the standard stuff of the first-year criminal law class. But it was a breakthrough to articulate so lucidly and powerfully a conception of culpability requirements comprehending all crime definitions, and it has been transforming in its impact on the law and on legal

> education and scholarship. Not all developments in American criminal law are looked upon with envy by our colleagues in other common law jurisdictions—hardly!—but this is surely one.
>
> The Model Penal Code, then, taught us to think clearly about the mens rea elements of crime.[69]

Though Kadish may be right that the new way may be by now old hat, I worry that the Code has come closer to replicating the sins of the past than to correcting them. One blaring defect in the old way, the Code's drafters tell us, is that there were "some 76 different methods of stating the requisite mental element in . . . federal criminal statutes. . . ."[70] Moreover, they add, to the extent that there *was* a consistent approach to "mens rea" in the pre-Code Dark Ages, it was "such an abiding source of confusion and ambiguity in the penal law" that the drafters, followed by a host of state legislatures, were happy to abandon it.[71] These are two quite different sorts of gripes with the pre-Code state of affairs, neither of which the Code has done much to rectify.

THE CODE DRAFTERS' FIRST GRIPE: TOO MANY MODIFIERS

The first gripe—that federal prosecutions used seventy-six different modifiers to describe the way actions are performed—implies that action is not susceptible to being described in seventy-six different ways. Four is plenty. Terms like maliciously, corruptly, wilfully, and deliberately apparently had survived for no good reason. Evidently the Code drafters did not take Austin seriously when he noted that "our common stock of words embodies all the distinctions men have found worth drawing, and the connexions they have found worth making, in the lifetimes of many generations" ("EXCUSES," 182). The drafters never go so far as to say that all modifiers other than purposely, knowingly, recklessly, and negligently are meaningless, precious, or redundant of the Code's four terms, though they do say that such variation in the way actions were described was confusing. But because actions are performed and go wrong in a wide range of ways, they excite a wide range of elaborations. Why compress the vocabulary if to do so threatens to distort or blunt our understanding of and response to what an accused has done? Where will that get us in our quest to come to grips with who is answerable for what and to what extent?

Take just one of the dozens of modifiers that the Code eliminated, "deliberately." As I quoted earlier, "I act *deliberately* when I have deliberated—which means when I have stopped to ask myself, 'Shall I or shan't I?' and then decided to do *X*, which I did. That is to say, I weighed up, in however rudimentary a fashion, the pros and cons. And it is understood that there must be some cons" ("INK," 286). It is thus quite possible, even common, that an action be done intentionally—even purposely—but not deliberately: "We walk along a cliff, and I feel a sudden impulse to push you over, and may even have devised a little ruse to achieve it: yet even then I did not act deliberately, for I did not (stop to) ask myself whether to do it or not" ("EXCUSES," 195).[72] And it is not just *any* kind of prior thinking that counts as deliberation. I may deliberate over moral pros and cons (or may not) or over what course of action I think is best or has most reasons recommending it. Indeed, thinking about ways and means may demonstrate forethought or premeditation, but not necessarily deliberation, which is a matter of decision (of whether to perform the action at all) not of planning (of how and when to perform the action) ("INK," 286). "That there should be slowness in moving into action or conducting it (so much relied on by lawyers) is the merest symptom [of deliberation]" ("INK," 286).

Nonetheless, while the Code's drafters have eliminated "graded" murder, that is, they no longer divide murder into first- and second-degree, the change was not for clarity. Instead, the change was to debunk the "premise that there exists some dependable relation between the duration of the reflection and the gravity of the offense."[73] The drafters saw no point in separating out killers who plan ahead from killers who act on impulse. The drafters justify the change on the ground that someone with the "tortured conscience" of a "mercy killer" can deliberate and still deserve milder punishment than a hothead who kills impulsively—even spontaneously—while doing something else, such as committing a felony like arson or rape.[74] Consequently, the Code has only one kind of murder, which covers all killings that cannot be fully or partially excused on grounds of accident, "extreme emotional disturbance," or some other extant excuse.

Something has gone wrong here. To begin with, the essence of a first-degree murder, whether it be described as the product of "a sedate deliberate mind and formed design"[75] or as a "wilful, deliberate, premeditated" killing,[76] is not "the duration of the reflection" (which is for Austin at best evidentiary), but the quality of it. A deliberate killer may suffer from "a tortured conscience," but for that very reason he poses a real problem to the world because he thinks about *whether* to kill; one might say that deliberate killers are sincere, that is, they are prepared to stand by later what they do now.[77] Killers who do not deliberate may plot their killings, but can do so without confronting the pros and cons, without, that is, choosing killing over not killing. A mercy killer (who may or may not think about whether to kill) may have a tortured conscience, but he has his own reasons for killing: reasons that supervene law. Mercy killers are moral actors; but so was anti-abortion fanatic Paul Hill, who claimed to be justified in killing a Pensacola, Florida "abortionist," who was about to "murder" unquickened fetuses.[78] Assessing what someone like Paul Hill deserves is not and never was a problem that depends on how much time he took before killing.

I do not mean to even hint that our attempts to interpret what constitutes a "wilful, deliberate, premeditated" killing cannot and do not go wrong. Far from it.[79] I mean only that economizing on the criminal-law vocabulary—on the vocabulary of responsibility—threatens to compress our ability to understand differences in what has been done and thus threatens to compress as well our ability to respond to who has done it. If deliberately performed actions (actions performed after deliberation) are not covered by the Code's four "culpability terms," then what we lose our grip on is not merely words or meanings, but more importantly, what those words are meant to provide: a sharpened perception of what has happened and perhaps some confidence in how to respond to it.

THE CODE DRAFTERS' SECOND GRIPE: WHAT'S AN INTENTION?

The second gripe that the Code's drafters raised is that to the extent that there *was* a consistent approach to "mens rea" in the pre-Code Dark Ages, it was "such an abiding source of confusion and ambiguity in the penal law" that wholesale reformation was in order. That approach, which remains the law in California, among other places, recognizes three, not four, classifications of criminal actions: those done with 1) negligence; 2) specific intent; and 3) general intent. Negligence—the failure to act reasonably under the circumstances—has never been a source of much difficulty, given law's familiarity with the concept in tort. Specific intent has certainly caused its share of confusion and ambiguity.[80] Two quite distinct, alternative notions of specific intent pervade. The first is "vertical," meaning that specific intent is located at the top of a hierarchy of fault, above knowledge, recklessness, and negligence. On this account, specific intent is that mode of action that the Model Penal Code identifies with its peculiar notion of purpose. That is, an action is done with specific intent when the actor puts himself to the task, including the outcome, that is carried out or realized. The second notion of specific intent is "horizontal" or temporal, meaning that one act (now), say, entering a building, is done with the specific intention of accomplishing something else in the future, say, stealing.[81] That the unjustified entry is done with an eye toward the future act or consequence of stealing is what makes the crime of burglary a "specific intent crime."

Like specific intent, general intent, too, was and remains a troubling notion for reviewing courts.[82] Troubling or not, the definition of general intent that the drafters quote sounds anything but foreign to their sensibilities:

> General criminal intent is present whenever there is specific intent, and also when the circumstances indicate that the offender, in the ordinary course of human experience, must have adverted to the prescribed criminal consequences as reasonably certain to result from his act or failure to act.[83]

This rolls into one the Code's formulations of purpose, knowledge, and recklessness. It is what common-law courts have for at least a century been equating with "malice."[84] If the Code's having segmented the notion of malice or general intent into purpose, knowledge, and recklessness is its virtue, then its vice is that it continued to condition liability on a notion of decision or choice that is incompatible with the way most untoward actions are performed.

Both the Code and pre-Code formulations *are* on to something crucial to the conditions of responsibility: that you have some idea of what you are doing—that you see far enough ahead to appreciate the implications of your actions. Austin likens this condition of responsibility to "a miner's lamp on our forehead which illuminates always just so far ahead as we go along" ("INK," 284).[85] Despite the good intuitions of the Code and pre-Code formulations in this regard, it is worth noting that Austin cautions that the lamp does not illuminate very well or far, since the circumstances of human action dictate that even when we take care, much remains outside of or incidental to our intentions.[86]

Kadish and Schulhofer present an excellent example of Austin's notion of the incidental in an excerpt from a British case:

> In fact people often intend something quite different from what they know to be the natural and probable result of what they are doing. To take a trivial example, if I say I intend to reach the green, people will believe me although we all know that the odds are ten to one against my succeeding; and no one but a lawyer would say that I must be presumed to have intended to put my ball in the bunker because that was the natural and probable result of my shot.[87]

Here we could say that the golfer had general not specific intent to hit the ball in the bunker; or, in the Code's terminology, the golfer was reckless to the bunker-as-destination. Both accounts (general intent and recklessness) conclude that a golfer who is aware of what can go wrong is responsible for the errant shot in a way that he would not be if he had no idea that the shot could land in the trap. If this is so, then what difference does it make whether we use the Code or pre-Code formulation so long as they get us to the right questions about responsibility? Either formulation asks: what was illuminated by the "miner's lamp"? What, other than the green, was accounted for in planning or executing the shot? The nearby sand trap, pond, trees? It is not as though one could ignore those hazards—those incidentals—and still be *playing* the hole, unless he were playing for the first time and had no idea how hard it was to hit the green. If these incidentals were outside the golfer's consciousness, then what do we do? What is our response? It is my understanding that the golfer lacks mens rea under *any* formulation. So does this mean we should not criticize the action because its consequences were not "chosen?"

I admit to being surprised by the staying power of decision or choice (of knowledge) in accounts of why the criminal law so strongly resists punishing the accident that is "negligent" but not "reckless." As Bernard Williams has summarized, "the idea of the voluntary is essentially superficial."[88] Superficial, he adds, to the extent that such a view of responsibility depends *uniquely* on "the product of the will."[89] Williams is right: the burden of action, of being equal to the consequences of our actions, must extend beyond the "voluntary," given that our victims are no less injured by our clumsiness than by our anger.[90] Accordingly, there is nothing about Watson's drunk-driving or the golfer's errant shot that suggests that either is an instance of non-responsibility. Sometimes "accident" is a sufficient plea; sometimes it is not. And whether accident is a plea that gets us off the hook is often only remotely related to whether we have "adverted to the prescribed criminal consequences" or "consciously disregarded a substantial and unjustifiable risk." Instead, the force of the plea has mostly to do with the background of the action: whether the accused was doing one thing when he should have been doing another; whether he knows better (generally) or had been warned (specifically); or whether he lived up to the standards we expect in such circumstances. In other words, the realm of responsible action is not so much a problem of predicating criminality on knowledge—let's take it as a given that knowledge is indeed a condition of criminal responsibility—but on identifying what we will *count* as knowledge.

Again, while the Code and pre-Code approaches both see responsibility as a matter of the responsible agent's decision or choice (his knowledge, in its most specific sense), the ordinary, infelicitous action does not follow a selection from among alternatives. Would we not be better off asking: *why* the other hazards (the incidentals) were not seen by the golfer? What types of precautions *was* he taking; that is, what *was* he was doing if not taking certain unhappy outcomes into account? Has the golfer plunked a similar shot in this trap before? If so, has he been practicing since? Adjusted his swing? His stance? Whether he appreciated all the incidentals of what he was doing *is* of great concern to us. But even when the actor is distracted or inattentive and fails to appreciate what risks are staked, that will not always be excusable, given that the standards for what we count as acceptable depend on the circumstances. ("We may plead that we trod on the snail inadvertently: but not on a baby—you ought to be looking where you are putting your great feet" ("EXCUSES," 194), although the "mental state" may be exactly the same in both instances.)

By criticizing the conventional view of responsibility, one which is based on mens rea, I am not arguing that more people should be convicted (or that they should not). Because "we are not, after all, quasi-infallible beings" (*S&S*, 52), liability without fault[91] is anathema in criminal law.[92] If the defendant is taking cost-justified precautions, then criminalizing an unhappy outcome may not be scapegoating, but it comes close. While this much seems unremarkable, Professor Mark Kelman has written that "[i]t may well be the case that if one looks only at the precise *moment* at which harm is consummated, the strictly liable actor may seem powerless to avoid criminality, but it is invariably the case that the actor could have avoided liability by taking earlier steps which were hardly impossible."[93] To demonstrate his thesis, which holds that negligence is fairer to defendants but almost as likely to yield convictions as liability without fault, Kelman analyzes

> the familiar problem of "reasonable" (non-negligent) mistakes as to the victim's age in the statutory rape setting. Is one's view of a "reasonable" belief to be ascertained solely by reference to perceptions available to defendant during the purportedly illegal seduction (she "*looked*" sixteen or "she told me she was sixteen"), or does one require that some checks prior to seduction be taken, such as checking birth certificates or asking parents? . . . [I]t is hardly conceivable that a defendant ought to attract serious sympathy as someone unable to avoid crime when he has certainly had the opportunity to check on the legal appropriateness of his companion as an object of sexual desire.[94]

The implication of Kelman's thesis is that it is always negligent to harm anyone; *all* harm is the product of an unacceptably low amount of precaution. Under Kelman's view, which he rightly calls "unorthodox," there is no such thing as an excusable mistake or accident.[95] This is precisely the sort of stingy notion of accidents that I earlier described as under-inclusive,[96] that is, a notion that recognizes far too few harms to be the result of accidents. "I didn't mean it" or "oops!" will never be good enough under Kelman's view because if we study the history of the event closely enough, we will invariably find evidence of the defendant's failure to pay (enough) attention.[97]

True: if we are *looking for* fallibility, we will be sure to find it. After the fact, it is altogether too easy and tempting for us to say "you ought to have paid particular heed here." Kelman's where-there's-harm-there's-foul theory threatens to make human action intolerable by refusing to acknowledge fallibility-as-excuse, though his theory certainly is the reverse of a superficial view of responsibility. To my mind the answer lies somewhere in between the skepticism and superficiality of a notion of responsibility that is based on decision or choice (on knowledge in its most specific sense) and the harshness of *ex post* refusals to acknowledge human fallibility. In between, I would hope, is a place where the excuses can be proffered free both from the sway of mens rea (of skepticism) and from a too-unforgiving ("you ought to have paid particular heed here") standard of the acceptable.

The law must reflect that "we are not . . . quasi-infallible" (*S&S*, 52). Cavell puts it this way:

> [T]here are many (specific) ways in which an action can go wrong (at least as many as the myriad excuses we are entitled to proffer when what we have done has resulted in some unhappiness); but it would be incorrect to suppose that we are *obligated* to see to it (to take precautions to ensure), *whenever* we undertake to do anything, that none of these ways will come to pass. Our obligation is to avoid doing something at a time and place or in a way which is *likely* to result in some misfortune, or to avoid being careless where it is easy to be, or to be *especially* careful where the action is dangerous or delicate, or avoid the temptation to skip a necessary step when it seems in the moment to make little difference. If for *all* excuses there were relevant obligations, then there would be no excuses and action would become intolerable. Any *particular* excuse may be countered with a *specific* obligation; not even the best excuse will always get you off the hook (That is no excuse; you should have known that was likely to result in an accident, you ought to have paid particular heed here, etc.). . . .
>
> [A] statement of what we *must* do (or say) has point only in the context (against the background) of knowledge that we are in fact doing (or saying) a thing, but doing (saying) it—or running a definite risk of doing or saying it—badly, inappropriately, thoughtlessly, tactlessly, self-defeatingly, etc.; or against the background of knowledge that we are in a certain position or occupy a certain office or station, and are *behaving* or *conducting ourselves* inappropriately, thoughtlessly, self-defeatingly. . . . ("MWM," 26–27).

Cavell is explicating the burden of action, which would be paralyzing were we expected to be quasi-infallible. As for what counts for knowledge in Cavell's scheme of responsibility, it is hard to tell from this passage. Is it sufficient that the background of knowledge he alludes to here is general (i.e., drunk driving is a dangerous activity)? Or must it be specific (i.e., *this* drunk driving poses a risk, *now*, to others)? While we know that the criminal law endorses the specific, contemporaneous mode of knowing (though even this is by no means clear), Cavell elsewhere intimates what this background of knowledge must include when he says that "[c]ertainly one can know a thing without bearing it in mind (fortunately—otherwise there wouldn't be room for much), or having it occur to you at regular intervals" ("MEANING IT," 233).

This more generalized mode of knowing provides a happier middle position between what I've been describing as the superficial and the intolerable. It acknowledges that much of what we are responsible for outstrips what we anticipate; to say otherwise reduces responsibility to a superficial concept. Yet at the same time, we must be able to avoid being held responsible for some harms that were indeed avoidable; to say otherwise stifles the excuses, and so, makes action intolerable. In sum, the problem of knowledge *is* the problem of mens rea. Criminal law conditions blame on the notion that those who have no idea what is staked when they act should not be criticized, or at least not in the same way as those who know what they are doing. But what does it mean to "know what you are doing?" Criminal law insists on a decision- or choice-based notion of knowing, which reserves blame for those who "adverted to the prescribed criminal consequences" or "consciously disregarded a substantial and unjustifiable risk." There may be good reasons—political reasons—for doing so,[98] but such a view of action is nonetheless false to our relation to our own actions and their "consequences, concomitants, upshots, effects, results, and so forth" (*A PITCH*, 233).

Excusing Mistakes

If what you did was by accident, then you are not to be blamed—at least not as severely as if you deliberately did it. That accident and blame are incompatible is a position about which there is much agreement.[99] But what about someone who makes a mistake? How good an excuse is that?

Our interest in mistakes, like our interest in all excuses, is in understanding what has gone wrong with an action in order to limit someone's responsibility for it ("MEANING IT," 236). A mistake involves the idea of a wrong alternative—either taking one thing for another, or taking one tack rather than another ("CRITICISM," 107). While with accidents something befalls (e.g., "I didn't mean to shoot the donkey—any donkey"), with mistakes you take the wrong one (e.g., "I meant to shoot that donkey, but thought it was mine, not yours") ("EXCUSES," 185 n.1, 200 n.1, 201–2). When you make a mistake you mean to do exactly what you do; it is just that you misinterpret your situation: you take someone else's property for your own, a minor for an adult, silence for consent, a harmless prank for a deadly threat.

The criminal law's response to mistakes is even bumpier than it is to accidents. While accidents almost always excuse,[100] mistakes operate something like this: mistakes of fact always excuse the defendant unless the legislature intended otherwise, which it can do only if the punishment for the offense is mild or the offense is not a pre-legal (*malum in se*) wrong.[101] In other words, when someone is accused of doing something a good person would not do, the accused must be given a chance to elaborate the factual background against which the act occurred. Thus an accusation of being a common thief (an instance of a pre-legal wrong)[102] or of anything involving a lengthy prison sentence (a proxy for a pre-legal wrong)[103] obligates a court to hear the accused's story about how the action misfired. Even then, whether a mistake will function as an excuse also depends not only on its subject matter (i.e., mistakes of fact count; mistakes of law do not)[104] but on the type of accusation (i.e., a general-intent crime as opposed to a specific-intent one), which in turn determines the quality of mistake (i.e., reasonable as opposed to unreasonable) that will let the accused off the hook.

This may not be the whole story, but it is enough of it to let me begin to establish that with mistakes the problem should not be deciding whether they should *count* as excuses (how could they not?), but rather, in identifying their criteria. The excuse of mistake should not depend on distinctions between fact and law, general and specific intent, or the reasonableness and unreasonableness of the mistake. These distinctions only deflect attention from what mistakes are to when we should acknowledge them or to whether the excuse-maker is a liar.

It is my position that mistake should always be an excuse. Paying closer attention to the criteria of mistakes—to whether law's use of the term conforms with its deployment in ordinary speech—should reveal that many actions that are passed off as mistakes really are not mistakes at all. I say this not because the putatively mistaken actor in those cases is a liar (I will assume he or she is not), but because what went wrong with the action is something *other* than its being traceable to a mistake. If we know what a mistake is—a misfired action performed by someone with the competence and commitment to get it right—then there should be nothing left for us to do *but* excuse. "We are not, after all, quasi-infallible beings, who can be taken in only where the avoidance of mistake is completely impossible" (*S&S*, 52).

Mistakes of Fact

EXCULPATORY MISTAKES

In *Regina v. Morgan*,[105] four members of the Royal Air Force participated in the rape of William Morgan's wife, Daphne. Morgan assured his three confederates that his wife would feign resistance as a cover-up for her kinky desire to be violated.[106] Since Morgan's liability as accomplice depended on their liability as principal rapists, the court initially examined whether the confederates had in actuality raped Ms. Morgan. Whether a woman consents to intercourse is considered a factual question, which is another way of saying that the excuse of mistake-as-to-consent does operate in rape cases. Although the trial court's conviction of all four men was upheld on appeal,[107] the House of Lords on further review held that the jury had been improperly instructed, given that under English law a mistake negated the intent to commit rape, even if the man's belief in the woman's consent was unreasonable.[108]

Morgan continues to reflect how the law of mistakes operates in the United States as well, not so much with the law of rape[109] as with specific-intent offenses[110] such as theft[111] and attempt[112] as well as some homicides[113] and civil-rights offenses.[114] Those laws hold that so-called honest mistakes demand acquittal if the jury accepts the defendant's belief *as* defendant's, however stupid, self-absorbed, or out of touch the defendant may be to so believe.[115] A defendant charged with a specific-intent crime therefore may be convicted only if his claim of mistake of fact is rejected and taken as a lie.

Unfortunately, courts are prone to this sort of analysis, which holds that when charged with a specific-intent crime, any relevant belief, however misguided on the part of the accused, is a mistake and as such a complete defense to liability. The courts' move in such situations tends to be to deny that the belief was held, not that the belief *even if held* does not necessarily constitute a mistake.[116] And nothing in the Model Penal Code's reforms makes such an approach any less likely.[117] To be sure, any law that is responsible for *Morgan* gives mistakes a bad name. While no one intentionally commits rape if he is mistaken as to what the woman wants, Morgan's confederates did not make a mistake about anything. And I am not suggesting that they were lying. That is the conventional criticism of the problem posed by "honest but unreasonable mistakes": allowing such pleas encourages conniving ("Believe it or not it's what I believed. And no one can tell me what I believed!").[118]

That sort of analysis of "honest but unreasonable mistakes," however, threatens to make the excuse (indeed, the entire notion of responsibility) *merely psychological*, that is, an internal phenomenon rather than something that occurs, is elaborated, and responded to in the world. The notion that mistakes are internal or "subjective" matters was indicated when just after *Morgan*, "[l]etters were written to newspapers complaining that no man could now be successfully prosecuted for rape; all he had to do was to 'persuade himself' that he believed the woman consented."[119] He doesn't, however, have to persuade merely himself; he must persuade others, too: those who sit in judgment. Whether a mistake occurs is not a matter for psychology, but for morality, that is, for the process of questioning others' intentions and demanding that they go on record by telling us what exactly they were doing (if not, say, raping), an account that we will accept or reject.

The defendant may or may not be lying. But ultimately it does not matter whether defendants whose "mistakes" are "honest but unreasonable" are lying (again, I will assume they are not) because they are not in any event *mistaken* about anything. Again, a mistake is taking one thing for another or taking one tack rather than another: you take dark navy for black or someone else's wood-handled umbrella for your own. Mistakes have their own criteria, which *cannot* include the realm of the honest but unreasonable. For example, Goetz was not mistaken that the four unarmed youths on the Bronx subway train were about to, as he put it, "maim" him.[120] Please recall that he 1) knew they were unarmed; 2) had not been threatened by them; 3) had warded off danger successfully in the past by drawing his concealed gun on aggressors; and 4) stalked the youths long after he had negated whatever threat he imagined he faced.[121] Although the jury acquitted Goetz of attempted murder, had the seriously injured youths died, it "is common in American jurisdictions" (though evidently not in New York)[122] that an honest-but-unreasonable belief that deadly force is in order reduces murder to manslaughter by calling the self-defense "imperfect."[123] In those jurisdictions, manslaughter would have been the appropriate charge if Goetz believed he was going to be maimed, however paranoid that belief might have been.[124] An act performed in self-defense would remain "perfect," however, not just when self-defense really *is* in order to repel an attack, but even when it is not, so long as the killer is reasonable in mistaking the situation for one that calls for deadly force.[125]

But what would it mean for Goetz to "believe" that those youths were out to get him? What would be the foundation for such a belief? Racism (i.e., a stake in their malevolence)? A prior mugging (like having been bitten by a dog)? Suppose he killed the youths and then was charged with murder, which his home state defines as a killing done "[w]ith intent to cause the death of another person."[126] If Goetz then defended that he genuinely believed that African-Americans are not persons, would not that negate his intent to kill another person? So if Goetz put on evidence of his adherence to the tenets of "polygenesis," a Civil War-era doctrine positing the subhumanity of African-Americans,[127] it seems then we would have no choice but to acquit him of murder, were we to believe his beliefs really to be his.

But that *cannot* be the law. The snag here is the so-called honest but unreasonable mistake, which in this case is to my mind not a mistake at all but either a pernicious *theory* about reality, or a fantasy: an instance where there is not even the appearance of things being the way the "mistaken" party claims them to be. If what Goetz was in possession of was a certain pernicious theory about African-Americans that manifested itself on the train that day, then he was not mistaken that his life was in danger because what he was missing was not a piece of information. One may say (as Cavell does of Othello) (*CR*, 484), that Goetz's failure was not one of knowledge: everything we know about the innocence of those four boys, he knew, too. Indeed, if we were there on that train with Goetz, what could we tell him to correct him or bring him out of it (as we would a child who is frightened by a play)? Tell him that they are just kids fooling around? But he already knows that. His failure, I am suggesting, is worse than a blank. It is a denial—a repudiation of what he already knows but cannot acknowledge. In other words, if mistakes occur when we are missing a crucial piece of information, Goetz was missing none. Again, what led him astray might well have been a certain theory about African-Americans. If so, then what went wrong was not the product of a mistake.

One could just as readily call this pernicious theory a delusion, but it was no mistake. As Austin has put it, illusions can be the basis of mistakes; delusions cannot. Examples of illusions could include when a ventriloquist's dummy appears to be talking, people who have limbs amputated still continue to feel pain in them, or a stick that normally appears straight looks bent when it is seen in water (*S&S*, 20–23). In these instances it is not that something totally unreal is conjured up. That would be a delusion, as in a delusion of persecution or grandeur (*S&S*, 20–23). Because delusions are completely without foundation, they are a much more serious matter—something is really wrong, *wrong with the person who has them*. There is nothing wrong with me personally when I fall for an optical illusion; it is public, anyone can see it, and we can develop procedures for producing and testing it. Furthermore, if we are not actually to be taken in, we need to be on our guard; *but it is no use to tell the sufferer from delusions to be on his guard*. He needs to be cured (*S&S*, 20–32).

This is not to say that there will be no hard cases once we separate the excuse of mistake from the excuse of delusion. For example, ghosts may be conjured up in the mind (delusion) or they may be just a giving-in to shadows, reflections, or a trick of the light (illusion) (*S&S*, 24). So too can we fairly characterize a mirage as invented by the crazed brain of a thirsty and exhausted traveler or as an instance of atmospheric refraction whereby something below the horizon appears to be above it (*S&S*, 24–25).

Most cases, however, are not so hard. Take Morgan's. Our response to his three confederates would be: "What made you believe *that*?" Ms. Morgan strenuously resisted the advances of the men, but was eventually overcome and carried, kicking and screaming, into the bedroom. There all three strangers had forcible intercourse with her, despite her repeated efforts to escape, even by screaming "Police!" to her eleven-year-old son, who slept in an adjoining room.[128] So why did the men rely so heavily on Mr. Morgan? Because he was "significantly older than the other three, and considerably senior to them in rank"?[129] Because they were strangers to the couple and thus misread both husband and wife[130] (a misreading worsened by alcohol)?[131] Because Morgan had supplied each of the younger men with contraceptive sheaths?[132] Because after "some degree of struggle"[133] Ms. Morgan seemed to "enjoy[] what was being done"?[134] Will any of that, alone or together, pass for argument?

That depends on standards:

> It is characteristic of excuses to be "unacceptable": given . . . almost any excuse, there will be cases of such a kind or of such gravity that "we will not accept" it. . . . The extent of supervision we exercise over the execution of any act can never be quite unlimited, and is usually expected to fall

> within fairly definite limits . . . though of course we set very different limits in very different cases. We may plead that we trod on a snail inadvertently: but not on a baby—you ought to look where you are putting your great feet. Of course it *was really*, if you like, inadvertence: but that word constitutes a plea, which is not going to be allowed, because of standards. And if you try it on, you will be subscribing to such dreadful standards that your last state will be worse than your first ("EXCUSES," 194–95).

Morgan's confederates could in our estimation be worse off for *saying* they were mistaken in that setting. That is, by pleading mistake, their "last state will be worse than [their] first." Because of standards (a baby cannot be trod on as casually as a snail), their entering an incompetent plea can make them worse off because our reaction may be to criticize them for failing to even know the stakes embedded in the setting that made their so-called mistake possible. When the intactness of Ms. Morgan's "giving and receiving self"[135] was staked, relying solely on the (too) fishy recommendations of the husband—*even if they really did believe him*—is not an instance of mistake.

This is true in the same sense that you cannot "inadvertently" tread on a baby. Not because you didn't really fail to see the baby, but because of standards: there is a limit beyond which claims of inadvertence or mistake will not be possible, even though the "internal state" of the actor is identical to cases where the pleas are allowed. There is a substantive moral limit on our ability to parlay our various mental states into the relevant excuses. As the snail/baby example reveals, it is the *stakes* that constitute the limit in each case.

It bears repeating that the Model Penal Code, too, criticizes "unreasonable mistakes," but not on the ground that they are something other than mistakes, but because they are "reckless" or "negligent" mistakes.[136] Under the Code, Goetz, for example, commits manslaughter or negligent homicide if he were to kill under a belief that was badly formed or arrived at. In other words, actions that misfire because they are based on faulty, poorly formed beliefs are only partially excused under the Code.[137] The residue of the action—that which is not excused—is a criticism of the belief itself. The Code does not deny that "unreasonable mistakes" are mistakes; it is just that they are mistakes that fail to make the same claim on us as reasonable mistakes do because we find the mistake itself to be subject to criticism rather than acknowledgment. Yet I reiterate that while the Code is consistent in its position that faulty, poorly formed (negligent or reckless) beliefs about the need for deadly force are "unreasonable mistakes" subject to partial excuse, it is revealing that none of the pertinent text or commentary contains a single example of such a situation.[138] I am inclined, therefore, to think we would be better off eliminating altogether the notion of the merely "honest" mistake—not because it is a lie (which it may or may not be)—but because it is more closely aligned with excuses (provocation, diminished capacity), if any, whose criteria are remote from those of mistakes.

INCULPATORY MISTAKES

Attention to the criteria of mistakes also could inform the way criminal law looks at so-called impossible attempts. Criminal attempts are punishable despite the fact that the intended harm is "unconsummated."[139] Although the intended crime fails because in one way or another the attempter gets caught before he can pull off the crime, the attempter remains partially on the hook, though less than if he had succeeded. Failure, accordingly, is a partial excuse. Attempts are said to be "impossible" when a criminal's efforts fail due to factors *apart from* his having gotten caught. That is, an attempt is impossible when the means selected for its execution are so shabby that we could have predicted the failure of the criminal effort *ex ante*.[140]

For example, a thief cannot pick an empty pocket. But if the thief does not know that the pocket is empty, does that mean he has not attempted theft? No. While theft in such a case could be *said* to be impossible from the outset, the would-be thief is still punishable for attempted theft.[141] Next time, the argument runs, he may figure out who has money and who does not. Thus for deterrence purposes he should this time be only partially excused. But what if someone intends to commit murder or rape, but fails because his victim is already dead[142] or is sleeping in another room when the "murderer" shoots a pillow, taking it for his roommate?[143] And what about someone who intends to take a deer out of season, but the deer is just a stuffed decoy?[144]

With the crime (or partial excuse) of attempt, in each case the question is whether the defendant is *trying* to commit (what really is) a crime. If so, then his failure—which tells us nothing redeeming about him—should be something for which he deserves only partial credit: bad intention; lucky result. If he *meant* to shoot or rape a dead person (not a live one), shoot a pillow (and not his roommate), or take a stuffed deer (not a real one), then he is not *attempting* anything. He *is* shooting or violating a corpse, shooting a pillow, or taking a stuffed deer, actions whose criminality, if any, has nothing at all to do with rape, murder, or preservation of deer from overzealous hunters.

Even if the defendant owns up to having tried to commit what really is a crime, there must be some instances in which he still should be let completely off the hook, if only because of the limits of the grammar of what it means "to try." It is possible that these would-be thieves, rapists, murderers, and lawless hunters go about things in such an unlikely way as to make their failure not merely inevitable,[145] but even worse, the product of fantasy or delusion, *not* mistake. Such "attempters" should give us deep doubt about whether they really did intend to commit a crime or take the requisite "substantial step"[146] toward its completion. They very well may be in need of some sort of reprogramming or warehousing, but they are not to be dealt with in the same way that we deal with fully responsible agents.

For example, what are the conditions under which someone could think that a decoy deer is a real one? A convincing decoy deer in the woods staged there by the game-warden should give us no trouble convicting someone who shoots at it of attempting to take a deer out of season:

> The State's evidence shows that conservation agents, about two weeks before the alleged offense, had procured the hide of a 2½ year old doe which had been killed by an automobile in Pulaski County. They had taken it to a taxidermist, who soaked it to soften it, stuffed it with excelsior and boards, inserted rods in the legs so it would stand upright and used the doe's skull in the head part of the hide so it would hold its former shape. For eyes, which had not been preserved, two small circular pieces of scotchlight reflector tape of a "white to amber color," had been placed over the eyeless sockets.[147]

But move the decoy deer to the end of a grocery store aisle or any other place where deer are unlikely to appear, or lower the quality of the decoy (so that it really *looks* like a decoy) and a conviction of attempt becomes manifestly absurd.

As for shooting a pillow, we would need thorough knowledge of the episode: did the would-be killer really think his roommate looked like a pillow? That again would be absurd. But if the lucky roommate had left his bedding carefully arranged like Clint Eastwood did to mask his late-night prison escape in the 1979 film *Escape from Alcatraz*, then thinking that one could murder by shooting into the bedding *would* be a mistake and thus an instance of attempted murder.

Though there is little attention to the matter of the so-called impossible attempt in Austin's written work, Pitcher reports that in the last meeting of Austin's seminar at Harvard, Austin posed to the class: "if a man hacks away with an axe at a pile of logs under the bedclothes, thinking it to be a man in his bed, isn't this attempted murder, despite the fact that the courts hold that it is not?"[148] Though I have no reason to doubt Pitcher's memory, without more than a (rhetorical?) question of Austin's to go by, I cannot imagine how Austin would have fit this peculiar action—on these barest of facts posed in the hypothetical—into the grammar of attempt. It sounds to me, well, distinctly un-Austinian, even though it is hard to glean a position from the following passage from "A Plea for Excuses." In it, Austin criticizes a judge whose instructions to the jury make the defendant/prisoner, "by contrast, stand . . . out as an evident master of the Queen's English" ("EXCUSES," 197):

> Not but what he probably manages to convey his meaning somehow or other. Judges seem to acquire a knack of conveying meaning, and even carrying conviction, through the use of a pithy Anglo-Saxon which sometimes has literally no meaning at all. Wishing to distinguish the case of shooting at a post in the belief that it was an enemy, as *not* an "attempt," from the case of picking an empty pocket in the belief that money was in it, which *is* an "attempt" the judge explains that in shooting at the post "*the man is never on the thing at all*" ("EXCUSES," 197 n.1, emphasis mine).

Austin is right: the expression may be meaningless at the literal level, but the judge does manage to get his point across somehow. What would make the man take a post for an enemy, anyway? Unless there were good grounds for taking the one for the other, then the man really "is never on the thing at all." The "thing" here refers to the completed action: the shooting of an enemy. It is never really threatened (he is never really "on" it)—not by *this* actor. His means (shooting at a post) are so poorly selected for the ends at which they are directed (shooting a man) that success is too unlikely from the get-go to treat the project as a (serious) attempt. There is something wrong with him, not with what he saw; he is not missing a bit of information, but much more seriously, he is at odds with reality. Before we could consider this shooting as an attempt at taking an enemy's life, we would need to learn much more about the background of the incident, much more than the stick-figure sort of sketch that Austin himself—a lover of facts—eschews. Only then could we be in a position to say that the man had a basis for taking the post for an enemy; only then could we be in a position to say that he shot at the post "by mistake."

And what would be the conditions under which one could take a dead person for a live one? They are narrow indeed, such as when the would-be killer shoots the victim immediately after he has been shot by someone else without verifying whether any signs of life remain.[149] But how, exactly, could someone *try* to rape a corpse? Raping a corpse is a perversion, but quite apart from anything like real rape. In fact, someone who violates a corpse very likely does so *because* the person is dead ("and I will kill thee, / And love thee after").[150] Such an action should excite some response from us, but not the same response we would make to someone who has put himself to the crime of rape and failed due to, say, impotence or resistance on the survivor's part.

The distinction I draw here between failing because something goes wrong with the criminal plan (a partial excuse) and failing because something is wrong with the criminal himself (potentially a complete, partial, or nonexcuse) may be what the Model Penal Code means when it says that attempt law should not punish someone who fails to demonstrate sufficient "dangerousness."[151] I am not by any means suggesting that the "something wrong with the criminal" is necessarily a case of psychosis or any other indicia of legal insanity, just that it is *not* a case of mistake. I take it that persons whom I have been calling "delusional" the Code could call "nondangerous." But they *are* dangerous. Anyone out of touch enough to take (just any) old pillow for a person is or at least can be dangerous.[152]

This is not to say that the criteria of mistakes are satisfied once we have ruled out instances of delusion or fantasy (or warped theories). In some instances when we are tempted to reject the excuse of mistake, neither a mistake nor a fantasy has occurred. Austin adumbrates such an instance when he speaks of a soldier who hears the order "'Right turn'" and then turns left ("EXCUSES," 200 n. 1). If the soldier does not even know left from right or was not paying attention to the order, then the wrong turn may or may not be excusable, but it is not excusable on grounds of mistake ("EXCUSES," 200 n. 1).

Although Austin does not elaborate, I think what he is getting at is this: a mistake can be made only by someone with the competence and commitment to have done otherwise, that is, by someone who could have and tried to get it right but did not. Someone who cannot get it right (except randomly) or does not care about getting it right is not mistaken when the action misfires. For example, if you tell me "fetch my umbrella," and upon seeing several similar ones in the designated area I grab one (just any old one), I am not mistaken if it turns out to be someone else's. First, in order for me to fetch the wrong umbrella by mistake, I would have to have a reason to know which one is yours. If I am merely guessing, then mistake drops out as a description of what has gone wrong. Indeed, it would be eccentric for me to say "I made a mistake" after guessing the wrong lottery numbers. When succeeding is random, mistake is never the explanation of the unhappy outcome. Second, even if I have reason to know which umbrella is yours, if I grab an umbrella (just any old umbrella), then *you* may have been mistaken to rely on me to fetch it for you: you took me for considerate and careful. But my lack of commitment to take the right one precludes my explaining that I have taken the wrong one by mistake. I cannot fail at something at which I have not even tried. (This, it seems to me, is our real objection to Goetz: he did not even try to get it right).

Still, we must be careful not to become too finicky in establishing the criteria for mistakes, or *nothing* would qualify and the word would cease to have any specific application in the world. An example of a too finicky, even impossible notion of mistake is provided by Thrasymachus, who challenges Socrates:

> [D]o you call a man who makes mistakes about the sick a doctor because of the very mistake he is making? Or a man who makes mistakes in calculation a skilled calculator, at the moment he is making a mistake, in the very sense of his mistake? I suppose rather that this is just our manner of speaking—the doctor made a mistake, the calculator made a mistake, and the grammarian. But I suppose that each of these men, insofar as he is what we address him as, never makes mistakes. Hence, in precise speech, since you too speak precisely, none of the craftsmen makes mistakes. The man who makes mistakes makes them on account of a failure in knowledge and is in that respect no craftsman. So no craftsman, wise man, or ruler makes mistakes at the moment when he is ruling, although everyone would say that the doctor made a mistake and the ruler made a mistake.[153]

To Thrasymachus, know-how fails when a mistake is made. When know-how fails, he goes on, then the activity to which the know-how pertains somehow ceases to occur. The craftsman (doctor, calculator, grammarian) no longer "is what we address him as" when he makes a mistake because if he deserves to be called (really is) a craftsman, then his knowledge will never fail. That is, knowledge is always infallible, so if you make a mistake you cannot have been acting "on the basis of your knowledge."

The implication of this, however, is that there is no such thing as a mistake. Someone who is *not* trained in medicine could not make a medical mistake (thus the humor of the Sprite soft drink commercial that asks whether you would want a pro basketball player performing surgery on you). Someone who *is* trained in medicine, contrariwise, could not make a mistake because at the moment of the lapse the practice of medicine is not occurring because a failure of knowledge is false to the activity itself ("you call yourself a doctor?"). According to Thrasymachus, therefore, "mistake" has no specific application in ordinary speech.

The entire idea of a success, however, depends on the possibility of a mistake. Thus, despite what Thrasymachus may say, we *do* "call a man who makes mistakes about the sick a doctor because of the very mistake he is making." Mistakes must be possible or it would mean nothing to refer to an action as "well done" or "successful" or "right."

For Austin, to understand what it means to say something in a "speech situation" is to understand what it means to do something much more generally, but also that understanding speech-acts and other acts entails studying "the doctrine of *the things that can be and go wrong* on the occasion of such utterances, the doctrine of the *Infelicities*" (*HTDTW*, 1–45, 136–61). The doctrine of the infelicities holds that what constitutes an action such as marrying can be discovered by identifying instances where the action fails or is "unhappy," such as where one purported spouse is married already, the person performing the ceremony lacks the authority to do so, or one purported spouse is underage, or a monkey (*HTDTW*, 1–45, 136–61).

When the criteria for mistakes are satisfied, however—when the claim of mistake is not fantastic and when it describes a misfired action that the actor had the competence and commitment to get right—then there is nothing left to do *but* excuse. I say this to reemphasize that one problem with the law's view of mistakes is that fantasies or actions that are the product of distraction (and so are performed under conditions where excuses other than mistake may be apt) are frequently passed off as mistakes.

Mistakes of Law

Another problem is that in other instances the excuse of mistake should apply, but does not. Those instances are when the excuse is that defendant was mistaken about a law instead of a fact. In *Cheek v. United States*,[154] an American Airlines pilot successfully argued that he did not "willfully" evade taxes if he thought he owed no taxes, a position he arrived at because "he truly believed that the Internal Revenue Code did not purport to treat wages as income. . . ."[155] Although mistake of law is normally no excuse, in this unusual case Congress had built the excuse into the offense by requiring not just a failure to pay tax, but a willful failure, which could not occur without the accused's sense of the obligation to pay tax. The Supreme Court agreed, "as incredible as such misunderstandings of and beliefs about the law might be."[156] So a new trial was ordered in which the trial court was prohibited from imposing a reasonableness requirement on Cheek's mistakes about the operation of the Internal Revenue Code.

But what made Cheek think *that*? "[A] group that believes . . . that the federal tax system is unconstitutional,"[157] we are told. But why believe *them*? What had Cheek learned from the six years he spent challenging, *inter alia*, the Sixteenth Amendment,[158] challenges culminating in his being sanctioned for bringing frivolous suits and appeals?[159] Nothing? Ultimately we see that there *are* procedures for evaluating the conditions under which a mistake is made, and Cheek would not survive them. When asked to elaborate the conditions of his "mistakes," what we would conclude is not so much that he is lying (again, I will assume he is not), but that there is something wrong with him—some lack of judgment so complete that it puts him (like Morgan's confederates, like Goetz) too far afield to be speaking in terms of mistake and still mean what we mean by it in ordinary speech. For Cheek (and others similarly situated) some other excuse may be apt (though I highly doubt it), but the excuse of mistake is not.

Cheek is seen as a product of an unusual drafting strategy by which Congress had explicitly made awareness of the law an element of the offense.[160] When defendants plead that they had put themselves to acting lawfully, much more typical is the law's response that "ignorance of the law is no excuse." But if the unlawful act really is due to a mistake—where the criteria for mistakes are satisfied—then why not excuse? Part of my confusion on this point owes to the fact that while the law insists that factual mistakes are excusable but legal ones are not, many paradigmatic factual mistakes are easily redescribed as legal.[161] As the Supreme Court is fond of saying, the application of legal principles to historical facts is neither factual nor legal, but rather, "a mixed determination of law and fact."[162] Because common mistakes about consent, age, status, ownership, or materiality are arguably as legal or "mixed" as they are factual, I see little profit in conditioning the excuse of mistake on such a shaky distinction between law and fact.

Relying on altogether different grounds, Dan Kahan has made out a strong case in favor of judicial recognition of mistake of law as an excuse. The maxim "[i]gnorance of the law is no excuse," he tells us, is meant to "maximize[] citizens' incentive to learn the rules that 'the law-maker has determined to make men know and obey.'"[163] But "if the goal is only to protect society from the legally stupid," Kahan argues, then a regime in which the but-I-thought-it-was-legal defense is always denied provides no payoff whatsoever for legal research: break the law and go to jail, even after diligent *ex ante* efforts to verify the lawfulness of an action. But in a negligence regime, Kahan concludes—one in which reasonable steps to ascertain the law are rewarded—more legal research will occur because researchers who really are mistaken can get off scot-free.[164]

For Kahan, the "strategically heedless," i.e., the intentional head burier, is only a bit player in the mistake-of-law drama. Kahan emphasizes this point through a close reading of *People v. Marrero*,[165] in which a federal prison guard was prohibited from pleading his quite understandable belief that he was a "correction officer[] of any state correctional facility or of any penal correctional institution"[166] and as such exempt from New York's concealed-weapons law. While New York's highest court insisted that excusing Marrero would encourage ignorance of the of law, Kahan insists that Marrero was far from heedless. Rather than "deliberately shield[] himself from legal knowledge," Marrero "had tenaciously attempted to ferret it out."[167] Other would-be head buriers, Kahan continues, hardly would be helped had Marrero's request for a mistake defense been accepted.[168] Indeed, Kahan makes a strong case that *Marrero* botched its stated intention of endorsing the utility of legal knowledge, not by denying a defense to the strategically heedless, but by denying a defense to the "impudently inquisitive" who pay "exacting attention to the law's fine points,"[169] but get the law wrong anyway.

Kahan then does a first-rate job of rehabilitating *Marrero*'s holding. Legal research performed by someone who is contemplating action of questionable legality is far from an unalloyed good, Kahan tells us. Whether we are talking about Marrero himself or a possessor of designer drugs, to condition the excuse on reasonable efforts to learn the law is to institutionalize "loopholing."[170] For example, drug manufacturers can avoid a jurisdiction's controlled-substances list simply by "alter[ing] the composition of . . . a substance slightly without changing its pharmacological effects."[171]

One way to fix the inevitable incompleteness of statutory definitions of crime is to draft laws at a level of abstraction sufficient to "remove offenders' temptation to look for loopholes *ex ante* by giving courts the flexibility to adapt the law to innovative forms of crime *ex post*."[172] This remedy for loopholing is what Kahan calls "prudent obfuscation." For such a remedy to work, Kahan posits, the law must deny *all* forms of mistake-as-excuse, *particularly* the excuse for reasonable mistakes. Otherwise, he points out, deliberately complex criminal laws would be thwarted by legal researchers whose efforts to keep current often would be understandably deficient.[173] Yet, as Kahan asks, "[i]f the law aspires to be deliberately vague and complex, and if it tries to discourage rather than reward inquiry into the fine points of law by punishing even reasonable mistakes, how can it expect individuals who want to be law-abiding to know what their legal duties are?"[174]

And so we arrive at the payoff of Kahan's essay: his "legal moralism," which he recommends to reward the diligent researcher (but not the loopholer) and to punish the strategically heedless. In a nutshell, legal moralism imposes strict, that is, no-fault liability on all agents whose actions are wrong in a pre-legal sense and punishes all negligent agents whose actions are *malum prohibitum*, that is, technically wrong, but not wrong in a pre-legal sense. According to Kahan, we all know right from wrong,[175] and so the law need not excuse the ignorance of law on the part of agents like Cleora King, who stashed drugs in a small foil package in her underwear, only to argue later that Minnesota's banned-substances list was too hard to keep up with.[176] Even Marrero, as almost-lawful as his conduct was, not only knew about "New York's . . . strong antipathy toward, and fear of, handguns,"[177] but he also, it turns out, had 1) violated his employer's internal gun policy; 2) unlawfully supplied others with guns; and 3) tried to pull a gun on the police who approached him in the nightclub where he was arrested.[178]

Kahan's legal moralism is meant to chill more borderline-lawful behavior than a negligence regime. This is a welcome result for Kahan, since we gain nothing by excusing agents like King and Marrero, who knew they were acting *at best* in a marginally legal way. So for Kahan the question is not just whether we (reasonably) believe in the lawfulness of our actions, but also whether those actions are independently "morally blameworthy." Kahan would have moral failings block the mistake-of-law defense, since it is "commonplace" for us to "condemn someone for being inattentive to moral obligations"[179] "with which the law-abiders and law-breakers alike *are* thoroughly familiar."[180]

The lines he asks us to draw are, he admits, "blurry."[181] So blurry, in fact, that even as early as 1822 the *malum in se/malum prohibitum* distinction was said to have "long since exploded."[182] Even if the distinction is not entirely spurious, then surely it comes close, as a glance at the Supreme Court's decisions on point betrays.[183] Examples that Kahan gives of laws to which the defense could apply include the technical sides of the laws of banking, broadcasting, and tax (including Justice Breyer's failure to know that the wages of his weekly maid were taxable),[184] as well as some possession-of-weapons laws.[185]

No doubt Kahan's contribution to the meaning and operation of mistakes is significant.[186] But rather than categorize offenses as susceptible to the mistake defense or not, were we to say instead that mistakes are always a defense, I suspect that Kahan's concern for the individual who is insufficiently tuned in to the true value of things would nonetheless be satisfied. Such a person would, after all, have a hard time elaborating what made him think that arson, rape, murder, theft, or selling drugs, just to name a few, was lawful. Thinking that such activities are lawful is either delusional or expressive of some sort of philosophical theory about the world (like thinking that African-Americans are not persons), but hardly a mistake. Our asking instead whether the criteria for mistakes are met would swap the unhappy activity of telling pre-legal from ticky-tack offenses (of deciding whether mistake *is* an excuse) for the activity of confronting what procedures, if any, defendant deployed to ensure his law-abidingness (of deciding whether a mistake took place).[187]

For example, in discussing *Cheek*, Kahan says that criminal tax provisions are the sort of ticky-tack laws that even a good person could unknowingly violate. Kahan goes on to distinguish failings like Cheek's (which don't impress Kahan as excusable) from Justice Breyer's (which do). To decide which offenses are even subject to the pleading of mistake, Kahan asks whether Cheek and Breyer failed us morally. I, contrariwise, would assume that mistake is always open to the defendant as an exculpatory plea. Instead of asking whether defendant is sufficiently morally sensitive, I would ask: what was the mistake? How could it have been corrected? Cheek could not correct his mistake because he wasn't mistaken at all—he was either delusional or more likely, giving in to a sort of political theory about the limits of government (just as polygenesis is a theory about what counts as human). As for Breyer, to correct his mistake, he needed just a bit more commitment (ability to know the laws of taxation is hardly lacking in his case). If in the course of his elaboration of what went wrong we become satisfied that he meant to abide by our tax laws but muffed it anyway, then his understanding really was mistaken and therefore excusable.

Summary on Mistakes

There will be a small number of cases in which paying attention to the criteria of mistakes *will* change the outcome.[188] But that is not the point, or at least not my point. The difference that this difference for which I have argued here makes is that people who do not like the *Morgan* case are attacking the wrong thing: by worrying to death whether Morgan's confederates were honest, they displace what is really wrong with those three men. This dichotomy between the reasonable and unreasonable mistake therefore generates an incredible blockage, which prevents our being able to see what our real moral objection to those three men is. And that objection is not that they were fudging their beliefs or even fooling themselves about what Ms. Morgan wanted. Rather, our real objection is to their failure to live up to a standard—not a standard that expects them to be able to tell whether she was consenting, but a standard that expects them to pay attention to the entire web of relations in which that specific question is embedded. (This I think is what Austin means when he suggests that at times entering a certain plea incompetently can morally compound the offense). That is, when one is engaging in an activity that looks and feels *that much* like rape, one cannot claim mistake without making one's plight worse. Just as Goetz's failure to try harder to assess his situation made his overreaction to the four boys something other than a mistake, for Morgan's three confederates to have been mistaken about Ms. Morgan's desires, they needed to demonstrate more interest than they did in getting the situation right.

So too is the problem with someone like Cheek not that he was dishonest, but that far from failing to know the ticky-tack, hypertechnicalities of tax law, he went so far as to disown the knowledge he had acquired about his obligations. That is, Cheek's stance toward his tax obligations was more a refusal to acknowledge the law than it was a blank about the law's coverage. This makes Cheek someone whom we may criticize or excuse for various reasons; but he is not in any event someone who has violated the tax laws by mistake. By trying to shoehorn his plea into the idea of a mistake, Cheek, like Goetz, like Morgan's confederates, really is worse off, if only for failing to live up to standards that would make a mistake even possible under the circumstances.

Whether the subject is laws or facts, the extent to which the law fails to consider the criteria of mistakes is reflected in the way in which the terms "mistake" and "belief" are mixed and matched, as though their meanings were identical. Take, for example, California's jury instruction on the operation of mistakes of fact on specific-intent crimes: "An act committed or an omission made in ignorance or by reason of a mistake of fact which disproves any criminal intent is not a crime. Thus a person is not guilty of a crime if [he or she] commits an act or omits to act under an actual . . . belief in the existence of certain facts and circumstances which, if true, would make the act or omission lawful."[189] The first sentence of this instruction speaks in terms of "mistake," while the second sentence speaks in terms of "belief." (So too does the *Cheek* case refer both to the notion of mistake and that of belief, lopsidedly giving forty mentions to "belief" and only three to "mistake"). Many wrong beliefs are not mistakes at all: they are fantasies or delusions, though the instruction quoted above certainly indicates that "mistake" and "wrong belief" are interchangeable. They are not. Just as Austin said of dreaming and waking, "[t]here are recognized ways of distinguishing between [beliefs and mistakes] (how otherwise should we know how to use and to contrast the words?)" ("MINDS," 87). The stake in seeing the difference between a mistake and a wrong belief is to avoid the pressure in moral encounters between accuser and accused to see questions of guilt or excuse as turning entirely on our ability to discern whether the accused is lying. In addition, coming to grips with the grammar of mistakes would allow us to give mistaken agents what they deserve: being let off the hook, in whole or in part, rather than blamed when, with the competence and commitment to get it right, they just took the wrong one on that occasion.

BLAMING VERSUS HOLDING RESPONSIBLE

Regardless of what we make of the precise operation of the excuses of accident and mistake in criminal law, it is a truth nearly universally accepted that being clumsy or misinformed is not as bad as being mean. But from this it does not follow that the clumsy or misinformed get off scot-free for the harm they do. If someone steps on your foot in the grocery store checkout line, do you not blame them? Well, that depends on the criteria of blaming. Maybe you just hold them responsible, summarily excuse them, or forgive them because they have no excuse. If, however, it turns out that you are willing to hold someone responsible but not blame them, then on what would the distinction turn? Judith Andre puts it this way: "to be responsible is to have an obligation to rectify bad consequences. If I break your vase, I must replace it. I can be responsible in [this] sense without being in the least blameworthy, although often the two coincide."[190] She does not elaborate. If Professor Andre is right—if "responsible" suppresses some feature of "blame"—then what exactly is suppressed? Suppose we were to say that you are responsible for the broken vase and that blaming you would express a stronger sense of disapproval than holding you responsible. Austin himself briskly states that blame goes to the *extent* of responsibility, but what does *that* mean? ("EXCUSES," 181 n. 1). Someone who kills someone else negligently is let partially off the hook,[191] but it is just as apt a description to say he is held partially responsible as it is to say he is held partially to blame. Yet I suspect that distinguishing blame from responsibility may implicate Professor Alexander's distinction between "wrong in the doing" and "wrong in the doer."

Blame may be code for "wrong," but even tort law, whose business is to hold negligent actors responsible but not to blame them, would be on shaky ground if it held someone responsible who had done no wrong. I cannot see how we could order a negligent driver to pay a plaintiff whom he has injured if the negligent driver committed no wrong. That would just be scapegoating. I am not suggesting that we err in making accident a way of getting out of being *held* responsible, or *entirely* responsible, for what we do. Everyone slips up now and then, to be sure. What I am suggesting is that we are responsible for what we do, even for our accidents.

Above I alluded to the ways in which Andre and Austin allude not just to blame, but to its separateness from responsibility.[192] I did so because there is, I suspect, a difference between blaming and holding responsible. But for me it is wrapped up not in the difference between "negligence" and "recklessness," but in the timing or circumstances (including the manner or style) in which the excuse is proffered. Blaming is a judgment made against those who refuse to accept responsibility for what they've done. By that I mean that blame is an action reserved for those whose excuses we reject, usually on the grounds that their excuses amount to rationalization or evasion of responsibility. For example, if I break your vase and offer to pay, I am in any event responsible for the breakage, but if you have to sue me to get me to acknowledge what I have done, then I get blamed. We could even say that the act of blaming is a continuation of the original harmful event to the extent that an elaboration that amounts to rationalizing or evading responsibility precludes our reclaiming the relationship that the untoward action ruptured in the first place. (This may be what Austin meant by blame having to do with the *extent* of responsibility. "Extent" goes not to size (bigger or smaller), but more like scope—extending beyond the actual incident generating the responsibility). It is at this point as if there is nothing left *but* to blame, in the sense that blaming marks the complete failure of a relationship.

It cannot, after all, be that the difference between blaming and holding responsible lies only in what is in store for you after we've concluded that you deserve one or the other. In other words, it cannot be that you are blamed if you go to jail but merely held responsible if you are ordered to compensate your victims.[193] While "[a] man is equally dead and his relatives equally bereaved whether he was stabbed or run over by a drunken motorist or by an incompetent one,"[194] that the first two killings (stabbing, drunk-driving manslaughter) are criminal and the third is not (when the risks the incompetent driver takes aren't that great) is uncontroversial. The actions of the stabber or drunk driver betray a "callousness,"[195] a contempt for others that justifies the noncompensatory, punitive remedies that "stigmatize," "censor," or "disgrace."[196] But if you are merely a bad but not callous driver, failing to pay attention when "you ought to have paid particular heed" (e.g., driving in a school-zone) gets you only partially off the hook. Although you remain partially on the hook for driving badly in this instance, your lack of "callousness" does, or at least can, exempt you from criminal punishment's "stigmatizing," "censoring," or "disgracing."

But *why* does the excuse that what you did was just an accident exempt you from *that*? When a drunk driver runs over a pedestrian, rarely does the driver intend to kill anyone. In such cases the driver is going to be held responsible or blamed because the death is what we might call an "inexcusable accident." If it were an excusable accident, then the driver would be responsible, but would not be held responsible or blamed. If the driver waits for responsibility to be allocated, then the driver runs the risk of being blamed. To fess up or to otherwise elaborate the action without rationalizing, evading, or being *forced* to elaborate the action means that the accused will be either excused or held responsible—depending on whether we accept or reject the elaboration—but in such a case the accused will not be blamed. In other words, *being* responsible is simply a function of whether you have participated in another's harm. It has little if anything to do with the excuses: it is, for lack of a better word, causal.[197] Being *held* responsible, contrariwise, depends not only on what was done—on whether you've harmed anyone—but requires as well the participation or consent of the accused in the determination of what was done. That is, being held responsible is in effect an act of *holding oneself* responsible or self-judging (in the context of community). The act of blaming, however, is reserved for an accused who not only is causally responsible for another's harm, but for an accused who refuses to hold himself responsible or answerable to others. In other words, blame is for those whom we must *judge* as responsible, for those who rationalize what they have done or failed to do or who evade responsibility if only by counting on us to demand an elaboration, which for that very reason we may be prone to reject.

Accordingly, a civil, wrongful-death suit arising out of bad but not callous driving will lead us to blame the driver, in part for waiting for responsibility to be handed out rather than accepting it from the outset. Just as an offer to settle can resolve the wrong by reconciling the parties in a civil case, a confession or guilty plea can accomplish the same end of reconciliation in a criminal case. Pleading guilty expresses that the defendant accepts responsibility and therefore the most common excuse—that he caused harm but didn't mean to—should facilitate the reclamation of the relationship. The problem with confessions and guilty pleas, however, is that they tend to fall on deaf ears.[198] It is safe to say that police, who receive confessions, and prosecutors, who receive guilty pleas, are for one reason or another disinclined to treat the defendant's acceptance of responsibility as an act of community:

> Studies show that suspects who confess are more likely to have charges filed against them, less likely to have charges dropped, and less likely to receive a plea bargain, that they receive worse deals if they do bargain, are more likely to be convicted at trial, and more likely to be convicted of serious charges.[199]

A police culture that punishes more severely those who accept responsibility on their own—who are held responsible in that they hold themselves responsible—denies the function and significance of excuses. Nonetheless, the fact that police or prosecutors *may* treat the suspect's or accused's acceptance of responsibility as grounds to excuse or forgive expresses that confessions and guilty pleas are at least potentially good not only for the soul, but for the community as well. Indeed, what victim, judge, juror, or observer is unmoved by the spectacle of the convicted killer apologizing to the victim's relatives in court?

Whether confessing or pleading guilty as a move toward reconciliation is to have any hold on us at all is largely a matter of timing. For example, after writing for over 250 pages about the crimes, capture, trial, appeal, and execution of Adolf Eichmann, Hanna Arendt closes her book in an imaginary colloquy in which she is a judge condemning Eichmann—the "hero . . . in the center of the play"—in part for *not* revealing himself:

> You admitted the crime committed against the Jewish people during the war was the greatest crime in recorded history, and you admitted your role in it. But you said you had never acted from base motives, that you had never had any inclination to kill anybody, that you had never hated Jews, and still that you could not have acted otherwise and that you did not feel guilty. We find this difficult, though not altogether impossible, to believe. . . . You told your story in terms of a hard-luck story, . . . [but] there still remains the fact that you have carried out, and therefore actively supported, a policy of mass murder.[200]

Suppose Eichmann had come clean at his trial. For him to acknowledge *at that point* his role in the Holocaust would do him little good—it's way too late for that. (This may be why it is the "cardinal rule" of celebrated defense lawyer Melvin Belli that "[i]f the guy's guilty, you don't put him on.")[201] Eichmann should have shouldered his responsibility much earlier. Therefore while what we will count as an act of accepting as opposed to evading responsibility depends on the circumstances, an early move toward reconciliation is certainly better than a late one. It is for this reason that despite the at times moving spectacle of in-court victim-accused encounters, [202] the problem with remedial stages of legal disputes, be they sentencing or damages stages, is that they are quite literally autopsies of relationships—as far from reconciliation as we could get.

Harmful versus Wrongful

Regardless of what we ultimately make of the significance of accepting responsibility in our exploration of the grammar of "blame," where "responsibility" begins to lose its sense is when we say that only those whom we hold responsible or blame have done *wrong*. I think it is worth reiterating that our recognizing accident as an excuse does not imply that "excuse" means "let completely off the hook." "[F]ew excuses get us out of it *completely*: the average excuse, in a poor situation, gets us only out of the fire into the frying pan—but still, of course, any frying pan in a fire. If I have broken your dish or your romance, maybe the best defense I can find will be clumsiness. . . . I do not exactly evade responsibility when I plead clumsiness or tactlessness. . . ." ("EXCUSES," 177, 181). To say otherwise would be to say that to have an excuse or a justification is to have done nothing wrong. That in turn would make responsible agency "a fairly superficial concept," one that cuts off much of what we do from what we are responsible for.[203]

Such a view of agency prevails, however. Take for example Professor Kadish's analysis of a real case in which

> a conductor signals to the bus driver that it is safe to back up when it is not, and someone is killed as a consequence. If the conductor was negligent in failing to see the danger, but the driver acted reasonably in relying on the conductor, could the conductor be found liable as an accomplice

> for a crime of causing a death through negligent driving? It has been argued that he could since he encouraged the wrongful but excused act of the driver. But it is hard to see how the driver can be said to have done a wrongful act when he simply backed up in reasonable reliance on the conductor, his driving being perfectly prudent and proper. Far from having done a wrong, he did what we want him to do. One might argue that his action could just as adequately be described as backing his bus into a group of alighting passengers. Even so, this would describe an action that caused a harm, not one that is wrongful, because wrongfulness, in contrast to harm, implies responsibility.[204]

This is a significant and troubling idea. Somehow, Kadish imagines two separate spheres of action: one is merely causal, and so as such is cut off from responsibility, and the other sphere is wrongful, and so as such is properly the office of responsibility. Does Kadish really mean that to redescribe this killing as "backing [a] bus into a group of alighting passengers" will somehow save the driver? Save his relationship with himself and with others? In what possible circumstances would "backing [a] bus into a group of alighting passengers" be anything *but* wrongful?

Now it becomes clear what Professor J. G. Murphy means when he says that accident, mistake, and duress are excuses, but in cases of seizures, convulsions, reflex movements, and sleepwalking, "talk of excuse here seems to make no more sense than would talk of excusing a rock for falling on one's head."[205] Like Kadish's position on the responsibility of the bus driver, Murphy thinks that having an excuse for what we do somehow makes everything alright or somehow separates us from what we have done or played some role in. (As if to deploy an excuse means you really didn't *do* it at all or *you* really didn't do it at all). I would think that Ms. Cogdon, the celebrated sleepwalker who while in a "somnambulistic fugue state" killed her daughter, is at best excused.[206] Indeed, she would be a monster if she felt she *needed* no excuse for, asleep or not, bludgeoning her daughter to death with an axe. When in practice Los Angeles Clippers' star basketball player Danny Manning blew out his knee when he inadvertently stepped on teammate Joe Kleine's foot, Kleine felt terrible.[207] Kleine's massive dose of "agent regret" persisted even though it was not really Kleine's fault—he was just standing there. But Kleine was right to feel regretful when he linked Manning's injury with his own (passive) role in the episode. Was he *responsible* for what happened?

Partly, maybe. Who else, if not him? Indeed, to say that Kleine should feel like an observer rather than a participant in Manning's suffering would cut off what we do and fail to do from what we are responsible for. Will we blame or hold Kleine responsible? No; we exculpate him on grounds of accident (or because Manning himself is more responsible), though Kleine may never forgive himself for having played some role, however minor, in the suffering of another.

I do not mean to suggest that the bus driver who backed into alighting passengers should be convicted of homicide. Even if charged with negligent homicide (a partial excuse), we still have good reason to fully excuse the driver because "stigmatizing," "censoring," or "disgracing" him merely for following the conductor's instructions would make action intolerable. But this view of responsibility is too hard on the bus driver for Kadish, who throws himself into a sort of moral no-man's-land where running over pedestrians is not only not wrong, but even worse, and this much I think is deeply troubling, "what we want him to do." Because we can't possibly want passengers to be mowed down, I take it that what we must want is for bus drivers (employees) to rely blindly on even fatal orders issued by conductors (employers). This sort of just-following-orders defense is hardly comforting, but even to treat it as a defense at all, that is, as a justification or excuse, presupposes what Kadish denies: that there is something wrong with what the driver has done that needs to be explained.[208] In Kadish's view, the bus driver needs no excuse, given that causing harm is not necessarily wrong, and harm without wrong does not entail responsibility.

Justifying versus Excusing

Kadish's position assumes the unfairness of criticizing someone who means no harm and who is reasonable in selecting what turns out to be a harmful course of conduct. In an effort to acknowledge our fallibility, however, he goes too far when he characterizes instances of fallibility as *unnecessary* to excuse. Kadish is not alone. His approach is shared by some leading legal philosophers who write thoughtfully about the distinction between extenuating explanations that justify as opposed to excuse our actions.

Kent Greenawalt generalizes "some of the typical features of justification and excuse" in the following way:

> Justified action is warranted action; similar actions could properly be performed by others; such actions should not be interfered with by those capable of stopping them; and such actions may be assisted by those in a position to render aid. If the action is excused, the actor is relieved of blame but others may not properly perform similar actions; interference with such actions is appropriate; and assistance of such actions is wrongful.[209]

This is certainly conventional. Leo Katz, for example, says that "[t]o acquit someone on grounds of necessity is to approve, support, applaud what he did. It is to find his actions *justified*."[210] So too, George Fletcher observes that "[w]e 'applaud' the justified actor's 'judgment' on choosing the superior value."[211] For Larry Alexander, because a justified act vindicates the actor's rights and violates no one else's rights, it is for that reason not "regrettable."[212]

The merits of these conventional positions notwithstanding, there is something odd about stripping all the wrongfulness from certain harms in a way that ignores that to justify an action is, as Austin puts it, "to give reasons for doing it, not to say to brazen it out, to glory in it, or the like" ("EXCUSES," 176). If we really support, applaud, and approve an action, then why do we ask the person who performed the action to justify himself at all? We would not, for instance, ask the Good Samaritan how, having found a man who had been beaten, robbed, stripped, and left for dead by the side of the road, he justifies tending the man's wounds, taking him to an inn, prepaying his bill, and offering him aid and succor.[213] What would it mean to ask the Good Samaritan to justify helping others in their true hour of need? Good Samaritans don't *need* to justify their actions because there is nothing *wrong* with being a Good Samaritan.

In a similar vein, consider the last lines of Terry Teachout's review of four books about Frank Sinatra: "But when the last standing ovation has died away and the fully comprehending biography is finally written, we will be left with something in which conventional notions of honor play no part: the records, those haunting testaments of passion and fear that arise from and explain his life—and, perhaps, justify it as well."[214] Teachout thinks Sinatra's life was fishy; otherwise there would be nothing for Sinatra's record albums *to* justify. The sort of demand Teachout makes of Sinatra is a demand we make when we feel we have the right to question what you have done because of our relation to you or to what you have done ("MEANING IT," 236). Unless Sinatra has done something wrong (fishy, untoward), there would be no *call* for justification.

The paradigmatic instances of justification relied on by Greenawalt, Katz, Fletcher, and Alexander—using deadly force to save your own or someone else's life—*do* need to be justified, and should hardly be applauded. There *are* actions that someone justified in using deadly force in a defensive posture could take that would be worth applauding: subduing or talking the suspect into turning himself in, even at considerable risk to the justified actor.[215] A warning shot or aiming low would be next best, but killing another person—even someone who in a sense now "deserves" it, is always at best a regrettable thing to do—something that could be *at best* justified.[216] Who would applaud a killing? (Conferring medals on soldiers and police who commit justifiable killings is more expressive of our relief that someone else is willing to do our dirty work for us than of our sense that what has been done—killing others, even enemies—is "good"). So when Greenawalt says that what characterizes justified acts is that everyone can help (pile on?) and no one can interfere (talk *either* party out of what they are set on doing?) he gives us a picture of human action that has very little to do with what we want to happen.

The stretch required to say that some harms are not wrongs because they are justified may explain why Paul Robinson notes in the first paragraph of *Criminal Law Defenses* that "the harm recognized by the justified behavior remains a legally recognized harm that is to be avoided whenever possible."[217] True, Robinson stops well short of calling the justified harm a "wrong," but Thomas Morawetz does take a step toward doing so when he urges us to accept a class of actions as "justified wrongs," where "the actor has good reasons for acting, but at the same time takes actions that society (for utilitarian reasons) is anxious to discourage."[218] Morawetz's notion of a justified wrong is illustrated by the following hypothetical of Greenawalt's:

> Employing the most advanced techniques for predicting wind patterns, Roger decides that a fire in a national forest that threatens human lives can be halted only by carefully burning out a section of the forest that is in the path of the fire. That section is burned on Roger's orders; shortly thereafter the wind shifts in a wholly unexpected way that halts the forest fire before it reaches the burned section.[219]

The concern here is whether it is the decision or the outcome that we justify or excuse. If it is the reasonable decision that counts, then

Roger is justified;[220] if it is the way things turn out that counts, then Roger is justified at the inception, but is at the end only excused.[221] According to Morawetz, both the decision and the outcome count: thus the term "justified wrong," which captures both crucial moments in the episode in which Roger had good reasons for his action (justification) that can't be fully approved of because that action ultimately misfired (excuse).

This is yet another example of the philosophical attempt to give "theoretical" answers to questions that are raised in a way that is divorced from an actual context of human action and concern. My reaction here is that neither decision nor outcome count *in themselves*. Our reaction to Roger all depends on what our concern in the situation is, what bothers us about what Roger did. Our concern may be whether he really did carefully calculate the wind patterns, if what decision he made really was the one that had to be made. Here it's the decision that matters. Or we may be concerned because even though Roger did do all the calculations carefully, the trees he burned down were particularly valuable—one of the last old-growth redwood stands in California—and we are asking, was this result (burning down *these* trees) worth it in light of what happened? Now it's the result that matters. What we focus on depends on what bothers us about what Roger did. But the way excuse/justification hypotheticals like ours are posed is in a vacuum—it's stipulated that Roger was reasonable, and we're not told enough about the result to raise any specific question about what happened. The hypothetical makes Roger's action seem not fishy from the get-go—so of course the question about whether he is excused or justified is hard to answer. The hypothetical is presented in such a way as to not allow us to get a grip on *why* a question is being raised about what Roger did. It is an *ex post* presentation of the problem, whereas the whole decision/result issue applies only in the *process* of our questioning what Roger did, a process we are told to take as a given.

Whatever we decide here has no practical influence in law, or none immediately felt, now that the historical difference between an absolute defense (justification) and the chance to be let off the hook (pardon or excuse) has dissolved.[222] But the difference between justification and excuse *does* matter in that what we make of elaborations tells us a lot about what we think about responsibility. If there is a difference between justifications and excuses, I think the now-dissolved historical explanation is right on: the difference is in the extent to which accepting the plea (reclaiming the relationship within community) is *up to us*. The justified actor is in a stronger position with us—there is nothing left *to* criticize, or, as Austin characterizes it, if I competently plea a justification to my accuser, "he will cease to disapprove of what I did" ("EXCUSES," 181 n. 1). (Nor is the withdrawal of disapproval tantamount to approval). If I am excused, contrariwise, I make an *appeal* to my accuser "so that he will cease to hold me, at least entirely and in every way, responsible for doing it" ("EXCUSES," 181 n. 1). That is, the excused actor makes an appeal to our shared fallibility, to our sense of community.

Whatever we make of the difference between justification and excuse, I am not persuaded that it is as sharp or binary as it is sometimes made out to be: both sorts of actions need to be explained. In Roger's case, a concern is that to call his action "excused" instead of "justified" amounts to "penalizing" his "justified" choice just because of its unhappy outcome: "Since the criminal law involves condemnation of individuals and efforts to affect future behavior, it is unfair to label the person who acted ideally, given all available information, as 'excused,' rather than 'justified.'"[223] Yet how will that redescription save him from responsibility for what he's done? Shouldn't Roger feel terrible about needlessly burning out a section of the forest? Whether we call it "justified," "a justified wrong," or "excused," it is by any other name a regrettable action for which Roger is responsible, but for which on these facts we will neither blame him nor hold him responsible.

A variation on Roger's plight is presented by Professor Robinson, who asks us to imagine that this time Roger "knows of the fire but responds to the information with indifference. He joins the project to seek revenge on the owner of the field who, he suspects, is sleeping with his wife."[224] Because this time the wind does not shift, Roger saves human lives by burning out the section of the forest.[225] Robinson insists that on these facts Roger is justified. So do Moore[226] and Alexander,[227] who say that someone in Roger's shoes "has done no wrong," but since Roger is nonetheless "very culpable," he has committed attempted arson.

But if Roger really "has done no wrong," then we have no business criticizing him *at all*, let alone "stigmatizing," "censoring," or "disgracing" him as an almost-arsonist. Furthermore, there is something atonal about calling the spiteful torching of someone else's land "attempted" arson. In this second scenario Roger has not tried and failed to commit arson; he *has* committed arson. In no sense has his intention to destroy his enemy's property fallen short. "Attempted" this or that is for would-be criminals who cannot pull the crime off because in one way or another they get caught. To be sure, the land in question may have "deserved" to have been set on fire, but only by someone who saw setting the fire as necessary, not retaliatory.[228]

That someone on whom morality has absolutely *no* pull (here, Roger) could have done no wrong or somehow did the right thing for the wrong reasons is an odd position indeed. Roger's intention to destroy property—not to save lives—should eliminate any interest we may have in his relationship to the imperiled lives that never even dawned on him. This explains why in his discussion of a version of the life of symbolist painter Paul Gauguin, Bernard Williams asks us to presuppose that the claims of family that Gauguin renounced in order to pursue his art *mattered to Gauguin*.[229] Williams sees that we need a reason to *care* whether Gauguin is partially redeemed by his becoming the "father of modern art"[230] after having kicked himself loose of the claims of morality. If Gauguin himself doesn't feel the pull of his family, then he is simply unredeemable and his case ceases to be of interest. (We could say the same of Sinatra, whose singing may convince us that he *must* have felt the pull of the claims of others—or he could not have sung like that—even though he fell short of acknowledging them in real life). Likewise do we want to know that Roger himself accepts that he should not out of spite start an arson fire on someone else's property, though it would be okay to do so if he thought it was necessary to save lives. If morality means nothing to Roger, then his plea will mean nothing to us.

2

Inchoate Criminality as Partial Excuse

WHEN I SAY THAT EVEN JUSTIFIED ACTS SUCH AS CORE CASES OF SELF-defense are, like excusable acts, both harmful and wrongful, I know I attribute more action to the domain of the wrongful than is customary. My concern, again, is to question a way of talking about responsibility that obscures the distinctions between being responsible on the one hand and being held responsible or blamed on the other. As Williams has summarized it, "the idea of the voluntary is essentially superficial."[1] Superficial, he adds, to the extent that such a view of responsibility depends *uniquely* on "the product of the will."[2] I agree that the burden of action, of being equal to the consequences of our actions, must extend beyond the voluntary. In fact it is to *avoid* reducing responsibility to a superficial concept that I insist not only that there are no wrongless harms, but that there are only a very few, if any, harmless wrongs. Here I'm not referring to so-called free-floating moral harms[3] such as gambling or smoking pot. Instead I am referring to the inchoate, anticipatory, or "nonconsummated"[4] offenses: attempt, solicitation, conspiracy, and complicity,[5] which betray what George Fletcher would call criminals' "subjective" (intended) or "manifest" (expressed), but not their actual, or harm-causing criminality.[6] Each of these offenses—failing, requesting, agreeing, and helping—is better understood as a form of partial excuse. As the Model Penal Code demonstrates, however, these offenses are legislatively approached as nothing *like* partial excuses. Although inchoate offenses risk rather than cause harm, they are too often approached in a way that has an *over*-inclusive view of responsibility that fails to properly accommodate the excuses. The following discussion therefore is a mirror image of the previous discussion in chapter 1, where I argued that the scope of responsibility is broader than it is acknowledged to be in the criminal law. That is, where chapter 1 maintained that we are responsible for more than criminal law tends to recognize, here I am going to depict inchoate criminality in a way that shows that in this area of criminal law, the scope of responsibility goes too far and the excuses not far enough.

The Equivalency Position

If we begin with two people who are doing the same thing or who mean to do the same thing, to what extent is our sense of their responsibility influenced by how things turn out? If you and I both back our cars out of our driveways carelessly, what difference does it make in a responsibility-sense if a child darts behind and is fatally struck by my car but not by yours? For Judith Thomson, we are equally "bad persons."[7] She would say the same thing of us were we both to put ourselves to committing theft, and while we both get caught, you fail at theft by luckily picking on a victim who is broke, whereas my victim hands over to me a pile of cash just before I am arrested for having unluckily completed grand theft. (Were neither of us to be caught, then I would be the "lucky" one when my intentions are realized in a successful theft and yours are not). A difference in outcome such as this, Thomson argues, "says nothing morally interesting"[8] about either of us. Thomson is not alone.[9]

But if human action that causes harm says nothing morally interesting about us that human action that avoids causing harm does not, then what, if anything, *does* the difference in outcomes say about us, except maybe that morality is not all that matters? "Nothing" is the answer from the "reformist"[10] position that has become known as "equivalency,"[11] which treats chancy outcomes that are outside our control as for that reason invariant to responsibility. Without endorsing the equivalency position, which legal philosophers have dubbed "Kantian,"[12] R. A. Duff doesn't exactly clear things up when he observes that

> [t]he equivalence theorist does not argue that the actual outcome of an action should make *no* difference to our response to the action or its agent, even if that actual outcome is to a significant degree a matter of luck; she allows that actual outcomes matter to us, and can properly affect our responses in various ways. She does argue, however, that we must distinguish our judgments of an agent's *culpability*, and the responses that directly express or depend on such judgments (blaming or morally condemning the agent, most obviously), from other kinds of response: whilst

> those other responses may be properly determined in part by matters of outcome-luck, judgments of culpability, and those that reflect them, should be independent of outcome-luck.[13]

This I take to mean that "blame," an aspect of "culpability," ignores the significance of outcomes (e.g., whether the putative theft victim has or parts with any property), though these outcomes may in some unspecified way be relevant or interesting to us or somehow part of "our response to the action or its agent." Duff does not elaborate.

We punish inchoate criminality for one reason alone: its relation to crime-in-fact. In other words, soliciting crime, conspiring to commit crime, trying but failing to commit crime, and helping crime are punishable acts *only* because of their relationship with or tendency to lead to or bring about "real" crime. Inchoate crimes therefore draw their authority from the other actions they threaten but which may or may not actually occur. When someone is accused of soliciting, conspiring, trying, or helping to commit crime "*A*," the accused's criminality is always evaluated in relation to a crime that either did not (attempt) or need not (solicitation, conspiracy, complicity) occur. Since the other crime that gives the inchoate criminal's actions their contemptible quality is not committed at all (when the planning stages stall or misfire) or if that other crime is committed it is committed by someone else, it makes good sense to see the legal meaning and operation of planning, failure, and help as traceable to the (partial) excuses.

For example, when charged with solicitation, conspiracy, attempt, or complicity, a defendant may respond with one of three exculpatory pleas: "But I did not do '*X*' [the target offense], I did something else: I merely requested, conspired, tried, or helped to do '*X*.'" (Similarly, "I meant to help crime '*Y*'—the principal departed from the common scheme or plan and did '*X*' all on his own."). Or he may respond, "But I did not *do* '*X*,' I merely solicited, conspired, tried, or helped to do '*X*.'" Or finally, in response to any of these charges except that of attempt, he may say, "But *I* did not do '*X*.' Someone else did." These pleas would in my view be pleas for partial excuse. Again, "few excuses get us out of it *completely*: the average excuse, in a poor situation, gets us only out of the fire into the frying pan—but still, of course, any frying pan in a fire" ("EXCUSES," 177). I realize that re-characterizing what we now see as the crimes of attempt, solicitation, conspiracy, and complicity as partial excuses may sound a little strange. It sounds strange because the entire *idea* of partial excuse is strange to law, particularly criminal law, where defenses tend to be catastrophic, all-or-none propositions by which defendants are fully acquitted or not, but only infrequently are they partially excused. Still I think that re-characterizing inchoate criminality as a mode of partial excuse will contribute to more fully confronting the relationships—both grammatical and moral—between those actions and the ultimate or "real" harms at which they are directed.

American law's position on equivalency is to always treat requesting, planning, trying, or helping crime as criminal, and to sometimes treat them as morally identical or adjacent to actually completing the crime yourself. An equivalency-regime meant to express an unwavering endangerment- or risk-basis of liability would ignore outcomes, and so would punish equally the defendant who puts the razor blade that is discovered in the Halloween apple prior to its being bitten into, and the defendant whose intended victim bites into the apple and suffers greatly. Accordingly, an endangerment- or risk-based regime would be concerned mostly with subjective or manifest (as opposed to harm-causing) criminality, and as such would tend mostly to prevent *potentially* harmful actions. (This is why Joel Feinberg says that he would eliminate the crimes of murder and attempted murder in favor of his invariant-to-outcomes invention: "Wrongful Homicidal Behavior.")[14] A harm- or outcome-based regime, oppositely, would be concerned mostly with harm-causing or outcome-oriented criminality, and as such would tend mostly to react to or condemn *harm-in-fact*.

As an illustration of the workings of harm and risk rationales, consider California's law of attempt.[15] That law punishes nothing preparative, virtually nothing less than a bungled or misfired action.[16] Consequently, California law reflects less concern for risk than does the Model Penal Code, whose attempt provision makes possible the punishment of even the slightest gesture toward crime.[17] At sentencing, California punishes attempts half as severely as completed offenses (which betokens a harm-orientation),[18] whereas the Model Penal Code punishes many attempts just as it does completed offenses (which betokens a risk-orientation).[19] But when it comes to solicitation and conspiracy, California's double-counting of the completed offense and either the request *or* the agreement is murderously risk-based.[20] The Model Penal Code, contrariwise, takes on a harm-orientation by allowing convictions only for the completed offense or its underlying request or agreement, but in any event *only* one offense of the three from which the prosecutor may choose.[21]

A truly harm-based regime would never punish for inchoate offenses. Indeed, a regime that punishes *any* attempts, solicitations, or conspiracies is at least *a bit* risk-based. There is no shortage of rhetoric in the Model Penal Code about manifest criminality—about the primacy of manifested intentions rather than outcomes in assessing blame:

> [W]here failure is due to a fortuity, like a misfired gun or a recalcitrant solicited party, exculpation on that ground would involve inequality of treatment that would shock the common sense of justice. Such a situation is unthinkable in any mature system designed to serve the proper goals of penal law.[22]

Despite the rhetoric, when push comes to shove, the Model Penal Code's equivalency position is abandoned for a compromise position on the importance of harm. While the Code purports to treat success, failure, planning, and carrying those plans out as equally "blameworthy" matters, it refuses to treat serious crimes that way.[23] Thus soliciting or conspiring to commit theft are punished identically to theft-in-fact,[24] but soliciting or conspiring to commit rape are punished less severely than rape-in-fact.[25] I do not see the makings of a unifying theory there.[26]

Can it really be that asking or agreeing with someone else to commit a crime are in any important sense just like trying (and failing) to commit a crime? Likewise, are requesting, agreeing, or failing just like actually pulling the crime off or helping someone else pull the crime off? And finally, is helping someone else pull the crime off anything like doing it yourself?

Soliciting someone else to commit a crime is a crime in itself, but only because it tends to excite the solicited party first into agreement, and then, much more significantly, into action: not because the social harm in the request is anything like the social harm in acting on the request. Criminal associations *tend* to succeed more than solo ventures do; and while whether or not this is true poses a complicated empirical question answerable only by laborious questioning,[27] absent evidence that too many cooks really do spoil the broth,[28] there is nothing wrong with treating criminal associations *as though* they create excessive risks of harm-causing criminality.

Certainly it is sound social policy to discourage criminal associations, to "give credit where credit is due—not merely to the ringleader—but to the ring" as well.[29] But we go too far when we conclude that soliciting[30] or conspiring[31] is close to, let alone identical to, real crime. The speech-act of the requestor is far too mediated by the will of the requested party to be treated "as though" the contemplated harm has taken or must take place. This is not to say that the target of the plot would be indifferent to the plot so long as it is never carried out. For example, parents who discover a razor blade in their child's apple *feel* harmed, though less so than if the parents were less vigilant.

Nor is asking or agreeing with someone else to commit a crime in any important sense just like trying (and failing) to commit a crime. Solicitation is punishable on its own, but not because it is an attempt or even like an attempt. It is neither. If, for example, I ask you to try to score a basket against Michael Jordan, it would be ungrammatical for me to say (provided that I have not placed such constraints on your will, or knowingly so exploited your *ex ante* lack of autonomy that it ceases to be your spontaneous act), "I have tried to score against Jordan." I have encouraged *you* to try to score against him. Whether a trying or an attempt is going to take place is at this point up to you, regardless of where the idea originates. Yet the law has at times held otherwise.[32]

The same criticism of solicitations-as-attempts is just as easily directed at redescriptions of conspiracies as attempts. This approach, discovered by Professor Philip Johnson,[33] overlooks that attempting entails *trying*. Conspiracies may demonstrate their members' bad intentions, but by agreeing to kill someone tomorrow or next month, the parties have no more attempted or tried to commit murder than those who engage to marry attempt to marry or those who register for a Bar Exam prep-course attempt to take the Bar Exam merely by registering. Professor Johnson forces his redescription of conspiracy into the Model Penal Code's definition of attempt,[34] which even without his help already makes a paranoid fantasy out of what it means to attempt a crime. Despite what the Code says, searching for a victim,[35] reconnoitering,[36] or possessing materials to be used in crime[37] do not by themselves depict what we think of when we think of someone who is *trying* to commit a crime. Equally ungrammatical is Professor Johnson's claim that *agreeing* to commit a crime is somehow trying to commit a crime.

It is hard for me to imagine a blame regime in which the distinction between intentions and outcomes, between manifest and harm-causing criminality, would *not* be acknowledged. (Who would see the defilement of Jimmy Carter, who lusted in his heart,[38] as comparable to that of Bill Clinton, who gratified his various lusts?) Like solicitation and conspiracy, attempt is an inchoate offense. Inchoate offenders do not bring about the harm they've set themselves to. That they don't is what it *means* to be an inchoate offender. Take an instance in which you and I both take aim and fire loaded guns at the President, whom each of us intends to kill to express our opposition to executive action taken abroad. I fail, whether it is the President's cigarette case, a nearby bird, bad aim, or a miraculous surgeon that accounts for the failure. You succeed in the killing, whether it is due to meticulous planning, good aim, or a lucky shot. When both of us are apprehended and our accounts of our actions are evaluated, it is plausible to say we have in a sense both done the same thing: we have both shot at the President. If that is a satisfactory description of our actions, then clearly I still have a ready excuse that you do not: I failed, I missed, I blundered, I was lucky; I killed no one.

It is this very idea that Peter Winch has in mind when he quotes a drunk driver who was "changed dramatically" after knocking down and killing a youth with his car:

> It's as if I'd been involved in one of the major mysteries of Life, as to Who gives it, and Who takes it away. To end another human being's life is a shocking thing. The most profoundly disturbing experience that can happen to anyone.[39]

Perhaps, Winch continues, it could also be said that

> [t]o (try to) end another person's life is a shocking thing. "The most profoundly disturbing experience that can happen to anyone." While we may still want to agree with what is said in the first sentence, our inclination will surely be to reply to the second that there is at least one more profoundly disturbing experience that can happen to anyone, namely to end another person's life (as in the original version).[40]

And so if I have (only) *tried* to kill the President, I should be, unless morality has absolutely no pull on me whatsoever, thankful, whether to God, to good fortune, or whatever. Thankful for what? That I did not become what I had in me and was ready to become: a killer. This profound difference between what I do become as opposed to what I could have become, or almost became, is expressed in Louis Menand's review of Steven Spielberg's *Saving Private Ryan*:

> What does [the film] tell us about war? That it is gruesome. Also that it is noble and necessary. The general view that *Saving Private Ryan* teaches revulsion for war because it contains revolting images of war seems to me to have the logic of the movie completely inside out. I have always thought that what makes war appalling isn't the possibility that someone will maim or kill you; it is the possibility that you will maim or kill someone else. War is specially terrible not because it destroys human beings, who can be destroyed in plenty of other ways, but because it turns human beings into destroyers.[41]

Regardless of my intentions, when I for whatever reason fall short of causing the harm I had in me to bring about—fall short of becoming what I had in me to become—then what was in me was not *realized*; I thus have avoided an outcome at the level of action that would have irretrievably altered my relation with myself and the world. That distinction matters; it is, whether oweable entirely to me or not, my excuse.

Merely Helping

The inchoate nature of the crime (or partial excuse) of attempt is undisputed. The dispute arises over whether criminal law should regulate risk taking and harm causing with equal punishments.[42] Unlike attempt, solicitation, or conspiracy, the crime (or partial excuse) of complicity is conventionally seen as a way of regulating harm, not risk. I think for this reason it is worth paying particularly close attention to whether complicity is, as it now is viewed, an instance where unwavering equivalency makes good sense.

Complicity rests on the premise that someone whom the law interchangeably calls an "accessory," "accomplice," "aider and abettor," "secondary party," or "helper" in his principal's offense is derivatively, not vicariously, liable for that offense. The difference between derivative and vicarious liability is that derivative liability is based partly on the defendant's own actions, not merely on his relationship with someone else. Derivative liability and therefore punishment is shared equally between principals and helpers. Proof of the helper's derivative liability is heavily mediated by the actions and intentions of the principal. If the principal commits a crime, then equal credit goes to the helper as well,[43] provided that the crime that occurs is one the helper knew about and whose success the helper intended when he provided his help.[44]

But in what way is it *as though* helpers who do not coerce or manipulate their principals commit their principals' offenses? The helper has merely helped. But helping, say, burglary, is not committing burglary; analytically, help can be withheld, or it wouldn't be helping at all.[45] Nor is helping burglary trying to commit burglary, any more than "'argue' is equivalent to 'try to convince,' or 'warn' is equivalent to 'try to alarm' or 'alert'" (*HTDTW*, 126).[46] Because helping crime is distinct from committing the crime that is being helped, complicity misspeaks by treating a helper as a principal.[47]

The law nevertheless treats a helper as a principal so long as the helper intentionally contributes to the principal's offense. "Contribute" in this sense is loosely like "cause," but not in its ordinary or strong sense that would be familiar to any first-year student of torts. That familiar sense requires that a condition be a *sine qua non* or at least a substantial factor in the occurrence in question.[48] Indeed, cause in the law of complicity doesn't mean cause at all, although some, like Professor Keith Smith (who wrote a very detailed treatise on the subject), characterize it as such.[49] At a minimum, a helper must render "actual"[50] aid that "mattered,"[51] "contribute[d],"[52] "made a difference,"[53] or "presum[ably] caused"[54] the principal's actions. Only when the helper's actions "could not have been successful in any case" is there no liability.[55] And it takes such an extended use of "cause" or "contribution" to support the conclusion that lending a man a smock to keep a battery victim's blood from staining the batterer's suit made enough difference to the batterer to justify our treating the smock lender as a batterer;[56] or, that an angry judge's interception of a telegram might have mattered in a murder because, had the victim received the telegram, he might have anticipated the gunman behind him when three gunmen stood before him and the wire had read, "Four men on horseback with guns following. Look out."[57] Even a door opened for a burglar "might possibly" make a difference to burglary through the window.[58]

While these are exceptional or borderline examples, even essential cases of complicity, such as where a helper lends his principal a crowbar for a burglary or drives him to the situs of the crime are not cases where the helper has caused the offense, even if the principal has no crowbar or cannot drive a car. So long as the principal might have acted anyway, even if by other means, then why say "caused" or even the less objectionable "made a difference" if we mean "helped" or in some cases, "tried to help"?[59] According to Smith, "cause" for purposes of complicity covers *any* influence on "an event's exact occurrence, including time, place, extent and type of harm, and so on."[60] Such an extravagantly loose notion of cause furnishes the law with a convenient way of passing through the mysterious workings of the principal, whom Professor Kadish calls a "wild card,"[61] whose will otherwise poses "a barrier through which the causal inquiry cannot penetrate."[62] So we say it is *as though* the helper committed the offense because it is *as though* he caused the principal to commit it.

Certainly one can perform an action by getting others to perform it. "We say, for example, 'Louis XIV built Versailles,' even though the actual construction was not done by him."[63] In fact, we can think of cases where the principal is not a principal at all, but is simply a tool, instrument, or means of someone else, such as when the helper recruits a lunatic or a child to do the deed. But those cases involve such coercion or manipulation of susceptible parties that the agent's act is fishy enough to be called "not responsible" or "not spontaneous." In such cases the crime can be entirely attributable to the helper/solicitor. Thus I find it unimaginable, although the law does not, that my providing a gun for a lunatic—I being *unaware* of his incapacity—to use to assault someone makes the assault mine and not his. For my agent's act to be mine, I must act in a way that shows that I *see* his act as such; it would be ungrammatical to say that someone could "use" someone else inadvertently. Apart from the exceptional circumstances in which the principal performs the action through an innocent agent, in evaluating the responsibility of the helper—who has positively associated himself with the principal's doings—*what difference does it make whether the helper makes a difference*?

The resilience of causal accounts of complicity may be due to the nature of derivative liability. For the helper's liability to flow backward from the principal's offense, the helper must have had something to do with the offense and not merely with the offender. Complicity requires that the helper be connected to his principal—since helpers must know the principal's plan and encourage or assist him—*and* to the offense, since the helper must intend to facilitate and then cause or make a difference in the principal's offense. The helper's relation to the principal reflects an endangerment- or risk-basis of liability, and the helper's relation to the offense reflects an outcome- or harm-basis of liability.

Not only is hornbook complicity concerned with harm, but it is as concerned with harm as with crime. Under the popularized "broad" view of complicity, most defenses that exculpate the principal are characterized as excuses that benefit only or remain personal to the principal.[64] This view would hold liable as accessory a sober helper who assisted a drunk burglar's entry and theft even if the principal burglar is acquitted on grounds that he was too drunk to form the intention to steal (and even if the helper is unaware of the principal's intoxication). This is a heavy tax laid on the helper, but it does leave intact the basic assumption that a helper's liability is mediated and unmediated at once. It is mediated in that the helper must help what he knows *his principal means to do*. It is unmediated in that, if their jointly intended harm occurs, however forgivably on the principal's part (usually because he is clumsy, mistaken, intoxicated, provoked, or exempt from prosecution in his role as *agent provocateur*), then it is *as though* the helper committed a crime that, paradoxically, is not a crime at all. So viewed, liability is derivative not so much of criminality, but of harmful results, even those harmful results that are brought about by excused or unconvictable principals. Thus it is as much the helper's association with harm as with other criminals at which the law of complicity strikes.

This state of affairs may express our belief that someone who helps an excused wrongdoer is just the sort of person with whom the criminal law should concern itself. I agree, but only because the helper has intentionally put himself to another's criminal purpose, which may or may not succeed. Judge Learned Hand put it best in a 1938 counterfeiting case when he explained that the doctrine of complicity demands that the helper "in some sort associate himself with the venture, that he participate in it as in something that he wishes to bring about, that he seek by his action to make it succeed."[65] The total absence of references to causal contributions or other attempts to measure the helper's input or aid indicates that Judge Hand sees complicity as largely a matter of the manifest intentions of the helper as opposed to the helper's influence on the principal or whether the principal can be convicted of a crime.

Complicity therefore presupposes that the principal has caused some legally prohibited harm, whether or not the principal has a full or partial defense that allows him to avoid all or some liability. Helping cannot exist in a vacuum. If the principal does nothing legally prohibited, then there is no wrong for which the helper could be held derivatively liable. The grammar of helping not only requires that the principal do something, but it also demands that the helper do something. Thus the Supreme Court correctly held over a century ago that a would-be helper who does not encourage or conspire with his principal, but goes along secretly ready to help if necessary (but never says so, and help turns out to be unnecessary), has helped nothing.[66] But fixating on the helper's relation to the principal's crimes or harms depends on a flimsy, rhetorical sense of "cause," even when it is toned down to "making a difference." Our instincts are correct about the propriety of punishing the helper, but not because we are satisfied that without the helper the crime would not or could not have occurred: the harm may have nothing that can be demonstrated, or even nothing at all, to do with the helper. The helper is an excessive risk taker who deserves punishment whether his aid or encouragement informs or merely glances off of his principal. As I said above, because it is fair to assume that criminal associations *tend* to succeed more than solo ventures do, we need to give credit not just to the ringleader, but to the ring as well. But we go too far when we conclude that, because helpers tend to add something to their principals' doings, helping is just like doing.

Here I am not talking about cases of "joint principality," under which two parties divide the elements of an offense; for example, two parties rob when one commits the assault and the other the larceny. Since both the force or threat of force and the taking of property are analytically, elementally, or definitionally necessary to *any* robbery, neither party is *helping* robbery; both are *committing* it. Nor am I talking about dangerous games like drag racing or Russian roulette, after which the lucky surviving participants are sometimes convicted of being complicit in the manslaughter of an unlucky participant or even unluckier bystander.[67] One cannot "help" drag racing or Russian roulette by *playing*. Certainly a buyer does not help a seller in the act of selling the goods by paying for the goods any more than a betrothed couple help each other get married by marrying each other, or someone helps someone else kiss simply by kissing them. However angry we may be at lucky survivors of dangerous games, multiparty game cases, like exchange transactions, do not instantiate helping by one whose participation is analytically necessary to the crime itself.

Manslaughter—the charge typically made against lucky survivors of dangerous games—has two elements: 1) excessive risk taking and 2) causing death. If the excessive risk for which the killer is being criticized was drag racing, then it is not an "element" which can be helped *by drag racing*. Manslaughter is not, analytically, a two-or-more-party offense; nor is it divided into one (you steer; I accelerate?) as obscene phone calling could be were one person to dial and the other to talk obscenely. To use someone's (statutorily, analytically) necessary participation as a means of describing their role as that of helping an unlucky dangerous-game player's actions papers over the grammatical and in my view moral distinction between helping and doing: again, *help can be withheld, or it wouldn't be helping at all.*

Oppositely, where the help of one party is necessary only as an empirical or synthetic matter—that is, where a helper does not fulfill a statutory definition of a crime or one of its elements, but his actions *happen to be* necessary for the crime to succeed *on these facts*, then he is helping and not doing, regardless of how he may characterize his own actions. For example, that a getaway driver may be necessary for a successful robbery must be observed to be known; getaway drivers are not analytically necessary to robbery. Consequently, getaway drivers are helpers, not doers or joint principals, regardless of how they may characterize their actions. Though American law insists on treating helpers and doers identically, getaway drivers and their analogues should have an excuse, albeit partial: they didn't really *do* it (or didn't really do *it*). They were *merely* helping.

I hope that the law of complicity—its notion of equivalency—is not as it is simply to avoid problems in separating principals from helpers. Because the principal's conviction was historically a necessary condition of the helper's conviction, *any* basis of the principal's acquittal precluded the helper's conviction, even when the prosecution otherwise had the helper dead to rights. Consequently, if the principal escaped, died, or came up with his own defense that worked at trial or even on appeal, the helper would be automatically immune from prosecution or entitled to an annulment of his conviction. To get around this snag in bringing helpers to book, courts began to subversively interpret the term "principal," extending it far beyond its grammar. Helpers became "constructive" principals who were held by fiction to be present and operating at the scene of the crime even if they were not. This way, if everyone involved in the offense could be called "principal," an escaped, dead, or exonerated principal would have no effect on the prosecution of other members of the criminal enterprise (other "principals"), even those members whose roles were comparatively minor. Parliament and Congress ratified this judicial charade over a century ago by eliminating the legal significance of the terminology that had plagued the prosecution of helpers: the legal fate of the principal would no longer influence that of the helper. Also cast aside was any notion that the roles that defendants played in an offense should influence the punishment that they deserved: all members of the criminal enterprise would be punished equally, regardless of what they did.[68] Accordingly, while the parties have in no sense done the same thing, nor are they necessarily even treated identically. In some cases, the principal does the dirty work and gets off scot-free due to a "personal" defense while the helper pays full price for someone else's actions.

But if the current state of complicity is symptomatic of our indignation at behind-the-scenes masterminds in gaming, counterfeiting, prostitution, drug manufacturing, and other far-flung enterprises that rely on hierarchy and division of labor, then this indignation expresses only that *we* think that "game," "counterfeit," "sell sex," and "manufacture drugs" describe actors and actions that the law does not. To answer who the real perpetrator is in these cases would require thorough knowledge of the enterprise, of who really has a stake in the outcome, of who, if anyone, exercises "hegemony over the act,"[69] and whether we think, for instance, that an underling's running a printing press is what we mean by "counterfeiting" as opposed to merely "helping counterfeiting." Making these hard calls is part of judging, informing them is part of lawyering, and being subject to them is part of being a criminal defendant who has treaded into areas of questionable legality.

Perhaps this argument I have been constructing here is just a sort of old-school reminiscence on the good old days of indeterminate sentencing, which, were it still the norm, would give judges significant leeway in selecting the appropriate punishment for participants based on the importance of the role that each played in the offense. Such an approach is now anathema in America, but examples of careful role-sorting-out can be found elsewhere. For example, Leo Katz summarizes a case that reached the German Reichsgericht in 1940 in which two sisters conspired to conceal their pregnancies from their tyrannical father, who threatened to put them both out of the house should they become pregnant. The dominant sister took her pregnancy to term; her submissive sister miscarried. After the still-pregnant, dominant sister somehow disguised her condition from their father, she secretly gave birth. Katz further recounts:

> The new mother implored her sister, who was just bathing the baby, to kill it lest their father toss them out on the street. After refusing for some time, the sister finally gave in and drowned the baby. Both were charged with murder. The court, nevertheless, found only the mother guilty of murder and convicted her sister merely as an accessory even though it was she who had actually carried out the killing.[70]

The court got to the bottom of this lopsided sibling relation by relying on the "hegemony" over the act exercised by the new mother (or dominant sister). That is, the new mother's "illegitimate" power over her sister characterized their relation and thus could in the court's eyes explain that while the ostensible perpetrator was the submissive sister (she after all is the one who drowned her newborn niece), a more thorough knowledge of their relation and of the episode supported a conviction of murder for the new mother. The submissive sister, meanwhile, was convicted of the much less serious offense of accessory to murder, thereby flipping the conventional application of the terms "perpetrator" and "accessory." A judge later explained: "If someone can be perpetrator without raising a finger in the actual execution, I don't see why someone can't be accessory, who executes the offensive act. If perpetration is to be defined exclusively in terms of whose will was controlling, I can see no principled difference between the two cases."[71]

If we know who the *real* principal is (the one who is running the printing press that produces the counterfeit bills? Or the one who set up the scheme?), then his helpers are punishable for one reason only: with an intention to associate themselves with a criminal venture, they increase the risk of criminality by bolstering or enlightening someone with encouragement, information, or materials. It is not as though they haven't done anything; they *have* done something that we should "stigmatize," "censor," or "disgrace." But given its essentially inchoate basis,[72] complicity, like all inchoate criminality, should be viewed as a form of partial excuse ("I *merely* helped," "I didn't do it—*he* did," "I was there, but . . .") in order to acknowledge the law's responsibility for making careful, refined, graded, even nuanced distinctions about who is answerable for what.

One response to this argument I have made against the equivalency position is that since "'tis not in mortals to command success,"[73] our inability to *control* the outcomes of the things we put ourselves to somehow makes those outcomes irrelevant in a responsibility-sense. This may be why Professor Ross says that all one promises when one promises to do so and so is only to do one's best to fulfill the promise, but not actually to fulfill it, since "we are under no obligation to effect changes, only to set ourselves to do so."[74] Such a way of responding to "luck"—to the fact that much of "[w]hat we do in the world depends on the world as well as on us"[75]—has led to our eliminating grammatical and moral distinctions between actions such as requesting, agreeing, trying, helping, and doing. Eliminating these distinctions caves in to a view of responsibility that suggests that the results of our actions are something *other* than the things that we do. If such a view is the one we accept, if manifested intentions are all that matter and results do not, then "it becomes gradually clear that actions are events and people things. Eventually nothing remains which can be ascribed to the responsible self, and we are left with nothing but a portion of the larger sequence of events, which can be deplored or celebrated, but not blamed or praised."[76] Therefore my stake in including inchoate criminality among the partial excuses is to preserve a realm for the responsible self where not only do results matter, but so does the difference between the results of *my* actions and someone else's: where we acknowledge that "[a] man's relation to his own acts is quite different from his relation to the acts of other people."[77]

3

Is Criminal Law (Especially) Moral?

The Domain of the Moral

It's safe to say that the epigraphs from Professor Arenella's work that opened this book are representative of an uncontested view that the criminal law is moral, makes moral judgments, or is in some important sense about morality. Our persistent zeroing in on criminal law's moral function evidently is meant to distinguish that function from, *inter alia*, allocating risks, enforcing expectancies, disgorging gains from the unjustly enriched, and coercing compliance with court orders. But it is an elusive notion of the moral that could make criminal law uniquely moral. In other words, it is not highly unusual crimes like murder,[1] even more unusual punishments like the death penalty,[2] or a public as opposed to private focus (a wobbly fiction even on a good day)[3] that makes criminal law moral whereas much of civil law is somehow not moral. References to criminal law's moral foundations *could* mean that criminal law is *more* moral than civil law. But what would that mean?

Consider the following comparison staged by Jeffrie Murphy:

> Is defamation treated as a tort and auto theft as a crime because the former is morally trivial (no serious harm, no major rights violations, nothing worthy of solemn moral condemnation) whereas the latter is morally important? Surely not. My life may be trashed utterly as the result of a believed defamation, and the cost to me of the theft of my auto is probably simply a bit of inconvenience while I wait for my insurance company to buy me another one.[4]

Although Jean Hampton concurs that "there are torts that constitute worse harms, from a moral point of view, than some crime,"[5] and that "some punishments can be milder than civil penalties,"[6] both Murphy and Hampton do identify and endorse a tort-crime distinction. Indeed, there must be such a distinction, and where it lies has been the topic of some recent symposia,[7] which have produced some impressive papers. I don't care to recite them here, but that the tort-crime line reflects in part that most criminal remedies are harder on the wrongdoer than most civil remedies (although less likely to be applied),[8] and that criminal punishment, unlike civil compensation, is designed for "stigmatizing," "censoring," and "disgracing"[9] in no way establishes that criminal law is moral but civil law is not.[10] Moreover, to say even *that* is an attempt to refute Stewart Macaulay's work showing that very few businesspersons need to sue to enforce contracts because someone who commits the civil wrong of breach of contract *is* stigmatized, censored, and disgraced.[11] Which, after all, would most Americans fear more: a brief jail stint or a permanently ruined credit rating?

There are, however, differences between civil and criminal law that we can classify as moral if by "moral" we refer to those undertakings that are *malum in se* or wrong in a prelegal sense—actions whose wrongfulness would occur to anyone who pays attention to "the values that would have motivated a good person to perceive the real value of things."[12] These prelegal wrongs, which are coterminous with much of the laws of crime *and* tort, are often put in opposition to *malum prohibitum* wrongs—those ticky-tack sorts of legal obligations that even a citizen attentive to the good, the right, and the true still may not be aware of. Not knowing that your weekly maid's wages are taxable, to crib an example of Dan Kahan's, is merely *malum prohibitum* in that it is an obligation, given the intricacies of the Internal Revenue Code, that even a good person could miss.[13] It is this type of wrong that Ronald Dworkin has in mind when he talks about how a legislature could take away the right to "drive either way on Fifty-seventh Street" or "vote for a congressman every two years."[14] But the tort of employment discrimination and the contract wrong of material breach, which are core examples of civil, not criminal, wrongs, are nothing at all like the minor, ticky-tack sort of regulations that merit the label "*malum prohibitum*." In other words, most defendants found to have offended a rule of civil law are as "inattentive to moral obligations"[15] as is, say, a common thief.

What is it, then, that urges us to refer to moral this or that? Why is accusing someone of theft or murder *itself* a moral act?

Judge Posner denies the importance of "adherence to generally accepted moral principles" except to the extent that it tends to "increase[] the wealth of society more than it reduces it."[16] For him, the justification of laws even against slavery[17] and rape[18] is merely a function of the fact that they reduce "transaction costs." Not willing to go quite that far is Justice Oliver Wendell Holmes, who while completely and deliberately emptying words like "negligence" of their moral sense, explicitly left criminal law aside in arguing that we not only have no moral obligation to obey the law, but we have no moral obligations, period.[19] So if criminal law is largely viewed as irretrievably moral, does that mean that accusing someone of breaking a promise or a vase, or of being inconsiderate—a contention that in Austin's view is "beneath the law, as too trivial, or outside it, as *too purely moral*" ("EXCUSES," 188, emphasis mine)—is an accusation that is somehow not moral at all or not moral enough?

When we refer to morality, we refer to responsibility, whose root is what you do and fail to do, and whose trunk and branch are what you are answerable for. A confrontation with what you are answerable for, in turn, occurs wherever your conduct raises a question that demands a specific response from you (as where your intentions fail, one way or another, in their execution). This response requires not only that you know what you do, what you are doing, what you have done and not done, but furthermore, it requires that you be able to *elaborate* the action: say why you are doing it, or excuse or justify it if that becomes necessary, even though the implications of your conduct—your responsibilities—are invariably not obvious to you (*CR*, 311–12). In morality, our interest in these elaborations—our interest in intentions, given the need to come to terms with another's conduct—is "to localize [your] responsibility within the shift of events" ("MEANING IT," 236–37). So when we ask you about your intentions, we ask whether you are meeting your responsibilities; we ask for an explanation of your conduct, which we feel we have the right to question because of our relation to you or to what you have done.

The point of moral discourse is not to pass judgments—that would be to moralize.[20] Nor is it even necessary to the success of moral discourse that we reach agreement. Rather, the point of moral discourse is to repair human relationships that have broken down. That is what I mean when I refer to the way in which morality's interest in intentions (in excuses) seeks "to localize [your] responsibility within the shift of events." We are located in relation to one another. Moral discourse therefore occurs in community, where civil obligations to keep your promises and keep your icy sidewalk shoveled are as much the domain of responsibility as is your obligation to keep your temper. Because civil *and* criminal laws raise questions of responsibility, the obligations they impose on us are legal *and* moral, whether they enjoin actions that are wrong in a prelegal sense or wrong just because the legislature says so. I say this because I cannot see how questions of whether we abide by or break the law are anything *but* questions of morality.[21] Indeed, not only am I unsure of what it would mean for an obligation to bind us legally and not at once bind us morally, but nor do I know, when we talk of "moral wrongs,"[22] what other kinds of wrongs there could be.

Criminal law may nonetheless be moral in a way that much of civil law, or at least contract law, is not. In contract law you are not answerable for breaking your promises. And how can we tell this? Because in contract law it normally doesn't matter at all why you broke your promise. Put another way: *in contract law there is no role played by excuses*, or not the same role they play in criminal law. Your elaborations do not mitigate your breach of a contractual obligation. Your elaborations can *relieve* you of your obligation, but usually on the theory that you never had an obligation in the first place, due, for example, to fraud,[23] duress[24] or unconscionability.[25] This powerfully reinforces the centrality of excuses to the morality of criminal law. And of course that you are not (legally) answerable for contract breaches explains why contract remedies are purely compensatory. Indeed, the recent importation of notions of good faith are making contract law more moral than before—more dependent then ever on the excuses of breaching parties.[26] This is especially true in the context of insurance law, where insurers are subject to punitive damages for the "tort" of breaching their contractual duty to defend or pay a claim to their insured.[27]

At the same time, however, even without the importation of notions of good faith into contract law, it may well be that contracts, if not contract law, are *more* moral than criminal law. While the excuses are unimportant to contract law, they are crucial to contracts, that is, to contractual relationships. Breaches of contract are typically healed extralegally by reestablishing or reworking the parties' expectations and obligations: by reconciling the problem of breach through the proffering of an excuse that is fully or partially accepted by the nonbreaching party. It is tempting to say that criminal law is more moral than contracts because criminal acts call uniquely for a legal or police response, while breaches of contract generally are handled without courts or lawyers. Yet it may be this very difference that makes contracts (again, not contract law) more moral than crime/criminal law. If contract law vanished overnight, the activity of contracting would be very little influenced. We would retain both the concept of a contract and the activity of contracts because "contract" does not have "legal enforceability" as part of its definition (despite what some law professors and lawyers may say). Were criminal law to vanish overnight, contrariwise, the activity of crime would most assuredly increase. And we would lose the concept of a crime (though not of a wrong) because "punishable" is part of the definition of "crime." There is consequently a sense in which criminal law is the *least* moral part of law in that it addresses harms where resolving questions of responsibility cannot be achieved *merely* though moral discourse. It may well be because relations in contracts tend to be self-repairing by adjusting existing relations that they *are* moral, or at least that they are handled through moral discourse, i.e., through the deployment of excuses. It may be equally true that it is because crime is highly unlikely to lead to extralegal reconciliation that it is *not* moral in that crime/criminal law is not about the working out of relationships, but an acknowledgment of their failure. Nothing highlights this better than the intense interest that crime victims and their families express in "closure," which they contend can be brought about only when the wrongdoer is legally punished.[28]

The Function of the Excuses in Moral Discourse

Questioning Intentions To Limit Responsibility

Aspects of this compressed explanation of the domain of the moral I glean from Stanley Cavell, who has carefully explicated the function of the excuses—of references to intentions—in moral discourse. Cavell holds that "in morality, tracing an intention *limits* a man's responsibility" ("MEANING IT," 236). This same insight was earlier adumbrated by Austin when he noted that accusations such as "you did that deliberately!" "may often bring in the very things that excuses, if we had any, would be designed to rule out" ("INK," 273). What Austin and Cavell mean by this is that all accusations—all requests for us to elaborate our intentions—ask, even demand, that we exculpate ourselves for the things we do or fail to do.

Indeed, it is hard to imagine how an utterance can *count* as an accusation unless it calls for an excuse from the accused. That is, it is definitory of an accusation that it call for an excuse. If we are interested only in an admission of responsibility, if we are not open to hearing and accepting excuses, then we would just hold others responsible or blame them rather than accuse them. For example, when Emile Zola published his celebrated letter in the newspaper *L'Aurore*, where he denounced the French general staff for falsely accusing a Jewish French army officer of espionage, his letter began, "*J'accuse*."[29] That utterance may be an essential aspect of Zola's holding responsible or blaming the French general staff for their role in the so-called *affaire* Dreyfus. But to accuse is to demand a response, which may take the form of an excuse, or it may take the form of a denial of responsibility or of a refusal to respond altogether. But unless Zola was open to reconciliation (to confronting and at least potentially accepting an excuse), then he has not really accused anyone; instead, he would be going straight to holding them responsible or blaming them while merely playing at accusing. Accusing without remaining open to reconciliation is a pose.

It is our response to the claim or demand that accusations make on us that Elizabeth Anscombe is getting at when she cites in one discussion the following two passages from Wittgenstein's *Philosophical Investigations*:

> I am not ashamed of what I did then, but of the intention which I had. And didn't the intention reside *also* in what I did? What justifies the shame? The whole history of the incident (*PI*, 165, para. 644).

> Why do I want to tell him about an intention too, as well as telling him what I did? . . . [B]ecause I want to tell him something about *myself*, which goes beyond what happened at that time. I reveal to him something of myself when I tell him what I was going to do. —Not, however, on grounds of self-observation, but by way of a response (it might also be called an intuition) (*PI*, 167, para. 659).

To Anscombe, in thinking this way about intentions Wittgenstein is "thinking of a response, or reaction." "[I]n the context of *our* interests," she goes on, "we can think of it as a response to our special question 'Why?' "[30] And that intuition to which she refers above—to reveal oneself—is expressed as an elaboration, an excuse, a move toward the restoration of a relation within community. This is not to say that our excuses cannot make matters worse for us. Sometimes what we reveal, or our refusal to reveal enough, excites indignation, not acknowledgment or compassion. Indignation may be a response to our being theatrical, that is, to our intending to just reveal, not to just explain ourselves.[31] In other words, if our plea is meant to have a specific effect on our audience, the excuse could fail *for that reason*. To intend to (just) reveal yourself has the overtone of controlling, manipulating, or scripting the reaction of others to you (instead of letting others make of you what they will, which is the precondition of ever really being acknowledged by them). To let others make of you what they will gives them the possibility of responding to you (accepting or rejecting you) when you proffer excuses, which connotes a recognition that they have a right or are in a position to question you.

Questioning Intentions: "No Modification without Aberration"

We question intentions when we question what was done. Most lawyers refer to intentions when they refer to various "mental states"[32] or degrees of "fault"[33] that characterize our "voluntary acts."[34] When we ask whether someone intended such and such, we insinuate that there was something fishy about what was done. For example, were I to ask you: "Do you wear your hair that way voluntarily?" my question would be incompetent unless I were searching for an explanation that, for example, you had been in a hurry, that the lights went out in your apartment, or that you had spent the night out late. This is what Austin means when he says "no modification without aberration" ("EXCUSES," 189). An adverb such as voluntarily, deliberately, intentionally, purposely, or thoughtlessly modifies only the aberrant or unusual action:

> Only if we do the action named in some *special* way or circumstances, different from those in which such an act is naturally done (and of course both the normal and the abnormal differ according to what verb in particular is in question) is a modifying expression called for, or even in order. I sit in my chair, in the usual way—I am not in a daze or influenced by threats or the like: here, it will not do to say either that I sat in it intentionally or that I did not sit in it intentionally, nor yet that I sat in it automatically or from habit or what you will ("EXCUSES," 190).

Accordingly, if you do not look *unusually* disheveled, then the question "Do you wear your hair that way voluntarily?" is empty. I would not ask you: "voluntary or not?" unless I felt entitled to and was prepared to accept an explanation. Indeed, not only does questioning what was done or the way in which it was done ask us for an excuse, but even more, much of what we say in response to that question is an excuse, e.g., "I've let everything slip since I've been feeling 'down in the dumps,'" "I just realized than vanity is a vice," or "I thought messy hair was fashionable—the latest craze." Some responses, of course, such as "My hair isn't messy!" would function more as a criticism of the accusation than as an excuse. This is so because deflecting responsibility altogether for the unhappy or untoward action that any accusation presupposes is a correction (even a criticism) of, rather than an attempt at reconciliation with, the accuser.[35]

Whatever your excuse may be, we *cannot* take my question as a dispassionate inquiry into whether a certain "mental state" regarding your hair existed when you left home this morning. In other words, an appeal to our intentions is meant to evoke a response sure enough, but *not*, contrary to the way criminal lawyers put it, by way of the revelation of secret "mental states":

> Descriptions of mental events or processes are not acceptable as answers to questions about what our intentions are. A request for our intentions is not a request for a description of something inside us, but a request for us to perform a certain act that requires us to go on record or to commit ourselves in a certain way that justifies the reliance of other persons on what we profess our intentions to be.[36]

Indeed, Paul Gudel's thoughtful repudiation of the prevailing view about human action is worth quoting at length:

> If intentions are not internal things or happenings, what are they? What sorts of things can fill in for the variable in the assertion, "My intention is *X*"? Most commonly, the place of the *X* is taken by a verb in the infinitive signifying an action or achievement. Therefore, the most general definition of an intention is "an action in prospect."
>
> It is not, then, that intentions are difficult to observe or to have "direct evidence" of. Intentions simply are not the sorts of things that *can* be observed, any more than one can observe the number five (not some particular written or printed instance of the number five, but the number itself). This does not mean they are necessarily hidden; it only means that the

> concept of "observation" has no obvious application to them. When we say something like, "The intentions of another cannot be directly observed," we have no coherent idea of what it would mean to "observe another's intention." If anything is meant by this phrase at all, it probably is something along the lines of "observe his intention as he himself observes it." But there is no such thing as this; there is no thing called "the intention" we observe by introspection just before every action we take. Intentions are not observed, either by ourselves or others.
>
> We use the language of intentions, and impute intentions to persons, *as a way of making human actions intelligible to ourselves*. We do not make actions intelligible to ourselves by adverting to an inner event that preceded that action. *Our interest in human actions is not usually in how they were produced, but in how they can be more fully understood.* Because this is what the attribution of intentions does, the language of intentions has reference to the public, observable world, not to an inaccessible world of inner events.[37]

"Voluntary or not?" "responsible or not?" "deliberate or not?" are not questions that we can competently ask of every action. Indeed, if from among all actions we subtract those that are voluntary and those that are not voluntary, not only do some actions remain, but most actions remain. What remains is that most pervasive class of actions: the ordinary.[38] Again, when I put the question: "Do you wear your hair that way voluntarily?" it may be tempting to see the answer as limited to "Yes" or "No." You must have done it freely or unfreely. What other response could be available? The answer is that most actions (ordinary actions) are done neither freely nor under constraint or out of ignorance. And not because they fall within that class of actions that Aristotle calls "mixed," that is, those actions that are both free and unfree, as in a ship captain's mixed action of tossing cargo overboard to keep the ship afloat in a storm.[39] Instead, ordinary actions are neither voluntary nor involuntary because they raise no question of voluntariness: there is nothing in "the public observable world" for us to make sense of.

One response at this point is to say that ordinary actions raise no question of voluntariness only because the voluntariness of ordinary actions is simply "too obvious"[40] to make pointing it out anything but redundant (*CR*, 211–21). In other words, wearing one's hair one way or another is typically so clearly a voluntary act that pointing it out is an unnecessary locution: a waste of breath. Every action, the argument runs, is voluntary or involuntary (or a mixture of the two). It is just that it is only the fishy actions whose voluntariness we doubt. Because with ordinary actions there is no such doubt, there is no payoff in establishing what we all know is true. Of course the ordinary action is voluntary! So it must follow that with *or* without our questioning the act, it retains its voluntary or involuntary quality, which in no way depends on what we make of those actions. *All* actions have those qualities quite apart from our acts of interpretation, quite apart from whatever explains our interest in those actions.

To the ordinary-language philosopher, however, the ordinary action is neither voluntary nor involuntary. Those labels do not describe inherent characteristics of action. Instead, they are descriptions we make only of actions of which we are attempting to make sense. An ordinary instance of arranging one's hair is not "obviously voluntary." It only gets its voluntariness from us in our role as interpreters of action in contexts in which we have reason to question what was done and thus are interested in the agent's excuses. To refer to voluntariness in any other context, Austin might warn, "is simply barking our way up the wrong gum tree" ("MINDS," 116). Cavell puts the matter this way when discussing the criteria for assertions of knowledge:

> Do I know (now) (am I, as it were *knowing*) that there is a green jar of pencils on the desk (though I am not now looking at it)? If I do know now, did I not know before I asked the question? I had not, before then, said that or thought it; but that is perhaps not relevant. If someone had asked me whether the jar was on the desk I could have said Yes without looking. So I did know. But what does it mean to say "I did know"? Of course no one will say that I *did not know* (that I wasn't knowing). On the other hand, no one would have said of me, seeing me sitting at my desk with the green jar out of my range of vision, "He knows there is a green jar of pencils on the desk," nor would anyone say of me now, "He (you) knew there was a green jar . . . ," *apart from some special reason which makes that description of my "knowledge" relevant* to something I did or said or am doing or saying (e.g., I told someone that I never keep pencils on my desk; I knew that Mrs. Greenjar was coming to tea and that she takes it as a personal affront if there is a green jar visible in the room . . . .) (*CR*, 205).

Asserting, like any other activity, has its conditions (*M&S*, 97–100). What you know or do not know—just like what you intend or not—is a question that arises only in very specific circumstances: when there is what Cavell calls "some special reason" that makes matters of knowing or intending relevant. Cavell imagines a response: "Perhaps no one would have *said* that you knew the jar was there, but you *did* know it. It makes sense to say you knew it" (*CR*, 215). To that he answers: "Certainly it makes sense. And that just means that we can easily imagine circumstances in which it *would* make sense to say it" as in " '[h]e ought to know better' (than to put a green jar in the same room with my pet bull)" (*CR*, 212).

When we rule out the excuses and conclude that the putatively voluntary action was indeed voluntary, the action is classified as such *only* because we raised the question. In the case of the ordinary, non-fishy action, the response to questions about what was done or its style of performance would be: "What do you mean by that?," "I'm not sure I understand," or "What are you insinuating?" The response "I did it voluntarily" or "I didn't mean for it to come out like this" is made either to deny or facilitate community: to mark the failure of, or preserve (or reestablish), a relation. Unless something has gone wrong or is in some way fishy or untoward, there would be no occasion for accusing—for demanding an excuse. Instead, once put on the spot with the question "voluntary or not?," the only response open to the accused in the absence of some reason to think the action extraordinary would be: "Huh?"

We ask you about your intentions because we are interested in your elaboration, your chance to exculpate yourself for what you have done. We ask because we have in "the public, observable world" observed something fishy about what you have done, something we would like to settle up or resolve with you. We are chasing after neither something inside you nor something we can infer about something inside you. An example of Austin's may help here:

> Suppose I tie a string across a stairhead. A fragile relative, from whom I have expectations, trips over it, falls, and perishes. Should we ask whether I tied the string there intentionally? Well, but it's hard to see how I could have done such a thing unintentionally, or even (what is not the same) not done it intentionally. You don't do that sort of thing—by accident? By mistake? Inadvertently? On the other hand, would I be bound to admit I did it "on purpose" or "purposely"? That has an ugly sound. What could the purpose have been if not to trip at least someone? Maybe I had better claim I was simply passing the time, playing cat's cradle, practising tying knots ("INK," 274–75).

What will defeat this claim of passing the time, playing a game, or tying knots is that it is something you "had better claim" (as if to put on or feign) rather than reveal or explain. It is, in a sense, self-refuting: why would you play *that* game *there*? Maybe you meant all along to do in your fragile relative, although even then we feel entitled to an elaboration. Perhaps the relative deserved it, or the boss had been running you down that day, or maybe inheriting under the will was not your motive: you did not know you stood to gain. In any event, when we ask about your intentions—when we feel entitled to an elaboration of your fishy or untoward actions—your excuses, your ways of getting out of it, are unavoidably wrapped up in or anticipated by the accusation ("you meant that," "you intended that," "you did that on purpose, didn't you").

It would be an exaggeration to say that "unintentionally" is the term on which the meaning of "intentionally" depends (as the meaning of "real" is parasitic on "fraudulent," "fake," "toy," "pretend," or "dummy").[41] But it would *not* be an exaggeration to say that a just-as-popular term of aggravation—voluntary—does get its sense or what Austin and Hart call its "cash value" (*S&S*, 18)[42] from our ability to rule out instances of the *not* voluntary. Indeed, well before drafting "A Plea For Excuses" ("EXCUSES," 190 n. 2)[43] and "Pretending" ("PRETENDING," 271)[44]—where this same relation is developed—Austin had already most carefully worked out the relation between the botched, or as he put it, "infelicitous" act and the ordinary, natural, successful act (*HTDTW*, Preface, v–vi).[45] Austin's *How To Do Things With Words* established not only that to understand what it means to say something in a "speech situation" is to understand what it means to do something much more generally, but also that understanding speech-acts involves studying "the doctrine of *the things that can be and go wrong* on the occasion of such utterances, the doctrine of the *Infelicities*." (*HTDTW* 14–45, 136–61). That doctrine holds that what constitutes an action such as marrying can be discovered by identifying instances where the action fails or is "unhappy," such as where one of you is married already, the person performing the ceremony lacks the authority to do so, or one purported spouse is underage or a monkey (*HTDTW*, 23–24). Whether we are studying speech-acts or other acts, only once we've ruled out the excuses that reduce or abrogate the agent's responsibility for a failed or unhappy action are we left with an action that is voluntary or intentional or some other "positive" term having no applicability whatsoever to the ordinary, natural, successful action. In other words, we cannot imagine a coherent use of "voluntary" other than by reference to what is left over after certain excuses such as "'under constraint' of some sort, duress or obligation or influence" ("EXCUSES," 191) have been ruled out.

So why slough off the importance of what Cavell has called "so homely, but altogether a central, moral activity as the entering of an excuse"? ("CRITICISM," 105). In other words, excuses are entered as a way of understanding and responding to the accusation itself: what was done, what went wrong. Yet hornbook criminal law and a host of leading academic lawyers see the relation between aggravating and extenuating adverbs quite differently from the way I have just described, or at least that is their official position. In their leading criminal-law casebook, Sanford Kadish and Stephen Schulhofer devote eleven pages of an early chapter to "Actus Reus—Culpable Conduct," which they say, with plenty of support,[46] imposes a "voluntary act" requirement that they put this way: "[T]he absence of an act precludes culpability. In such a case, there is physical action, but it is discounted because there is no mental disposition to take such action, let alone a criminal disposition."[47] So it seems they suggest that the "voluntariness" of an act depends on a precedent "mental act" which pre-dates, as it were, the entire activity of questioning/responding (accusing/excusing) and is analytically separate from them. Yet Kadish and Schulhofer's treatment of voluntary acts is invariably trained on the excuses. (This same relation between accusing and excusing may explain why Aristotle interprets voluntary acts *first* by eliminating from the realm of the voluntary any action performed under constraint or out of ignorance).[48] Though a voluntary act is a prerequisite of "culpability" (another special criminal-law word) the meaning of "voluntary" is demonstrated by Kadish and Schulhofer through instances of nonaction, e.g., sleepwalking, seizures, shock-induced frenzies, and hypnosis. But Kadish and Schulhofer nowhere confront this internal affinity between aggravating and extenuating language; in fact, such a confrontation is blocked by an explanatory note that the text never contradicts. In that note, J. G. Murphy says that accident, mistake, and duress are excuses, but in cases of seizures, convulsions, reflex movements, and sleepwalking, "talk of excuse here seems to make no more sense than would talk of excusing a rock for falling on one's head."[49]

I already said what I have to say about Murphy's account of what we need and need not excuse ourselves for.[50] For now, I mean only to point out that Kadish and Schulhofer set out to define criminal conduct by conditioning it on the concurrence of physical action and a mental disposition, but they cannot manage to get underway establishing instances of action *except* through instances of nonaction, which Kadish and Schulhofer choose to locate outside the domain of the excuses.[51] Because in their view a "voluntary act" means little without a guilty "mental state," Kadish and Schulhofer proceed to define the pertinent "mental states" of "purpose," "knowledge," "recklessness," and "negligence,"[52] to which they periodically attribute a "special sense" that they never explain.[53] But again, the aggravating mental states are analyzed mainly through court cases that conclude that: 1) accidents generally are not "culpable"; and 2) mistakes—the idea of a wrong alternative (either taking one thing for another, or taking one tack rather than another) ("CRITICISM," 107)—strip the culpability from the mental state. It is not until near the end of the book that Kadish and Schulhofer devote a whole chapter to justifications and excuses—the "reverse" of the inculpatory or aggravating part of criminal law—that appear as somehow though not entirely[54] external to the previous one thousand pages on various ways of getting into trouble.

4

The Ghost in the Machine

Doing an Action

A Primer on Ordinary-Language Methodology

My concerns here are not with a casebook's table of contents. Rather, I am puzzled by just how profoundly the language of the criminal law departs from ordinary language. For example, to Professor Michael Moore, whose view is quite companionable with Kadish and Schulhofer, the act "portion" of what makes us responsible for unhappy outcomes entails a "willed bodily movement," which he cautions us not to confuse with Justice Holmes's description of a human action as a "voluntary muscular contraction" (*A&C*, 81).[1] To Moore, we are responsible for the harms traceable to our willed movements if those harms and movements are caused by certain "mental states" that make the movements "moral wrongs" that are recognized as such by legislatures. This, in turn, is for Moore essential to what he endorses as a "univocal act requirement," the key ingredient to his "hidden systematization" of "moral responsibility or legal liability" (*A&C*, 40–43).

I suspect, however, that giving into such a picture of human action—this "fetishization . . . of inner and outer"[2]—may distort our evaluations of who is answerable for what, no matter how committed we are to getting to the bottom of things. In other words, while it may seem innocuous enough to say that criminality is bifurcated into "bad acts and guilty minds,"[3] I wonder how we establish who is responsible for what if we do not get a faithful picture of what it is that people really *do*? How can we acknowledge others, confront them, their cares, their commitments, and hold them responsible or let them off the hook ("localize [their] responsibility within the shift of events") if we literalize what Austin called "the machinery of doing actions"? ("EXCUSES," 193).

Moore's four hundred-page monograph on the implications of the philosophy of action for the criminal law is meant to rescue his theory of action by which the mind causes fingers to squeeze triggers (*A&C*, 200), pelvises to move rhythmically (*A&C*, 90), tongues to move (*A&C*, 129), lips to touch (*A&C*, 237) (or make contact) (*A&C*, 371), and toes to push off (*A&C*, 152) as "useful [and] true" (*A&C*, 109) redescriptions of killing, raping, talking, kissing, and walking. But rescue it from what? From the "influence" of "high-handed" ordinary-language philosophy, which "is still felt in criminal-law theory" (*A&C*, 91–92).[4] In other words, Moore seeks to rescue the "voluntary act requirement" from the damage that Austin and company have done to Moore's view of the world. If Moore has a fear, it is that his theory of action, which owes largely to eighteenth-century legal philosopher John Austin (no relation), will "be dismissed as 'really nothing more than an outdated fiction—a piece of eighteenth century psychology which has no application to human conduct'" (*A&C*, 165).[5]

What has gone wrong here is that Moore assumes that ordinary language reflects a certain theory about human action—one among many possible theories, including his. But ordinary-language philosophy provides no theory at all, but rather, a way of looking at or evaluating *all* theories, namely, a way of considering all the statements of philosophical theories *as* ordinary assertions and then asking: what would their grammar be? What would be the criteria of their use? Cite an instance of what is ordinarily said ("We say . . . but we don't say . . ."), or offer an explication of what is implied or meant when we utter sentences of the first type ("When we say . . . we imply . . ."; "We don't say . . . unless we mean . . ."). Ordinary language is not a kind of language that is set in opposition to "philosophical language." An ordinary-language philosopher accepts philosophical arguments *as* ordinary utterances. For this reason, Cavell takes Austin to task for excluding the philosopher from the *we* when Austin speaks of "what we should say when. . . ."[6] What we gain from philosophizing in such a manner is a way of talking that makes agreement *and* disagreement possible ("K&A," 240–41). Moore gets off to a bad start by profoundly misreading Austin on the methodological or "metaphysical" level. He doesn't seem to take seriously Wittgenstein's statement in the *Investigations* that "[i]f one tried to advance *theses* in philosophy, it would never be possible to debate them, because everyone would agree to them" (because they would be trivial or obvious) (*PI*, para. 128).[7]

What, then, does the ordinary-language philosopher do if not come up with theories about reality? The term "Ordinary Language Philosophy," synonymous with "Oxford Philosophy" and "Oxford Analysis," identifies a way of approaching philosophical problems. It began in Thursday evening discussions among a small group of philosophers (no more than seven) under the direction of Austin from spring 1937 until summer 1939 in the rooms of Isaiah Berlin at Oxford's All Souls College.[8] Most notable about these gatherings were the often testy exchanges between Austin and A. J. Ayer, who did all he could to defend his sense-datum theory against Austin's relentless attacks. Wittgenstein's unpublished but illicitly circulated views in the "Blue" and "Brown" books were then available, but there is no evidence that they had reached Austin's circle, except indirectly by way of the work of Wittgenstein's student—John Henry Wisdom—with which Austin was no doubt acquainted.[9] Once these meetings were recommenced at Oxford in the 1950s on Saturday mornings in sometimes makeshift quarters, Wittgenstein's *Philosophical Investigations*, published in 1953, were, along with Aristotle's *Nicomachean Ethics*, the most frequently discussed texts, when texts were discussed.[10] These meetings, it is reported, "were not occasions on which philosophy was talked about, or taught, or learned—they were occasions on which it was done, at which that actually happened, there and then. . . ."[11]

If these ordinary-language philosophers were not theorizing in the manner of say, a Michael Moore, then what were they doing? The ordinary-language philosopher "is himself speaking as an ordinary man" (*MWM*, xl) in possession of "a view of words free of philosophical preoccupation" ("K&A," 238). For him, "what we ordinarily say and mean may have a direct and deep control over what we can philosophically say and mean" ("MWM," 1). Thus the ordinary-language philosopher's office is "to bring words back from their metaphysical to their everyday use" (*PI*, para. 116; "LATER WITTGENSTEIN," 62).

If the ordinary-language philosopher insists that

> we need to remind ourselves of *what we should say when*[,] . . . what is the point of reminding ourselves of that? When the philosopher asks, "What should we say here?," what is meant is, "What would be the normal thing

to say here?," or perhaps, "What is the most natural thing we could say here?" And the point of the question is this: answering it is sometimes the only way to tell—tell others and tell for ourselves—what the situation *is* ("MWM," 20–21).

The goal of ordinary-language philosophy is to better understand the world, where human action (including speaking) does of course play a central part. Attentiveness to ordinary language is hardly an end in itself, however. In the end, who cares what we call things? What matters is what they are:

> When we examine what we should say when, what words we should use in what situations, we are looking again not *merely* at words (or "meanings," whatever they may be) but also at the realities we use the words to talk about: we are using a sharpened awareness of words to sharpen our perception of, though not as the final arbiter of, the phenomena ("EXCUSES," 182).

Asking "'what we should say when' gives us not 'knowledge of our language.' Knowledge of our language is something a Martian linguist on a field trip might acquire: for him, our language would be a field of empirical data. By asking ourselves 'what we should say when' we acquire knowledge or awareness of our language, our world, ourselves.[12] One could call it wisdom" (*M&S*, 58). Cavell specifies this wisdom:

> It is true that [Austin] asks for the difference between doing something by mistake and doing it by accident, but what transpires is a characterization of *what a mistake is* and (as contrasted, or so far as contrasted with this) what an accident is. He asks for the difference between being sure and being certain, but what is uncovered is an initial survey of the complex and mutual alignments between mind and world that are necessary to successful knowledge. He asks for the difference between expressing belief and expressing knowledge (or between saying "I believe" and saying "I know") and what comes up is a new sense and assessment of the human limitations, or human responsibilities, of human knowledge; and so on ("CRITICISM," 104).

Cavell goes on at some length in "Austin at Criticism" to demonstrate that Austin's procedures are hardly a scholastic fascination with words or meanings. Instead, Austin's distinctions "penetrate the phenomena they record—a feeling from within which the traditional philosopher will be the one who seems to be talking about mere words" ("CRITICISM," 103). Ordinary language, Cavell elaborates, happily can lead us to "dispossess" ourselves of distinctions "lying around philosophy" and replace them with distinctions that are "finer, . . . more solid, having . . . a greater natural weight; appearing normal, even inevitable, when the others are luridly arbitrary; useful where the others seem twisted; real where the others are academic; fruitful where the others are cold ("CRITICISM," 103). In making fine distinctions, so often through the use of revelatory examples, Austin demonstrates "the hang" or knack of "tell[ing] what a given word is about. . . ." The payoff? For Cavell, "what we will learn will not be new empirical facts about the world, and yet illuminating facts about the world" ("CRITICISM," at 104).[13]

In this way ordinary-language philosophy is not really about language, not in any sense in which it is not also about the world. That is, "ordinary language philosophy is about whatever ordinary language is about" ("AESTHETIC PROBLEMS," 95). It is not composed of data, or, as Moore suggests, "observations" (*A&C*, 42, 92–93, 256), which suggests that ordinary-language philosophers gather evidence about ordinary usage (but very unsystematically). They don't: not because they lack evidence for "what we should say when . . .", but because asking "what we should say when . . ." raises no question of evidence ("MWM," 13–14). When taking positions on what can be said in a given speech-situation, "[a] native speaker's utterances are the corpus on the basis of which (descriptive and prescriptive) grammars and rule-books are constructed—they are not themselves based on such a body of rules."[14]

How people speak has little interest for ordinary-language philosophers; what interests them is an explanation of *why* people speak as they do ("CRITICISM," 99). Put slightly differently, evidence of how other people speak is not the pressure to be applied against a speaker; rather, "the most characteristic pressure against him is applied by producing or deepening an example which shows him that *he* would not say what he says 'we' say" ("AESTHETIC PROBLEMS," 95). So it is essential to the procedure that while he asks what *we* should say when, the ordinary-language philosopher is not interested in how other people speak, "but in determining where and why one wishes, or hesitates, to use a particular expression oneself" ("AESTHETIC PROBLEMS," 95).[15] So how does he go about it? Cavell puts it this way:

> The appeal to "what we should say if . . ." requires that we imagine an example or story, sometimes one or more less similar to events which may happen any day, sometimes one unlike anything we have known. Whatever the difficulties will be in trying to characterize this procedure fully and clearly, this much can be said at once: if we find we disagree about what we should say, it would make no obvious sense to attempt to confirm or disconfirm one or other of our responses by collecting data to show which one of us is in fact right. What we should do is either (a) try to determine why we disagree (perhaps we are imagining the story differently)—just as, if we agree in response we will, when we start philosophizing about this fact, want to know why we agree, what it shows about our concepts; or (b) we will, if the disagreement cannot be explained, either find some explanation for *that*, or else discard the example. Disagreement is not disconfirming: it is as much a datum for philosophizing as agreement is ("AESTHETIC PROBLEMS," 95).

Let's suppose that you apply this pressure to me—pressuring me to justify my use of a particular term that strikes you as inappropriate to the particular speech-situation in which I have used it. I could, I suppose, answer that "I can say what I like. . . . I can speak in extraordinary ways, and you will perfectly well understand me." Yet the only reason you will understand me is that language provides conventions for speaking—in some situations—strangely or in extraordinary ways: speaking, for instance, metaphorically, cryptically, loosely, personally. In other words, you *cannot* just say what you like (speak strangely, speak in an extraordinary way) and make yourself understood *except* in ways provided for in the language ("MWM," 33).

This is all a bit dogmatic, to be sure, the dogma operating as an injunction against speaking however you like. Who, after all, is Austin to say "you can't say *x* (in ordinary speech) and mean *y*"? How can he seriously lay claim to such a "universal voice"? ("AESTHETIC PROBLEMS," 96). I may insist that my way of speaking is different—not a sort of private (therefore unintelligible) language—but instead, a view or version of our language shared by some but not all others.

Cavell illuminates this question of who can speak *for* others (determine or act as an authority on what we can say when) by recharacterizing the question instead as a matter of speaking *to* others. He argues that to deny me the right to speak for my community is to deny me the capacity for speech, period.[16] Still, ordinary-language procedures "do not presuppose universal agreement among native speakers but rather constitute a means of exploring or mapping the extent of that agreement. This follows from what one might call the essentially democratic nature of the speech community."[17] Cavell's point is made by imagining a question, which I summarize as: Are, say, professors' ordinary uses of words the same as, say, bakers'? ("MWM," 32–33). Talking together is a difficulty for *anyone*: "otherwise the only threat to communication would be acoustical" ("MWM," 12). It is for Cavell a given that the professor and the baker can talk together ("MWM," 34). "Nice day"; "The pumpernickel is good, but the whole wheat and the rye even better"; "I'll have the darker loaf there"; "Careful of the step"; "Be back next week": these are just a few exchanges in the intricate activity of talking to one another. In this way the professor and the baker communicate to each other just as professors communicate to each other (or bakers to each other). As Stephen Mulhall has put it, "[c]ommunication hangs together with community."[18]

But what about, for example, Austin's claim that "voluntary means fishy." Would a baker know or agree to that? Or is that just a mode of professor-talk? Suppose the baker claims that he never uses voluntary (and involuntary) in the way that Austin recommends. Suppose that in "his" language, every action is voluntary that is not involuntary: that all action is either one or the other (or mixed). Or suppose that the baker insists that "inadvertently" and "automatically" mean the same thing. Then what? That is, suppose that when the baker breaks the decanter, he says that to him it makes no difference in meaning to say that the breakage was inadvertent as opposed to automatic.

First, Cavell admonishes, it is important to rule out a loose description—perhaps the baker says there is no difference between the two descriptions; but the baker may (really) mean that he automatically grabbed the cigarette and inadvertently knocked the decanter over. But what if the baker insists that he would mean the same thing whether he used the word "inadvertently" or the word "automatically"? What do we say to him then? That he cannot say that "inadvertently" and "automatically" mean the same thing because *I* say they don't? At this point, pushed to madness, Cavell says he would be tempted to tell the baker: "'If you cooked the way you talk, you would forgo special implements for different jobs, and peel, core, scrape, slice, carve, chop, and saw, all with one knife. The distinction is there, in the language (as implements are there to be had), and you just impoverish what you say by neglecting it. And there is something you aren't noticing about the world'" ("MWM," 35–36). Unlike the cook, who even with only one knife can prepare food, the philosopher in possession only of "voluntary or not" as a way of dividing out actions "can scarcely begin to do his work" of knowing "what it is to do something and to say something" ("MWM," 36).

It is true that none of us is impervious to erring now and then in the same way as the baker has here. "Few speakers of a language," Cavell continues, "utilize the full range of perception which the language provides. . . . But to neglect it deliberately is foolhardy" ("MWM," 37). Wittgenstein has famously noted that "[o]ne human being can be a complete enigma to another." This mystery of others is what Austin was alluding to when he observed that deception and other modes of misunderstanding, including our difficulty at times in telling inadvertently from deliberately caused harm, can account for that feeling of loneliness we have all experienced. Not saying what you mean only compounds the sometimes enigmatical nature of others. We will be hard-pressed to understand what they do, what they say, and identify how to respond to them if they make no attempt to get across how things are with them, but instead, hide behind non-claims such as " 'inadvertent and automatic' mean the same to me (in my language)."

I have now managed only to expose another aspect of the putatively dogmatic side of ordinary-language philosophy. After all, language changes; meanings "*will* of course, stretch and shrink, and they will be stretched and shrunk" ("MWM," 42). But a private meaning may be more arbitrary than one arrived at publicly. That language inevitably changes is no reason to change it just for the sake of change. "Here we need to remind ourselves that ordinary language is natural language, and that its changing is natural" ("MWM," 42), not home-made or arbitrary ("CRITICISM," 102). To attend to its nature can, as Cavell puts it, not only reveal a changing culture in a changing language, but "coax" us out of subjectivity and private definitions back, through the community, home ("MWM," 43).

Moore's Act and Crime: The Flight from the Ordinary

> For we are sometimes not so good at observing what we *can't* say as what we can, yet the first is pretty regularly the more revealing.
>
> Austin, "A Plea for Excuses"

Having set forth my sense of the nature and aims of ordinary-language methodology, we are ready to confront legal doctrine and theory, the state of which would in my view be improved by a steady dose of that methodology—of "what we should say when." Initially, I have selected Moore's *Act and Crime* as representative of the doctrinal and theoretical content of the criminal law. I have made this choice not only because of the uncommon care that Moore has taken to explain criminal law's causal, mind-body orientation, but also because Moore himself is a member of the tiny minority of prominent figures in criminal law (indeed, in legal philosophy) who have taken a position on what they perceive to be the function of ordinary language in the field. Because I want to be fair to Professor Moore, I want to attend as carefully as possible to presenting and analyzing what I take to be the central points of his book.

Moore's project, as best as I can tell, obliquely has as its target H. L. A. Hart's 1968 monograph, *Punishment and Responsibility*, which, *far* more than Hart's coauthored *Causation in the Law* (1959), reflects some sensibilities shared with Austin, with whom he taught a class at Oxford in 1948 on law, action, and responsibility.[19] Moore takes Hart's positions as expressive of the "high-handed" sort of philosophy that Moore equates with Austin. Moore's stake in the project is, at least in part, theory: "human actions," he sets forth, "do form a natural kind whose nature thus demands a theory" (*A&C*, 135). Accordingly, he sets out "to formulate a plausible theory of what the nature of that kind is" (*A&C*, 135). He insists that while others have come up with a theory similar to his, they admit that their theory is more a useful fiction than a truth, whereas Moore fully believes in its truth as well (*A&C*, 109). For Moore, the truth he urges us to accept is that actions "'are bona fide entities'" (*A&C*, 60 n.1)—"a class of action things about which we could have a theory" (*A&C*, 62). It is a "hidden unity" (*A&C*, 42–43) in the world of actions that *Act and Crime* pursues.

What is never altogether clear is why a theory of action is so important. Here I am reminded of Timothy Gould's recent description of Austin's allusion to the "descriptive fallacy," which Gould describes as "the sense that our conceptual scheme must apply everywhere if it is to be valid. . . ."[20] Gould characterizes Austin as

> challenging—more or less explicitly—the model of conceptual analysis that had dominated English philosophy at least since Russell. Here [Austin] chips away at—among other things—the idea that if we have a concept, we must be able to ask about every item in the universe whether our

> concept applies or not. . . . He will also come to challenge more explicitly the idea that for every concept and every item in the world, there is some statement linking the concept to the item or denying the existence of such a link.[21]

Moore argues for a unifying theory of action of the very sort whose value Gould (and Austin) are questioning.

As for the intended payoff for our seeing things his way, over halfway through his book we are given the impression that a stake in his theory of action is to solve some unusual, technical, even far-fetched problems unlikely to have ever arisen in the practice of even the most experienced criminal lawyer. Without a unifying theory of action like Moore's, we wouldn't know how to solve cases like this one, involving a criminal prohibition against "'killing a correctional officer within a correctional institution'" (*A&C*, 247):

> Suppose . . . Smith was a California correctional officer working at a California correctional institution located in California on the border with Nevada. As Smith leaves work for his home in Nevada, he is shot by Jones from within the prison. Smith staggers home, goes into a coma, and eventually dies. He was on the verge of retirement anyway, and at some point between Jones's finger movement on the trigger and Smith's death Smith was automatically retired from California's correctional service; in addition, during this same period the California statute criminalizing the killing of a state correctional officer within a state correctional facility was repealed.

Here, I take it, is the stake in the above classroom hypothetical:

> If the killing of Smith by Jones is identical to the moving of the trigger finger by Jones, then there are no barriers to prosecuting Jones in California under California law making it a crime to kill a state correctional officer within a state correctional facility. If the killing of Smith by Jones is not identical to this movement event, then the killing presumably has greater spatio-temporal boundaries (perhaps even including the death of Smith), and these may well give rise to jurisdictional, choice-of-law, venue, legality, and other technical objections to prosecution. It thus matters to such issues (as they are currently framed) whether complex actions like killings are identical to bodily movements or not (*A&C*, 247–48).

Certainly Moore did not write *Act and Crime* as a device for resolving exotic, unlikely-to-occur-in-the-world conundrums like this. Should this bizarre "spatio-temporal" difficulty ever confront a real court, I suppose the court would have to explore the grammar of the statutory term "killing" in order to fix the killing either in California where the deadly act was committed, or in Nevada, where the victim expired.

Yet while I doubt that Moore sought merely to address unusual hypotheticals in *Act and Crime*, no matter how hard I push his text, I cannot figure out what his interest in action *is* or what it is meant to reveal. There are glimpses of concerns with ascriptions of responsibility (what I would think any book on human action would inexorably focus on), but they are only glimpses. Chapter 3, for example, which explains why criminal law largely (but not without exception) punishes us for the bad we do rather than for the good we fail to do, can be interpreted as having responsibility at its center. There Moore intermittently makes his interest in responsibility explicit, one such instance being a reiteration of his point that omissions liability (holding one responsible for failing to prevent harm) is a bad thing:

> It is probably . . . true that some of the attraction of . . . the idea that omissions can be causes stems from a moral judgment: that people can be as morally responsible for harms they fail to prevent [as] for harms they cause. . . . But however much reason there might be to hold people morally responsible for harms they fail to prevent, such reason is no justification for gerrymandering one's metaphysics in order to make one's moral conclusions look more palatable. Omitting to save is not causing death, and no view of moral responsibility gives us any reason to pretend otherwise (*A&C*, 278).

In addition to this rare glimpse into Moore's sense of the importance of making a case for a "univocal act requirement" (presumably in order to preserve causation as an element of responsibility), there is a subsection specifically designed "to show why we should care about such a requirement" (*A&C*, 46–59). There we learn that an act requirement is all that separates us from being punished for mere status, mental acts and mental states, involuntary movements, and, once more, omissions. I cannot tell whether this was a sort of constitutional line of argument holding that due process/fundamental fairness requires that we be judged by what we do, not by what we think or what we are. Because this argument is already reflected in American constitutional law, I cannot tell what makes Moore think that punishment for status or thought-crimes is a live threat to our system of criminal law. Moreover, other than these brief attempts to hook up his interest in action with agents (with responsibility), we never get much on the basis of the interest that human action holds for him.[22] We do know beyond peradventure that *defining* action is crucial to *Act and Crime*. But we also know that the need for definitions (along the lines of the sort of overarching conceptual schemes that Gould describes above) arises only in very specific situations. As to why criminal law is one of those situations, I remain unsure. Accordingly, most of *Act and Crime* explains, even defends, Moore's theory of action, though the entire project is rather weakly justified. But this could just be my projecting on to his book (whose cares and commitments are more aligned with the philosophy of mind than with criminal-law theory or philosophy of law) my own demands that an interest in human action is by definition an interest in the conditions and scope of responsibility.

As the hypothetical problem of Smith's killing by Jones makes clear, Moore's theory of action is meant to make sense of the role and relation of essential criminal-law vocabulary such as shooting, killing, and dying. This is worthwhile enough, but he does so by introducing into that vocabulary otherwise peripheral terms such as bodily movement, or in this specific instance, finger movement. Moore's theory—which is mapped on to the entire field of criminal law and is therefore by no means limited to this hypothetical inside the correctional facility—is meant to eliminate any (meaningful) distinction between verbs like shoot, kill, and finger movement. This, in a nutshell, is Moore's theory: *basic acts (like finger movements) are the stuff that make up complex acts (like killing), which in turn are legislatively proscribed (through statutes punishing murders and manslaughters)*. Any other view of things, for Moore, is at best misleading, and at worst, a threat to the continued vitality of an "act requirement" as the foundation of criminal liability.

I am going to do my best here to reconstruct Moore's theory of action, which he has labeled the "equivalence thesis," the meaning of which can be captured from this boiled down version with which he opens chapter 10: "all . . . actions are (identical to) bodily movements" (*A&C*, 245). A more elaborate statement of the equivalence thesis appears early in the book:

> This thesis asserts that any complex action description used in the special part of the criminal law is equivalent to (and thus can be replaced by) a

> description of some simple act [e.g., raising one's arm, moving one's tongue, finger, or hips] of the accused causing a prohibited state of affairs (*A&C*, 46).

Thus Moore claims that murder is "a prohibition equivalent to a prohibition that forbids 'any simple act that causes the death of another'" (*A&C*, 46). Moore's focus on simple acts and causation is, in a word, relentless. A simple or basic act such as a finger moving, tongue moving, knee flexing, or hip thrusting is also, under the proper conditions (causing death, emitting sounds that accord with the rules of English, taking place in hiding with the intent to remain hidden, or nonconsensually penetrating a woman by force or fear), a complex act of killing, saying, concealing, and raping. In other words, for Moore, "Jones killed Smith," "Jones caused Smith's death," and "Jones's finger movement caused Smith's death" are all, well, the same. They are all bodily movements that cause a prohibited state of affairs, but each is at bottom just a simple or basic act of finger moving that is for one reason or another being alternatively described.

It gets more complicated. These simple acts (however described) are both caused and causal. They are caused in the sense that they are traceable to "volitions," which are, in Moore's terminology, "a kind of intention" (*A&C*, 121) that plays an "executory role . . . , executing our motivating wants and their accompanying beliefs into the actions that serve them" (*A&C*, 120). Intentions are for Moore "*causes* of actions" (*A&C*, 382). For example, the sport or activity of "fishing is not done simply by dangling one's line in the water where there are fish in the circumstance that one desires fish to be caught; in addition, such dangling is fishing only if one's desire for fish *causes* one to dangle the line" (*A&C*, 198). (Even though it is quite plausible that my desire to fish causes me to catch fish, when, say, I intend to throw them back for the sport of it). Volitions are for Moore part of all actions, whereas intentions are not (*A&C*, 382). Evidently intentions, unlike volitions, are the causal force *behind* actions but are not *part* of actions. Actions, in turn, "are partially identical to bodily movements, partially identical to volitions, and only fully identical to the causal sequence volition-causes-bodily-movement" (*A&C*, 85). Under our current limitations, Moore notes that the objects of our volitions can at this point in our development be achieved only through bodily movements (as opposed to through mental willings) (*A&C*, 105).

Bodily movements need not be obvious, either. Take, for example,

Moore's invented "reluctant executioner," who can cause a guillotine to activate and kill a condemned prisoner by rigging the guillotine to drop in response to changes in the executioner's skin conductivity, which he can alter by fantasizing. Because the executioner

> has used his body as the means to effect a change in the world which he desires to bring about, . . . it shouldn't matter whether the means involve a literal motion of a whole limb or only the microscopic motions within some limbs or other organ. All such willed changes of bodily states, when used as a means to change the world, are actions (*A&C*, 265).

Ultimately, Moore's theory of action—his equivalence thesis—can be stated formulaically: "*X V*-ed if and only if some basic act of *X* caused state *S* to obtain in circumstances *C*" (*A&C*, 213). What, then, are these "states" and "circumstances" that are caused by a putative criminal's basic acts? It is easy to see that, for example, the "state" of killing is necessary for murder, maiming for mayhem, hitting for battery, confining for false imprisonment, and that the circumstances of non-consent are necessary for rape and theft (*A&C*, 216–17).

But what about so-called inchoate criminality? How are crimes like attempt (trying and failing to commit crime), solicitation (asking someone else to commit a crime), and conspiracy (agreeing with someone else to commit a crime) in any sense causal? What is caused in or by inchoate crimes? I thought the whole *idea* of inchoate criminality presupposed that nothing happened beyond planning other than, at most, an unsuccessful gesture toward realizing the plan: the attempted thief obtains no property (or it has been abandoned) while the crimes of solicitation and conspiracy are completed when requests and agreements are made whether or not the plans are ever put into action.

Moore holds his causal theory together not by acknowledging that inchoate criminality is an exception to his theory, but rather, by saying that attempt, solicitation, and conspiracy somehow *are* causal. Attempters do not cause the harms they put themselves to (or theirs would be fully realized crimes, not attempts), but they do cause changes in "states" in that they have taken substantial steps toward the completed offense. Thus the gesture of, say, attempted theft, includes the "result" of coming close to pulling it off. So too does a would-be conspirator cause a change in states by reaching a criminal agreement with another, *even if*, argues Moore, his agreement is with an undercover police officer who has no intention whatsoever to carry out the "plan." The existence of the agreement (or apparent agreement) puts matters in a different "state" than they were in before, and so this state can be said to have been "caused" by the agreement (or apparent agreement). A solicitor also would have some causal upshot in Moore's view, even if his request got lost in the mail, was not understood, or was taken as ironical. And what, exactly is "caused" in these examples? "[A] proximity to success" (here, a proximity to successful communication, not the crime it contemplates) (*A&C*, 220–23).

These strike me as somewhat extended uses not only of the term "causal," but in the case of a stillborn solicitation or "unilateral conspiracy," abuses of what it means both to request and to agree. This is to my mind an important juncture in any study of *Act and Crime*, because it entails a confrontation with Moore's stance toward ordinary-language procedures. As fate would have it, Austin took a position that Moore himself recognizes as applicable to the meaning and operation of "solicit" or "conspire." In *How To Do Things With Words*, Austin made the radical move of establishing a closer relation between physical action and speech than previously acknowledged in or out of philosophy. A well-known aspect of his development of that relation is his development of three different types of speech-acts: 1) the "locutionary" act or what is said; 2) the "illocutionary" act or what is meant; and 3) the "perlocutionary" act or what is achieved or brought about, if anything, by the speaker. Thus when we hear the locution "Shoot her!" the illocution can be read as "He urged (or advised, ordered, &c.) me to shoot her," while the perlocution can be read as "He persuaded me to shoot her" or "He got me to (or made me, &c.) shoot her" (*HTDTW*, 101–2).

As with physical action, however, speech, too, can misfire. In other words, what I intend in doing something is up to me in a way in which the results of my doing it are not, or not merely, up to me (or not up to *just* me).[23] Not only is speech subject to "the ills that all action is heir to" (*HTDTW*, 105), but speech is also vulnerable to ills that physical action is not, such as "aetiolations, parasitic uses, [and] various 'not serious' and 'not full normal' uses"[24] (*HTDTW*, 104). For example, "it is always possible . . . to try to thank or inform somebody yet in different ways to fail, because he doesn't listen, or takes it as ironical, or wasn't responsible for whatever it was, and so on" (*HTDTW*, 106). To demonstrate this point, Austin notes that we say

"I warn you that" but we do not say "I convince you that" or "I alarm you that." Convincing and alarming someone are perlocutions that may or may not occur since how we are taken by others is largely out of our control. Our audience could remain unconvinced or unalarmed even if they've heard and understood us perfectly well.

Moore cites these same passages from *How To Do Things With Words*. He even concedes that the difference between urging or commanding someone to do something and actually getting them to do it, once mapped on to the concepts or crimes of solicitation and conspiracy, indicates that it would be peculiar to say that someone who has solicited, say, a deaf person (who does not read lips), has committed the crime of solicitation. Likewise, Moore acknowledges the peculiarity of saying that someone who has "agreed" with an undercover agent who intends to thwart, not pursue the plan, has entered a conspiracy. What is remarkable is what Moore does with Austin's insight about the difference between illocutions that have their intended (perlocutionary) effects and those that do not:

> Surely Austin's ear accurately captures ordinary, idiomatic usage of the illocutionary-act verbs that are used to define solicitation and conspiracy. Yet distinguishing attempted communications from successful communications does not answer the question of legal liability, and here the criminal law is clear: such attempted communications are both solicitations and conspiracies (*A&C*, 222–23).

Moore may be on to something here: the law may be impervious to ordinary-language procedures in the same way that some other fields (such as "time") are ("EXCUSES," 182), on the ground that those fields are, in Austin's own view, "too much trodden into bogs or tracks by traditional philosophy, for in that case even 'ordinary' language will often have become infected with the jargon of extinct theories, and our own prejudices too, as the upholders or imbibers of theoretical views, will be too readily, and often insensibly, engaged" ("EXCUSES," 182–83). Austin nowhere suggests that the law is outside ordinary language on the grounds of having been infected in the ways described above, though I suppose that he could have. But Austin does make explicit that ordinary language and the law do have at least one conflict, quite apart from jargon (or apart from having been exhausted by the philosophies of Kant, Plato, and Aristotle):

> In the law a constant stream of actual cases, more novel and more tortuous than the mere imagination could contrive, are brought up for *decision*—

> that is, formulae for docketing them must somehow be found. Hence it is necessary first to be careful with, but also to be brutal with, to torture, to fake and to override, ordinary language: we cannot here evade or forget the whole affair. (In ordinary life we dismiss the puzzles that crop up about time, but we cannot do that indefinitely in physics) ("EXCUSES," 186).

Austin here acknowledges that the pressure to rule in a legal case may necessitate our deviating from "what we should say when."

While Austin offers no examples, they wouldn't be hard to find. The law's fondness for doctrines of "constructive possession" or "constructive knowledge" allows us to hold people responsible for having and knowing things that we cannot exactly prove they had or knew. Specifically, who possesses the items found in a car with several occupants or found on the common-area coffee table of a jointly occupied apartment? And does a courier who knows of a secret compartment in the car that he is loaned to make a delivery, but who intentionally avoids learning what is in that compartment, *know* that it contains drugs? The law in both instances allows jurors to impose on the accused "constructive" possession or knowledge of the goods or facts at issue.

This reminds me of a talk I heard Harvard's Frank Michelman give while I was in law school. There he was discussing a pre-constitutional doctrine of "virtual or constructive representation," which sought to assure the American colonists that, although they were not entitled to vote for members of Parliament, their political interests would be voiced for them by those who could vote since those voters would do what was good not just for themselves, but for the colonists (whose burden they shared) as well. Michelman enjoined his audience that, in law, whenever we hear the word "constructive" used as an adjective, we should substitute for it the word "not."[25] In other words, "constructive possession" means "not possession." The ordinary conditions of possession, of knowledge, and in his example, of representation, had been overridden by law.

Whether there was a need for it, however, is a separate matter; one would think we would require some justification on the part of the party who would override, fake, torture, or be brutal with what we can ordinarily say. Moore is right that the law (at least the Model Penal Code—the legislation he cites) does call a failed solicitation a solicitation nonetheless and a conspiracy where you are in fact agreeing with no one a conspiracy nonetheless. But why would the Model Penal Code do that? Isn't the first case—where the intended subject of your request fails to hear, understand, or take you seriously—an *attempted* solicitation? If not, then why not? Is it because we have no such crime? Why is that? Because it contemplates two layers of inchoateness? The first layer is that with any solicitation, the requesting party's will is heavily mediated by the will of the solicited party, who may or may not carry out the request. The second layer here is that not only is the solicited party a potential wild card who may not want to commit the crime for whatever reason, but we cannot even reach that question if the solicitation does not even register with the solicited party. This makes the intended harm terribly remote and perhaps for that reason in no need of a coercive, that is punitive, response from the law. That, of course, is not just a recognition of the double-layered inchoate crime of attempted solicitation, but it is also an argument against calling attempted solicitations "solicitations." As for the case of the unilateral conspiracy (where only one party really has the intention that the contemplated crime or crimes occur), isn't this, too, a sort of attempt? We do have a law of attempted conspiracy—it's called "solicitation." So where is the need here to override what we ordinarily can say? What is the pressure on our language that the Model Penal Code and Professor Moore perceive to tamper with the ordinary meaning of "solicit" and "conspire"?

Moore's brief nods to ordinary language have a tendency both to acknowledge that he puts things in a way that may stretch terms all out of shape, and to follow up these stretchings-out-of-shape with what I consider to be somewhat unsatisfactory justifications for doing so. Above he noted that questions of legal liability are not dictated in inchoate criminality by the limits of ordinary language. That is not an explanation, however, of *why* the question of legal liability would cut against ordinary language. Much earlier in *Act and Crime*, Moore does hint that legal liability is an extraordinary context where we are freed from the limits of what we ordinarily can mean by an utterance:

> Ordinary usage of the verbs of action developed for ordinary uses, including the ascription of moral responsibility. Among those ordinary uses was not an attempted systematization of the conditions of either moral responsibility or legal liability. It is thus quite open to the moral or legal theorist to propose such a hidden systematization, even if the concepts and principles employed in doing so are quite alien to ordinary ways of thinking and

> speaking. No observations about the bountiful diversity of ordinary usage of action verbs can preclude the claim that underneath such diversity there is none the less a hidden unity. It is surely *not* a "fatal defect in any account of action" that it is "quite at variance with the ordinary man's experience and the way in which his own actions appear to him," or that it ignores "the simple but important truth . . . that when we deliberate and think about actions, we do so not in terms of muscular movements but in the [quite different and diverse] ordinary terminology of actions." To think that this is a fatal defect would be like thinking that the quite diverse things ordinarily said about the planet Venus prior to the discoveries of Babylonian astronomy—things like "It is the star that appears in the morning," and "It is the star that appears in the evening"—could preclude someone discovering a hidden unity, namely, that these "stars" were in reality one and the same thing, namely, the second planet from the sun (*A&C*, 42–43).

What is the pressure that this "systematization" places on ordinary language? Is it, as Austin says, that the field has been corrupted by theory or by the pressure to decide live cases? Moore never says. That is, Moore makes no attempt to justify criminal law as an extraordinary speech-situation where ordinary conventions will no longer do. As Austin has written elsewhere, "[t]here may be extraordinary facts, even about our everyday experience, which plain men and plain language overlook" ("A WORD," 69). Furthermore, in his own philosophical practice, Austin created his own share of technical terms, of which "constative" and "performative" are only the best-known examples.[26] But Moore nowhere argues that questions of legal liability apply such pressure to our language.

Even the example he chooses to acclimate us to the idea that ordinary language simply has not had sufficient opportunity to absorb and reflect his vocabulary is a curious one. I can imagine how astronomy could bring us to accept the discovery that the Morning Star (really) is Venus. And so I can imagine as well how this discovery would then lead to our changing the way we refer to Venus: no longer as a star but now as the second planet from the sun. What I cannot imagine, however, is what could bring us to see killings as *generally* reducible to finger movements (actions as bodily-movements-caused-by-a-volition), or feigned agreements as reducible to agreements. What sort of discovery could prompt that sort of move strikes me as occurring on a totally different plane from the factual discovery that astronomers presented us with in the case of Venus. Yet Moore relies on this identical example some fifty pages later into his book to support his claim that "[n]o amount of linguistic observation . . . should convince us that acts are not in fact identical to bodily movements. That such an identity should lead to some linguistic oddities should not be surprising if the identity itself has not been widely enough known, for a long enough period, to get reflected in ordinary-usage patterns" (*A&C*, 93).

The oddity to which Moore refers here was criticized as such by, among others, A. I. Melden, who argued that when we speak of motives, intentions, and reasons, we are explaining actions. It would be terribly odd to speak of a motive for arm raisings, but not as odd to speak of motives for raising one's arm. (I hope that my discussion of motives in the first chapter demonstrates why, except in extraordinary circumstances, it would be odd to speak of motives *even* for raising one's arm). For current purposes, however, whether it be Melden's point that arm raisings are distinct from actions, or Wittgenstein's related point (also alluded to by Moore) that the difference between one's arm going up (a bodily movement) and one raising one's arm (an action) is that one is not surprised when one raises one's arm, Moore's only intelligible response is that we need to get accustomed to seeing actions as movements, however bizarre it may strike us.

Hart was right when he stated that our relation to our own actions is *not* that of a physiologist.[27] Nor are we (normally) surprised when we raise our arms, though our arm-goings-up would give us more than a little pause. Does Moore not see this gap between the world of action and the descriptions he attributes to it? There is sufficient evidence to conclude that he does see this. Repeatedly, in fact, Moore attempts to justify our reducing (all) actions to mere bodily movements by referring to the experience of learning to do something:

> Undeniably we learn to string together various of our bodily movements into complex routines with such dexterity that, once we have mastered the routine, we can literally not pay attention to what we are doing (at the level of bodily movements). . . . [T]o learn how to play the piano is to learn (among other things) how to move one's fingers; to learn to speak English is, among other things, to learn how to move one's tongue. Remembering that we seek phenomenal clues to the nature of those mental states that execute desires into action, a good place to look for such clues is at the mental states we had to acquire in order to acquire our various

> skills of action. The objects of those states were bodily motions. It is a reasonable . . . hypothesis that those same states exist to cause those same motions when they occur later in life as part of speaking or playing, even though awareness of those states has receded (*A&C*, 129–30).

Moore has chosen the experience of learning as representative of one's relation with one's own body. That is, he reminds us that at some point the development of certain skills (playing piano, speaking) amounts to little more than making movements of the fingers and the tongue. Yet learning is a very specific context in which action takes place, a context in which we are (if the skill is demanding enough) not really *doing* it at all. Instead, we are at that stage just learning it, where consciousness of the need to control our bodies in specific ways is what separates doing from learning. But as Moore sees it, mastering an activity just shifts the control over the body from the core to the periphery of our consciousness. That does not for him nullify the notion that when we act we are nevertheless making bodily movements. It's just that after proficiency in an activity develops, we *forget* that what we are doing is making a complex series of bodily movements, which are

> pre-conscious in the sense of easily called to mind if attention is focused on [them], and so remain part of a person's mental states. . . . At some point as we descend in our descriptions of even smaller bits of bodily movements, we reach the sub-personal level where the scripts that guide movements are not accessible to our consciousness. This argument about volitions is thus only an argument about degree: do the contents of our bare intentions reach the fineness of detail of discrete bodily movements like moving one's arm, or are they limited to larger goals like throwing a strike or walking downtown? If we take our learning experiences into account, conjoined with the accessibility of the scripts we learned even later in adult life when we have mastered many complex motor skills, the evidence strongly favours the former answer even for seemingly "automatic" or habitual actions like throwing a baseball pitch, saying a sentence, or playing the piano. Motor skills that are not nearly so routinized, such as moving one's finger on a trigger so as to execute one's intention to kill another person, are *a fortiori* cases for supposing volitions with such finely grained propositional objects to exist (*A&C*, 154–55).

Moore's view is an attempt to defeat the intuition that bodily movements are the subject of intentions only in specific situations. Yet

Moore shares this intuition, at least superficially; otherwise he would not rely so heavily on the experience of learning to do something: "if you include learning experiences in one's evidential base, and if you make the reasonable assumption that the states needed for such experiences continue after learning has occurred even though such states are no longer noticed, then the phenomenological evidence is pretty good for the existence of volitions" (*A&C*, 164). This is a curious statement for at least two reasons. First, it emphasizes Moore's view that Austin (and others) rely on a view of action that repudiates the existence either of actions or of volitions (*A&C*, 60–61). In Austin's work I find no textual basis whatsoever for the idea that Austin denies that actions "exist." His work does strongly suggest, however, that the *question* "Do actions exist?" itself is empty (just like "What is the meaning of a word?" or "What is a real thing?"). Actions exist as concepts—constructions of language—deployed to make sense of the world *in specific speech-situations*. Yet Moore has reified actions (and volitions) without regard for the particular situations in which concern about or reference to their "existence" arises.

Second, learning experiences ultimately demonstrate the reverse of what Moore uses them for. From the fact that in some (extraordinary) situations actions are bodily movements, Moore concludes that in all situations actions are bodily movements; our mastery of those minute movements simply functions to obscure that fact from us. In a brilliant piece published in the *New Yorker* in 2000, Malcom Gladwell analyzes (in a distinctly Austinian way) the difference between doing and learning. The occasion was his plan to delineate two different modes of failure: choking and panicking. To depict what constitutes choking, Gladwell details the late stages of the 1993 Ladies' Final at Wimbledon. Jana Novotna held a commanding lead, just points from victory over the game's dominant player, Steffi Graf. Suddenly, Novotna's game fell apart in ways unrelated to the play of Graf. Unimaginable bonehead moves, playing the ball directly to Graf, unforced errors of various sorts, and balls inexplicably sailing out of play characterized Novotna's play in the final seven uncontested games. From serving at 4–1 40–30 in the final set to sobbing on the Duchess of Kent's shoulder took just a few minutes.

What happened, Gladwell asks? Novotna choked, he explains, relying on the difference between implicit and explicit learning. Explicit learning, Gladwell reports, citing a University of Virginia psychologist, is evident when, first having learned to hit, say, a backhand, you "think it through in a very deliberate manner. But as you get better the implicit system takes over: you start to hit a backhand fluidly, without thinking." Gladwell goes on to say that the implicit system gradually takes over so that after several thousand backhands, "you don't really notice what your hand is doing at all."

"Under conditions of stress," Gladwell elaborates,

> the explicit system sometimes takes over. That's what it means to choke. When Jana Novotna faltered at Wimbledon, it was because she began thinking about her shots again. She lost her fluidity, her touch. She double faulted on her serves and mis-hit her overheads, the shots that demand the greatest sensitivity in force and timing. She seemed like a different person—playing with the slow, cautious deliberation of a beginner—because, in a sense, she was a beginner again . . . relying on a learning system that she hadn't used to hit serves and overheads and volleys since she was first taught tennis, as a child.

Choking, therefore, in its most boiled down form, is thinking too much (whereas panic is the opposite—not relying on explicit learning when you should—that is, thinking too little, as in a pilot's attempt to keep his wings level by looking into the night's blackness for the lights of Martha's Vineyard instead of reading his instruments).

I raise this here to support the idea that once we have learned something, the entire notion of bodily movements drops out (rather than recedes, yet continuing to operate as our mode of acting as Moore would see it). Only in extraordinary circumstances—for example, facing the world's greatest player in front of thousands of fans, millions more by television, with the respect of colleagues (and the Duke and Duchess of Kent) in the balance—can doing be redescribed as making a series of bodily movements. This is not to say that the body is irrelevant to the practiced performer. Novotna still was thinking about execution—about the movements of her body—when she turned things around and finally won the Wimbledon title in 2001. But reminding oneself of the importance of maintaining good form, concentrating on a few weaknesses, tendencies, or especially difficult maneuvers hardly turns the entire activity into a series of self-conscious, intentional, individualized exertions.

And how do we know this? Because of the absence in ordinary language to references to bodily movements except in specific, even extraordinary, speech situations. As I have stated, the peculiarity of the actions-are-merely-bodily-movements mode of expression is not totally lost on Moore. For example, his theory impels him to decouple a killing from the death it causes, apparently because the death is not the action (the bodily movement) of the killing, or definitory of the killing, but instead, is just a consequence of the killing. Putting the matter this way no doubt sounds strange, even to him:

> It is decidedly odd to say "A killed B and then B died" or "A's killing of B caused B to die several hours later." Yet the oddity here too is only a pragmatic feature of this usage, not affecting the semantics of the verb "to kill." . . . Analogously, it is less odd to say "The movement of Jones's finger caused Smith's death" than it is to say "The killing of Smith by Jones caused Smith's death," but the truth values of the two sentences are the same. . . . (*A&C*, 288). There are many pragmatically odd things that people can say that are none the less perfectly true. "Jones killed Smith, and then Smith died" is one of them (*A&C*, 292).

What Moore seems vexed by is the specific case in which the death takes place after the killing, such as where Smith languishes in a hospital before perishing. "When was Smith killed?" is a question of particular importance for Moore. (Just the sort of unusual technical legal problem that characterizes *Act and Crime*). It is conceivable that the meaning and operation of the verb "kill" is tested in such a case, but one would think that such a difficulty is handled by saying that Jones, say, shot (stabbed, poisoned) Smith on Monday and that Smith then died on Thursday. To my mind that description captures—within the conventions of our language—the lag between the act and the consequence better than Moore's description.

The distinction that Moore would have us draw between what words mean (their semantics) and how they are used in speech (their pragmatics) is an evasion of how emptied out a word like "semantics" can be when cut off from its "pragmatics." What Moore suggests is that while no one would (except in the most extraordinary circumstances) say "A killed B and then B died" or "The movement of Jones's finger caused Smith's death" let alone "The killing of Smith by Jones caused Smith's death," they are all equally true. Pragmatically, they may be mostly useless as utterances, but still they are as semantically sound as an utterance that would actually be deployed in speech.

But what would you say to someone who told you that "a killing caused a death"? I doubt that you would say that it is true, because true or not, the fact that something is true is not, without more, a reason for saying it. The question is, true or not, why say that it is true *here, now*? Without being able to elaborate that (beyond "because it is as true as other statements, though it says, *practically speaking*, nothing"), it is hard to get a sense of what role the word "semantics" is supposed to have in speech:

> [T]he pragmatic element of an utterance's meaning is not something secondary to its semantic element, not something grafted on to the latter only as a result of the speaker's decision to use those words to say something—as if using words to say something is not of their essence, as if the words of a language might be detached from their modes of employment and still be regarded as meaningful. On the contrary, the semantics of an utterance are merely one aspect of what is meant in saying it.[28]

This semantic-pragmatic distinction, so important to Moore's justification for linguistic oddities, is one that Cavell addressed a half-century ago in *Must We Mean What We Say*:

> [S]omething *does* follow from the fact that a term is used in its usual way: it entitles you (or, using the term, you entitle others) to make certain inferences, draw certain conclusions. (This is part of what you say when you say that you are talking about the *logic* of ordinary language). *Learning what these implications are is part of learning the language*; no less a part than learning its syntax, or learning what it is to which terms apply: they are an essential part of what we communicate when we talk. Intimate understanding is understanding which is implicit. Nor *could* everything we say (mean to communicate), in normal communication, be said explicitly—otherwise the only threat to communication is acoustical. We are, therefore, exactly as responsible for the specific implications of our utterances as we are for their explicit factual claims. And there can no more be some general procedure for securing that what one implies is appropriate than there can be for determining that what one says is true ("MWM," 11–12).

In this sense is it impossible not only to avoid the implications of our speech, but so too is it equally impossible to avoid *being implicated* by the "pragmatics" of our speech.[29] This presence or burden of responsibility in speaking may be what accounts for Cavell's so recently having recast the subject of ordinary-language philosophy as "the justice of speech" (*CITIES*, 356), a term that designates notions of fairness and responsibility—how we cannot fairly attribute any meaning we want to our utterances or avoid responsibility for the implications of our speech—in a way that "ordinary language philosophy," or even worse, Austin's own label, "linguistic phenomenology," cannot.

I hope by now it is evident that Moore acknowledges that much of what he suggests for the law is at odds with what people actually say. At times, however, I am not sure that his assessment of where ordinary-language procedures would lead us in a given case is altogether faithful. For example, Moore makes much of the fact that Hart uses action verbs like sleepwalking to describe what people in unconscious states sometimes "do" (*A&C*, 252–56). To Moore, whatever happens at the hand of an unconscious person is, properly understood, a non-action. And about that he's right. But I doubt that he has been quite fair to Hart, who qualifies his observation that action verbs are sometimes used to describe happenings or occurrences while the "actor" is, for example, sleepwalking, suffering a seizure, under hypnosis, or hit on the head by a rock or stung by a bee. Moore is correct in saying that Hart notes that in ordinary language when we describe these quite extraordinary occurrences, we use action verbs such as driving (while asleep or while in a state of automatism). But nowhere does Hart even intimate that in his view or in the view of the courts whose opinions he reviews occurrences owing to "St. Vitus Dance, automatism, epilepsy, uncontrolled reflexes"[30] and the like are in any sense actions. Far from it. As for the use of action verbs, their presence is carefully qualified. The cases in which Hart states that we describe these happenings with action verbs are cases that really do look like ones where the agent did in fact act. Hart explains:

> The phrase "sleep-walking" is alone sufficient to remind us that if the outward movements *appear* to be co-ordinated as they are in normal action, the fact that the subject is unconscious from whatever cause does not prevent us using an active verb to describe the case, though we would *qualify* it with the adverb "unconsciously," or with the adverbial phrases "in his sleep," "in a state of automatism," etc. So in the case of "driving" it would be natural, as a matter of English, to distinguish those cases where the movements of the body are wild or spasmodic or where the "driver" simply slumps in his seat or collapses over the wheel, from cases where, though unconscious, he is *apparently* controlling the vehicle, changing gears, steering, braking, etc. In the latter case it might well be said that he drove the vehicle, changed gear, braked, etc. "in his sleep" or "in a state of automatism." Such cases can certainly occur.[31]

In some cases, Hart clarifies, the nonaction is juxtaposed to the action it resembles in order to reveal something about it—that the nonaction has all the outward trappings of action—but really is just at bottom a mere happening or occurrence. No one would say that wild or spasmodic movements due to, say, a seizure, closely resemble a mode of driving, because the only feature they share with driving is that the subject is in a car. Where, however, the driver is handling the car in a way consonant with driving (with seeing himself and being seen as driving), but is in actuality in a state of somnambulism, then our description is meant to note both the similarity to driving (he looks like he's driving) and what separates it from driving (but he is really just driving in his sleep).

Moore never notes Hart's qualification, however, even though Moore himself recognizes that these unconscious happenings or occurrences—these movements—"look like actions" (*A&C*, 255). Instead, he concludes that

> Hart seems to think that the sleep-walker indeed performs the action of walking, the unconscious driver indeed drives, the hypoglycemic assaulter indeed hits his victims, the hypnotized subject told to raise his arm, and who does so, does indeed raise his arm. Hart's reason for thinking that involuntary bodily movements such as these are actions is that it is idiomatic in ordinary English to describe them with ordinary verbs of action. Ordinary usage certainly seems to be with Hart here (*A&C*, 253).

Moore then cautions us not to take ordinary language too seriously, given that much of it is merely metaphorical, e.g., "the tree shed its leaves"; the sleepwalking Lady Macbeth "rubs her hands". The following summary Moore offers on this matter, including the role that ordinary language should play in where we end up, should be unsurprising: "In any case, the questions whether sleep-walking is a kind of walking (as an action), or whether post-hypnotic movement with death as its consequence is a kind of killing (as an action) are only answered by one's best theory of action. Ordinary-language observations cannot overthrow such a theory, no matter how ordinary and idiomatic may be the employment of our verbs of action to describe such phenomena" (*A&C*, 256). Had Moore not redacted or perhaps misread much of what Hart had to say on point, I think we could reach agreement promptly that Hart and Moore themselves agree that sleepwalkers don't exactly walk.

Despite Moore's skepticism concerning the value of ordinary language in the interpretation of action, I struggle to see what mischief ordinary-language procedures could possibly do, even if given a chance. While Moore would rescue criminal law from ordinary-language philosophy, the rescue he has in mind either has already been performed or never was needed. No criminal code, court, or casebook known to me sees human action as anything *but* the union of bodily movements and hidden mental states whose meanings are inferred. I selected Kadish and Schulhofer's casebook as an example of the prevailing view of human action *because* it is so representative.[32] One would not have to look far into the Supreme Court Reports to find this sort of expression: "The state of a man's mind is as much a fact as the state of his digestion. It is true that it is very difficult to prove what the state of a man's mind at a particular time is, but if it can be ascertained it is as much a fact as anything else."[33] Nor would one encounter much difficulty in finding legislatures or courts that condition criminal liability on "the concurrence of act and intent."[34] In other words, Moore's view *is* the law. And criminal-law legislation and cases show no sign of being informed by even a casual reading of Austin. As for academic lawyers, the jumbo issue that the *University of Pennsylvania Law Review* dedicated to reactions to Moore's book betray leading legal philosophers suffering no "anxiety of influence" from Austin's shadow whatsoever. The only place Austin's name shows up in the entire symposium is in one of Moore's footnotes.[35] More recent legal literature on point, as little of it as there is, follows suit.[36]

While Moore would like to refute ordinary-language philosophy—not reconcile himself with it[37]—he leaves us in a fog as to what he thinks it is. He refers to it here and there, that is, he cites it, but his book makes no serious effort to confront it. While at times Moore seems willing to give ordinary language the mere "First Word" Austin granted it (*A&C*, 227–35) (whatever Austin meant by that) ("CRITICISM," 102),[38] still Moore finds it "remarkable that an entire generation of analytic philosophers took this style of argument seriously" (*A&C*, 91).[39] He repeatedly calls Austin a "sceptic" (*A&C*, 11, 196, 213, 246), that is, someone who craves but doubts the possibility of knowledge or insists that it is obtainable only with great difficulty and precaution. Yet Austin is a *response to* if not a refutation of skepticism (indeed, to epistemology).[40] It is Moore's work that is skeptical in that it converts questions of responsibility (who is answerable for what?) into questions of knowledge (how can we know what the defendant was thinking?). In other words, what I am offering is a view of skepticism by which it is *any* view that converts questions of human response into questions of knowledge no matter what the ultimate answer to the question of knowledge is. The real danger that Austin poses, Moore tells us, is that "[t]o pursue Austin's query very far would be to dissolve any general act requirement running throughout the criminal law into the special act requirement of each statute that prohibits actions of mayhem, rape, arson, etc" (*A&C*, 8). Moore worries that Austin means for us to draw an "inference" that "there is no act requirement": "only as many act requirements as there are distinct verbs of action in . . . some jurisdiction's criminal code" (*A&C*, 42).

I cannot figure out what would motivate Moore to say this or why a "dissolving" of the "act requirement" is staked in ordinary-language philosophy's approach to questions of responsibility. Could Austin possibly dissolve the act requirement by asking "*what we should say when* . . ."? It bears repeating that ordinary-language philosophers take philosophical statements *as* ordinary statements, which amounts to asking for philosophical use of terms (like Moore's use of "will" as a verb) to conform to the criteria of ordinary utterances (i.e., that they be speech-acts rather than nonclaims). To do otherwise is really what it means to use ordinary words in that "illegitimate" way I referred to at the start of this book.[41] There *is* a way to give sense to "willed bodily movement" (or "bodily-movement-caused-by-a-volition") (*A&C*, 169), as in "I made a willed bodily movement" so that it does conform to the criteria of ordinary utterances.[42] For example, in a tennis match I may mean to serve an "American Twist," which requires a severe bending of the knees and back in order to strike the ball on its inside edge with a peculiar topspin that bounces the ball unpredictably. Because only rarely can I pull this action off, it makes sense there—and *only* there—to speak of my "willing a bodily movement" since there the normal criteria of the word "willing" and the words "bodily movement" would be present. And why is this so? It has to do with the fact that just like "voluntary," "willed" is not a term the application of which can even be raised with regard to ordinary actions. For example, I take a sip of wine and you ask: "Did you will that movement?" Me: "Huh?" Terms like voluntary and willed get their sense from being used in specific speech-situations that do not arise in the case of the ordinary action. This is meant to illustrate again that what's at stake in ordinary-language philosophy is trying to provide criteria for philosophical statements (like Moore's) as if they were ordinary assertions themselves. I see little evidence that deploying ordinary-language procedures would dissolve Moore's act requirement, though they may no doubt provide a basis for criticizing what *counts* for him as an action.

Moore's Examples: The Problem of Representativeness[43]

Another hitch in our understanding the relation between ordinary language and Moore's philosophy of action (an act is a "bodily-movement-caused-by-a-volition") is that many of his examples are so unrepresentative of the concepts they are meant to illustrate that it is hard to see their point or be taken in by them. ("Taken in" in that I felt as though I was *meant* to be taken in, as in tricked or fooled). Consider again the case of the "reluctant executioner":

> A state executioner who has read thus far into this book wishes to do his job yet not perform the action of killing. He accordingly connects the guillotine that is used in his line of work to a device that reads the electrical conductivity of his skin. He learns how to use the device in two stages: in stage one, he learns that by fantasizing about something very pleasant, he can raise the conductivity of his skin; in stage two, he learns to dispense with this fantasy and simply to will his skin conductivity to increase. At either stage, the increase in skin conductivity causes the guillotine to drop, killing the condemned prisoner. In each case has not the executioner killed, even though he did not move his body in order to do so?
>
> The second stage of this . . . example (of the squeamish executioner) is easy. If the executioner can simply will a change in the conductivity of his skin, and that change in conductivity can have real-world effects, then we should construe bodily movements to include such changes in conductivity. For he also surely kills when he wills such a change of bodily states in order to release the guillotine, which is in fact released and beheads its victim. He has used his body as the means to effect a change in the world which he desires to bring about, and it shouldn't matter whether the means involve a literal motion of a whole limb or only the microscopic motions within some limbs or other organ. All such willed changes of bodily states, when used as a means to change the world, are actions (*A&C*, 264–65).[44]

There are more where these came from (e.g., "the act of signing a contract can be done through the movement of one's toes as well as by the movement of one's fingers, as long as you can grasp a pen with either") (*A&C*, 90),[45] including this: "Suppose [a] doctor runs the patient down with his Lincoln Continental, hitting the patient in just the way that causes his appendix to fly out of his body. Has the doctor caused a removing of the appendix? Has he removed the appendix?" (*A&C*, 231).[46] Credit for many of Moore's characteristic examples is given to others,[47] though he is no slouch at inventing them himself:

> X wants to scare Y and realizes that an effective way to do so is to manifest the behavioral features of his trying to move his non-existent leg (for Y will believe X is darkly angry or mentally disturbed, since that is how X looks during such times). X accordingly tries to move his phantom limb while he faces Y. This effort of will causes the eye, lips, and facial movements earlier described; these in turn cause Y to be frightened. Has not X performed the action of frightening Y by moving his facial muscles, lips, and pupils? (*A&C*, 107).

Another Moore original asks us to imagine if Squeaky Fromme, who tried to assassinate President Ford, "woke up finding that her hand had been wrapped round a loaded pistol that was pointed at Ford, decided for the first time at that moment to kill him, and moved her finger with that intent" (*A&C*, 218–19).

Moore nicked "the reluctant executioner" from Leo Katz. In Katz's 1994 article "Crime, Consent, and Insider Trading,"[48] he takes up "a moral argument against insider trading" to be developed "with the help of some studiedly ridiculous examples," whose ridiculousness he delivers,[49] but never "makes up for" with the "clarity" he promises.[50] That same year, for the University of Pennsylvania's symposium on Moore's book, Katz authored an article in which he cooked up a dozen of his self-described "stylized,"[51] "twisted,"[52] and "extraordinarily contrived"[53] examples, including these two doozies:

> Septimus is a surgeon who has been curious about what it would be like to operate on someone while he, Septimus, is in a slight state of intoxication. Realizing that to do so would be criminally reckless, he never actually goes through with the experiment. Instead, he makes painfully sure to be quite free of alcohol when he is actually on duty. But when he is off duty, he maintains a constant state of slight intoxication. His reason for doing so is somewhat devious. He hopes that some day an emergency will arise in which he is the only person with surgical skills far and wide, and de-

> spite his intoxication, his help will be eagerly sought. This does indeed happen. In the course of operating, Septimus's hands shake quite violently and the patient suffers a good deal of damage which he would not have had Septimus been sober. I would say about this case: Septimus's policy of maintaining a constant state of light intoxication so he could find out what it would be like to operate drunk constitutes an act (or many acts, if you prefer) that proximately caused the patient's injuries, but that nevertheless Septimus is beyond reproach, at least legal reproach.[54]

> Ethelbert sees someone drowning in the middle of the lake. He jumps in to rescue him, takes hold of him, and starts for the shore. He then discovers that the victim is someone he has long regarded as his mortal enemy. Before reaching the shore, he sloughs him off, as it were, and swims back by himself. His act of sloughing off the victim proximately caused his death. All the same, I do not believe he would be liable for any kind of homicide.[55]

In a talk I heard Katz give in 1997, he presented this second problem with a slight twist. This time Katz asked whether a "libertarian" would let Ethelbert and the drowning victim enter a contract under which the victim assents today to being someday thrown back in the water after having being fished out (should he ever find himself in such a pinch) in exchange for valuable consideration—I believe it was $100.[56]

These unrepresentative examples are part of a mode of talking about criminal law. Their most obvious shared feature is their self-conscious extraordinariness—their complete foreignness to the sorts of problems that confront real people with real problems, cares, commitments, and responsibilities in the real world. And what good are examples like that? Are they designed to remove the "blinkers" of ordinary language? ("A WORD," 68). Katz recommends their "clarity," but he never addresses whether or why the clear is conditioned on the fantastic. Why would it be? Each example that I've reproduced here, be it Moore's or Katz's, imagines human beings cut off from the normal "burden of action, of being an agent in the world, . . . the burden of being equal to the consequences of our actions" (*M&S*, 75). That is, just like the thought-experiments that they imitate, these examples take place, quite literally, in a vacuum.

The "reluctant executioner" whom Moore borrowed from Katz imagines such a vacuum: a world in which the yoke of responsibility thrust on and accepted by the executioner who acts for the state (or through whom the state acts) is faced not at the level of action (what do I do? what can I do? what have I done?), but merely at the level of thought. To be sure, killing the prisoner by altering his own skin conductivity cuts him off from action, or at least from movement, as we know it. But why imagine *that*? Because for Moore you can perform a bodily movement without moving your body? In what way will those exotic conditions save the executioner from responsibility for killing prisoners? What is the point of talking about our responsibility for things like "changing your skin conductivity," twitching your "facial muscles, eyes, and lips" and your nonexistent limbs in order to frighten someone, "removing" someone's appendix with a Lincoln Continental, or paying someone today to waive his or her right against being drowned by you in the future? At one point Moore observes that sending a nerve impulse would be an action if only we knew how to do it (*A&C*, 103).

What is he getting at? If I can squeeze anything out of this way of talking about responsibility, it would be this: even when we imagine a world in which we are converted into beings who somehow *seem* to have avoided the (unbearable) burden of action, still we cannot escape that burden even after reorienting ourselves to such an other-worldly notion of action whereby we alter our skin conductivity, etc. Maybe it is Moore's point that even if we were to somehow wake up with a gun strapped to our hand and aimed at the President, still we are on the hook for what we then do despite our somehow having isolated ourselves from the normal grammar of "assassinate," since absent, among other things, is the premeditation and deliberation we would expect from such an action. Is *that* it? Is *that* clear? If that is in fact the point, it is true enough, but nonetheless strikes me as a too-indirect way of resolving the moral problems that Moore and Katz mean to address.[57] In other words, that I suspect that Moore and I are ultimately in agreement on his point (but that I cannot really tell), is much more a criticism of the examples he has selected to illustrate his point than of the point itself.

"[A] Vague and Comforting Idea"

There must be—indeed there is—a connection between the penchant for examples that are unrepresentative of the dilemmas we really do face and the view of human action as "bodily-movement-caused-by-a-volition" (*A&C*, 169). Take what I consider to be Moore's central example, the relevance of which I *can* grasp: that "'Jones killed Smith'" is an alternative description both for "'Jones caused Smith's death'" and "'Jones's movement of his finger caused Smith's death'" (*A&C* 192). For Moore, which of these three utterances we deploy depends on our being able to tell "the difference between the various mental states required by the mens rea requirement and the single mental state required by the act requirement" (*A&C*, 173).

So there are two "mens reas" per action? One act of "willing" gets the body going in a certain way and another pursues its objectives? No wonder Gilbert Ryle called such an account of human action "ghostly."[58] No one talks that way, in or out of court. How could they? "'Caught in the act,' for example, conjures up a picture of the burglar creeping away with the swag over his shoulder; of the murderer standing over his victim, bloody knife in hand: not of a criminal contracting various muscles."[59] Gudel summarizes the case against "bodily-movement-caused-by-a-volition" this way: "This picture of action as consisting of two causally related components, one mental and one physical, is false to the way we normally talk and think about human acts. When we observe our fellow humans, we do not see mere bodily movements [to which are attached inner events]. We see *actions*."[60] Anyone accused of speaking, say, in a disrespectful tone, would reveal little by elaborating about making movements of the tongue.[61] Rarely will references to contracting muscles tell us anything about what someone has done. Thus Moore's having broken down "killing" into its component "contracting the finger" is unlikely to get us any closer to understanding human action. Even when in a rare case the accused *has* tried to pull the trigger, "attempted to shoot" would be a much more helpful description than "contracted the finger."

We can begin to learn something about whether and when "Jones killed Smith" is an alternative description both for "Jones caused Smith's death" and "Jones's movement of his finger caused Smith's death" from Austin's *Sense and Sensibilia*:

> Suppose that I look through a telescope and you ask me, "What do you see?." I may answer (1) "A bright speck"; (2) "A star"; (3) "Sirius"; (4) "The image in the fourteenth mirror of the telescope." All these answers may be perfectly correct. Have we then different senses of "see"? *Four* different senses? Of course not. The image in the fourteenth mirror of the telescope *is* a bright speck, this bright speck *is* a star, and the star *is* Sirius;

> I can say, quite correctly and with no ambiguity whatever, that I see any of these. Which way of saying what I see I actually choose will depend on the particular circumstances of the case—for instance, on what sort of answer I expect you to be interested in, on how much I know, or on how far I am prepared to stick my neck out (*S&S*, 99).

So too, if asked "What did you kick?," whether I answer "a piece of painted wood" or "Jones's front door" depends on, among other things, our "interest in this aspect or that of the total situation," that is, on the circumstances in which something is said (*S&S*, 101). Or put another way, no one description of an action is more "fundamental" or "basic" as opposed to "derived" than any other.

This limit on interpretation does not constrain Professor Moore, however. "Suppose," he proposes, "that John kisses Mary tenderly on the cheek at noon of a given day. How many events took place?" (*A&C*, 370). For Moore, this is a "thorny issue" (*A&C*, 370), given that an answer either of "quite a few" or "only one" strikes him as "absurd" or "false" (*A&C*, 370). Moore therefore recommends that we count "kisses" rather than "events," adding that "lip-touching" "counts" as a "kiss-making property," "but tenderness and on-the-cheek-ness do not count in making an event a kiss, . . . [a]lthough they are properties of kisses" (*A&C*, 371).[62]

I wonder how many events or kisses Moore thinks took place. Whether we call Sirius "Sirius," "a star," "a bright speck," or "the image in the fourteenth mirror of the telescope" depends on *why we are being asked*, "on what sort of answer I expect you to be interested in." As P. F. Strawson has argued,

> the context of utterance is of an importance which it is almost impossible to exaggerate; and by "context" I mean, at least, the time, the place, the situation, the identity of the speaker, the subjects which form the immediate focus of interest, and the personal histories of both the speaker and those he is addressing. Besides context, there is, of course, convention;—linguistic convention.[63]

When John kisses Mary, I cannot imagine how "how many," abstractly, just like that, *without* context, could be a question at all. The modifying adverb here, tenderly, suggests that there may be some question about the *way* the kiss was performed ("no modification without aberration"). But that hardly is aberrational. Most kisses are tender. Does calling attention to such an action indicate that John normally is abusive? Is that the point of the sentence? Why it is said? That this time John kissed Mary tenderly as opposed to brutally, impatiently, indifferently? The kiss may have followed a disagreement. John may want to bury the hatchet. Or perhaps John himself is tender. But tender how? Soft and caring? Or is he raw, as if recovering from a painful experience? These are the sorts of elaborations that would be responsive to an inquiry into the meaning of "John kissed Mary tenderly on the cheek. . . ." To convert that particular action into an inquiry into "how many" events took place is an interpretation that is simply not open to us. To respond to Moore's example in the way I have tried to here is to my mind what Cavell means when he admonishes us to treat philosophical statements—like Moore's—*as* ordinary utterances.

Similarly, when Jones is being accused of killing Smith, is it quite extraordinary to say that "Jones caused Smith's death," and even more extraordinary to say that "Jones's movement of his finger caused Smith's death." Accusing someone of "causing death" rather than "killing" excites an altogether different picture of human action. When I hear "Jones *caused* Smith's death," I picture him doing a subpar job repairing the brakes on Smith's car before Smith's fatal car crash, or introducing Smith to psychoactive drugs, cigarettes, mountain climbing, or any other high-risk activity that ultimately does Smith in. That is, we say "Jones caused Smith's death" only when we suspect that "killed" (let alone "murdered") would overstate Jones's role in Smith's demise. If what you really saw was that Jones shot Smith dead, then just say so. And to describe the killing as "Jones's movement of his finger caused Smith's death" makes matters worse, even unintelligible. Do you mean that Jones was sleepwalking or acting in response to posthypnotic suggestion as in *The Manchurian Candidate*? If not, then why talk that way? Again, if you mean that Jones shot Smith, killed Smith, or if you really want to stick your neck out, murdered him, there is nothing useful about blocking your meaning. No doubt Jones did move his finger, but the fact that something is true is not, without more, a reason for saying anything (*CR*, 206).

Indeed, you *cannot* say "Jones moved his finger . . ." and mean the same thing in ordinary speech as "Jones murdered Smith." The criteria for the application of these two sentences are different, as they were in my attempt to give a sense to "willed bodily movement" sentences by describing my efforts to serve up an American Twist in tennis. You would *only* make sense talking about moving fingers to describe a murder in exceedingly unusual circumstances.

But what is lost when we talk in a loose or eccentric way? If the context is one in which we accuse someone of burglary, arguably it makes no difference whether we say a burglar is someone creeping around with a swag over his shoulder or instead is someone whose "mental state" urges his body to make certain "burglarious"[64] movements. What harm, exactly, is done by breaking down actions into firing synapses and twitching muscles à la Michael Moore? The harm in "this vague and comforting idea that . . . doing an action must come down to the making of physical movements with parts of the body" ("EXCUSES," 178) is that the notion of an action as "bodily-movement-caused-by-a-volition" has very little basis in human experience. It decouples the human from the action. As an interpretive strategy, therefore, it defeats the whole point of an accusation: to elicit an elaboration that will allow us to reclaim the relation—the community—that the accused has threatened. In other words, what is lost is our ability to really understand the internal (rather than contingent) connection of excuses to crimes, i.e., the connection that establishes that excuses are constitutive of what count as crimes. This is my stake in objecting to Moore: that his approach (criminal law's approach), which I hope now to establish as skeptical, negatively influences what is entailed in making judgments about responsibility.

JUDGING AN ACTION: THE PROBLEM OF SKEPTICISM

Accusing someone of *anything* is an act of neck-sticking-out. It simply cannot be done, as Austin would say, in an "incorrigible" way. An incorrigible utterance is one that takes no chances and makes absolutely minimal commitments so as to wipe out the risk of making a mistake (*S&S*, 112). But what makes questions of responsibility so daunting is that in making our rulings on who is answerable for what, we must stick our necks out a bit, given that in law, again, "there is the overriding requirement that a decision be reached, and a relatively black or white decision—guilty or not guilty—for the plaintiff or for the defendant" ("EXCUSES," 188). In law "we cannot . . . evade or forget the whole affair" ("EXCUSES," 186), even though the implications of what we do, of who is answerable for what, are invariably not obvious. ("Actions, unlike envelopes and goldfinches, do not come named for the assessment, nor like apples, ripe for grading") (*CR*, 265).

Nonetheless, Moore's interest in the mechanics of human action is a quest for the incorrigible. He knows that interpretations of action can go wrong. It is his view on *why* interpretations of action go wrong that is skeptical. Take this perfectly conventional position of Moore's: "My own intentions are usually known to me in a way different from how they are known to a third-person observer, the latter having to make behavioural inferences since he lacks my first-person experience" (*A&C*, 94).[65] Moore says we must "infer," to him a second-rate way of *knowing*, but if close enough attention is paid to the data—to the way the body moves and what the mind must have willed it to do—we can discover a "useful and true" view of "mental states." It is precisely Moore's interest in what he calls "first-person experience" of others' intentions that accounts for his redescribing "Jones killed Smith" as "Jones's movement of his finger caused Smith's death." Because for Moore human action is boiled down to bodily movements, evaluating those actions entails close study of the movements to see if they support the necessary inference about the crucial mental state. That inference takes place because, under such a view, our responses to others are conditioned on our knowledge of them, knowledge of what they have done.

To treat our responses to others as based on knowledge of them, however, where knowledge is a function of certainty, shows that a skeptic's notion of who is responsible for what demands the penetration of the private (demands "the denial of the otherness of others").[66] Due to the fact of their separateness—they are in their bodies and we in ours—others *are* private. Certainly we can "know" them, but the way we respond to what they do and fail to do, whether we reconcile with them, is outside the realm of knowledge, at least to the extent that we equate knowledge with certainty. Rather, it calls on our capacity to acknowledge others, which is a capacity to respond to the claims they make on us, claims that are not mediated by our capacity to know, again, not that mode of knowing which is equated with certainty.

When I ask you to excuse me for stepping on your foot, and you do by saying "It's okay; I know you didn't mean it," you don't actually *know* what I meant to do (how would you know that?). Rather, you acknowledge that my hurting you was inadvertent. But if only I know what I was (really) doing, then why would you say that you know it was inadvertent? For Cavell, this distinction between my knowing something (which I may acknowledge or refuse to acknowledge to you) and my acknowledging something (which I "know," but not in the sense that I am certain about it or am experiencing it as you are), is the difference between a piece of data (knowing it) and doing or refusing to do something about it (acknowledging it) ("K&A," 254–66).

If a skeptic's responses to the world are mediated merely by knowledge, then Moore's approach, like the conventions of criminal law more generally, indulges us in what we would like most to do: exempt ourselves from the responsibility of confronting (being prepared to acknowledge) the gun-wielding Jones—of making something of what he has done "in the public, observable world." In other words, the inferences Moore would have us resort to about others' mental states (since their intentions are not known to us the way our own are) are a reaction to the problem of the privacy of others, but in no way a solution to it. Since we cannot penetrate the private—even inferentially—all we can do with the accused is respond to him by relying on or rejecting his account of his actions when he commits himself by going on record about what he has done and why.

Indeed, so struck is Moore by our powerlessness to know the interior "secret" selves of others that I would venture to say that his entire project of rescuing the "act requirement" may just be veneering. Moore's real concern, if I may venture, may not be that the "act requirement" is in danger or that it needs justifying. Rather, it is that Moore's attempts to rescue the "act requirement" are really expressions of his own impulse toward community—to *know* others rather than *merely* acknowledge them—as though acknowledging them, that is, responding to their claims on us, is somehow inferior to knowing (beholding?) them. But the power and demand of the excuses is that excuses themselves are claims on us to respond to—claims that we accept or reject—*not* things that we know or do not know or judge as true or false. Accepting or rejecting an excuse is critical to our moral judgment on what has been done. And when we accept or reject an excuse in whole or in part we make no claim of knowing anything. Moore, however, reduces the question of whether to accept or reject an excuse down to a set of true/false judgments of whether the facts corresponding to a list of elements of crimes have been proved.

If Moore's causal theory of human action really is directed at preserving an "act requirement," then I think it is safe to say that Austin had no interest whatsoever in threatening or even addressing it. Austin's goal—that of ordinary-language philosophy—is *not* to make crime an actionless phenomenon. How would he do that? Rather, it is to better understand action (including speaking) itself. Again, "when we examine what we should say when, . . . we are looking . . . not *merely* at words (or 'meanings,' whatever they may be) but also at the realities we use the words to talk about: we are using a sharpened awareness of words to sharpen our perception of, though not as the final arbiter of, the phenomena" ("EXCUSES," 182).

But suppose for a moment that Austin really did want to eliminate the "act requirement" from the criminal law. Let us suppose the repeal of Model Penal Code, section 2.01, which conditions criminal liability on "a voluntary act" or certain duty-based "omissions" to act, or of California Penal Code, section 20, which requires "a union, or joint operation of act and intent." Now what? Who would be criminally liable who should not be? It is hard to see what a "univocal act requirement" preserves. Is it the requirement that criminals do things before we call them "criminals"? Do things as opposed to what? There would be no coherent concept of "the actions of mayhem, rape, arson, etc."[67] or any other crime that could be understood *without* human action (or lazing around—omitting to act—when it is your duty not to). How else could one commit "the actions of mayhem, rape, arson, etc." if not by putting oneself to the task? Individual statutes[68] and jury instructions[69] describe in great detail the proscribed actions; it is a curiosity to think that the only thing preventing legislatures from punishing criminals for nothing at all is the preservation of an overarching "univocal act requirement."

Nonetheless, Moore's rescue of the "act requirement" lines up in its sights Mark Kelman's famous article, "Interpretive Construction in the Substantive Criminal Law."[70] There Kelman posits that the voluntary-act requirement, like so much of criminal law, obscures important "policy" decisions by neglecting, among other things, the importance of deciding how thick a story to tell at criminal trials, how far back in time we should go before the prohibited harm in question occurs. Kelman wants us to see that the "time framing" of an episode determines the doctrine we use and its application in our evaluating criminality. He reveals the importance of time framing in a range of contexts, one of which is *Martin v. State*,[71] where an appellate court reversed Martin's conviction of being drunk and boisterous in public. Martin had gotten drunk at home where police arrested him for an unrelated offense before dragging him into public where he "appeared" in a drunk and boisterous condition. Pointing out the potential arbitrariness of how to time-frame the issue, Kelman writes that Martin

> may have done *something* voluntarily (before the police came) that posed a risk that he would get arrested and carried into public in his drunken state. While it is plausible that Martin was arrested on an old warrant and could not foresee that he would wind up in public on this occasion, it is quite possible that the defendant was arrested for activity he was engaging in at home: for instance, beating his wife. Why did the court not consider saying that the voluntary act at time one (wife beating) both posed a risk of and caused a harmful involuntary act at time two (public drunkenness) and assessing the voluntariness of the alleged criminal act with reference to the wider time-framed scenario? It cannot be that the involuntary, harmful act at time two was unforeseeable. . . . One of the risks one (voluntarily) takes when one performs acts for which one ultimately may be arrested is that one will someday be forced to go places with the police, when *they* want to go and not when the individual wants to. . . . Ultimately, the *Martin* finding of voluntariness "works" not because it is "right," but because all the hard points disappear in the initial interpretive construction of the potentially relevant facts.[72]

To Moore, "[t]he presupposition of Kelman's entire analysis is simply (and obviously) false" (*A&C*, 35). "Every competent teacher of elementary criminal law," Moore wagers, knows that "[t]here is no 'time-framing' choice here. If there is *any* point in time where the act and *mens rea* requirements are simultaneously satisfied, and from which the requisite causal relations exist to some legally prohibited state of affairs, then the defendant is prima facie liable" (*A&C*, 35). For Moore the problem is simple: "those earlier acts of Martin were not the proximate cause of his being drunk in public. The police officers' intentional placing of Martin in a public place constitutes an intervening cause on anyone's reading of that notion, making Martin not a proximate cause of the legally prohibited state of affairs" (*A&C*, 36–37).

While we could perhaps get something valuable out of debating whether Martin's crime caused his arrest (didn't it?), I suspect that the value of what Kelman has done would be diluted by such a debate. Despite Moore's attempt at "dispatching" Kelman's time-framing of Martin's case (*A&C*, 35 n.46), Kelman's disquisition on the openness of the act requirement, quite apart from its left-wing quality, asks us to confront what we make of the operation of the excuses in criminal law. Given that action must always be assessed in the context in which it takes place, Kelman alerts us to the fact that accepting something as part of that context is itself a crucial act of interpretation. This, it seems to me, would be a very hard thing for anyone who cares about responsibility *not* to care about. Is getting drunk at time-one, not in unrepresentative cases like *Martin*, but in much more ordinary cases involving vehicular manslaughter, part of the drunk driver's responsibility for running over a pedestrian or smashing into another car at time-two?[73] In what instances does getting drunk pass for an acceptable excuse?[74] When does it not only fail as an excuse, but actually make matters worse for the excuse maker?[75]

In my view, Kelman's article is a thoughtful meditation on the excuses: on what sorts of elaborations will be heard, will count, and why. As Kelman demonstrates, the success of Martin's excuse, which was that he did not *do* anything, depends, as the success of any excuse does, on how the episode is bracketed: where it begins and ends. If Martin's actions that brought police to his house are included, then his conviction at trial starts to make more sense than it would if we were to ignore that and begin with his (subsequent) decision to drink in the privacy of his own home. In establishing how crucial these "time-framing" decisions are to guilt-innocence decisions, Kelman covers just about every defense in the book and is clearly aware of the stakes in that it is the point of his article to demonstrate that deciding which aspects of an elaboration we deem relevant frequently will determine our judgments about the defendant's responsibility. Kelman's concerns about time-framing are concerns about the function of the excuses generally: how excuses are structured and explained, and what those who hear them should pay attention or respond to. In fact, Moore's argument that "proximate cause" wipes out the relevance of time-framing is responsive to what Kelman wrote only to the extent that Kelman's article could easily be cast as in part a critique of the notion of "proximate cause," which is porous and shot-through with "policy considerations."[76] This is not to say that Kelman's writings about human action are incontestable.[77] It is, however, to say that he is definitely on to something when he writes that establishing what we will count as an elaboration is a central function of criminal law.

Conclusion

In Joseph Conrad's *The Secret Agent*,[1] Alexander "Tom" Ossipon, anarchist, nicknamed "the Doctor," author of a medical (and improper) pamphlet ("Future of the Proletariat"), made his living by manipulating women. He appeared "free from the trammels of conventional morality"[2] as he swindled Winnie Verloc out of her pigskin pocketbook "flush of safe banknotes"[3] after she had killed her husband (more like her father) for, among other things, having somewhat inadvertently killed her brother (more like her son). When soon after the swindle, Ossipon read in the news that just after he had abandoned Winnie she had hurled herself overboard on a cross-Channel boat, he "was menaced by this thing in the very sources of his existence."[4] Indeed, because insanity was "lying in wait," it was clear he "could no longer issue forth to meet his various conquests."[5] Over and over and over the newspaper's report refrained in Ossipon's head: "*An impenetrable mystery seems destined to hang forever over this act of madness and despair.*"[6]

Why, exactly, would a man like Ossipon, whom his anarchist boss accused of being completely without "force"[7]—of being incapable of killing even a fly[8]—fall to pieces over one of his conquests? He got her money, after all, which is just what he wanted. Wouldn't it be more like Ossipon to not care a bit about anyone but himself?

The answer may be that Ossipon never even imagined that he could ever be responsible for *anything*. Despite his bad intentions, he had to that point been, or at least he had seen himself as, utterly inconsequential. Once confronted with his responsibility for Winnie's death, he suddenly saw himself as an actor in the world, who *did* have force, who could hurt, even destroy something, something much greater than a fly. His responsibilities were not apparent to him when he abandoned her, but they were his responsibilities nevertheless. Will his elaboration get him off the hook? What would his elaboration *be*? That he had no idea he was an agent in the world? Could *that* ever be an excuse we could accept? How? Ossipon no doubt is headed straight for the fire.

Being equal to the consequences of what we do and fail to do is accepting responsibility for those consequences, even though what precautions we need to take—what can go wrong—isn't always apparent to us, just as it wasn't to Ossipon (though inexcusably in his case). Since action would be intolerable if we remained on the hook for *everything* we do and fail to do, the excuses are there to create a context for establishing how things were with us so that localizing our responsibility in relation to one another can take place. By proffering excuses we reveal not so much what was "in our mind" at some crucial juncture, but what we were doing, whether we appreciated what we were doing, and whether it was just an instance of being less than quasi-infallible (of being hasty or preoccupied) as opposed to a weakness of the will (of being greedy or brutal). Thus it is important to remember that the excuses typically do not *defeat* our responsibility, even though it is too often suggested that they do. Rather, they relieve us of the burden not of *being* responsible but of being *held* responsible or blamed (being responsible being a *condition* of not being held responsible). But while the excuses mitigate responsibility, not all pleas or responses we offer our accusers can count as excuses: "I've done harm without wrong," "I'm not to blame," "I've done a 'good' thing" may or may not get us off the hook, but they are not pleas of excuse.

Our elaborations—our excuses—are our opportunity to make things right again, to confront, and be confronted for, what we have done. If not for our interest in excuses, an accusation would mean nothing, since to trace an intention is to limit, not merely establish, another's responsibility. To say otherwise, that is, to give in to the notion that criminal law is a matter of getting at the relation between the mind and the body explains the sort of skepticism (scholasticism) that characterizes so much contemporary criminal-law theory, court cases, and legislation. Through the skeptical lens, human action is a mysterious expression of secret selves, whose hidden agendas must somehow be penetrated by careful observation of the bodily movements that reveal the presence or absence of guilty minds. While skepticism describes *an* alternative to evaluating human action, its major drawback is its tendency to impede an ex-post confrontation with and response to the excuse, a confrontation that puts on us as accusers the burden of responding ourselves, as opposed to our just observing what happened from a "God's eye" perspective. Skepticism—a refusal to accept the limits of knowledge—may be well motivated by the very strongest sense of community, by a longing to really "know" others, to really "know" the world. As well motivated as it may be, a skeptic's notion of responsibility tends to stifle the making of moral evaluations, that is, the reconciliation that emerges from our responding to others' responses to questions we put to them about whether they are meeting their responsibilities.

Notes

Preface

1. For an interesting reading of Austin's stance toward importance as a good, see G. J. Warnock, *J. L. Austin: The Arguments of the Philosophers*, ed. Ted Honderich (London: Routledge, 1989), 7–8.

2. See G.J. Warnock, "Saturday Mornings," in *Essays on J. L. Austin* (Oxford: Clarendon Press, 1973), 32–33 ("Quite apart from the fact that he enjoyed philosophical argument, Austin liked jokes—sometimes really silly jokes, real farcical fantasy [of which the most representative instances in his writings are to be found, I think, in his paper 'Pretending']").

3. William Rothman and Marian Keane, *Reading Cavell's The World Viewed: A Philosophical Perspective on Film* (Detroit: Wayne State University Press, 2000), app. 263.

4. Sir Isaiah Berlin, "Austin and the Early Beginnings of Oxford Philosophy," in *Essays on J. L. Austin* (Oxford: Clarendon Press, 1973), 8.

Introduction

1. Peter Arenella, "Convicting the Morally Blameless: Reassessing the Relationship Between Legal and Moral Accountability," *U. C. L. A. Law Review* 39 (1992): 1511 (emphasis mine).

2. Ibid., 1527 (emphasis mine).

3. E.g., *Morissette v. United States*, 342 US 246, 250 (1952) ("The contention that an injury can amount to a crime only when inflicted by intention is no provincial or transient notion. It is as universal and persistent in mature systems of law as belief in freedom of the human will and a consequent ability and duty of the normal individual to choose between good and evil.").

4. E.g., *Staples v. United States*, 511 US 600, 605 (1994) (quoting ibid.); John S. Wiley, Jr., "Not Guilty by Reason of Blamelessness: Culpability in Federal Criminal Interpretation," *Virginia Law Rev.* 85 (1999): 1021–1162.

5. Ernest van den Haag, "The Ultimate Punishment: A Defense," *Harvard Law Review* 99 (1986): 1662–69.

6. See H. L. A. Hart, *Punishment and Responsibility: Essays in the Philosophy of Law* (Oxford: Clarendon Press, 1968), 210–30 (cited in Michael S. Moore, "The Independent Moral Significance of Wrongdoing," *Journal of Contemporary Legal Issues* 5 (1994): 241; Joel Feinberg, "Action and Responsibility," in *Doing and Deserving: Essays in the Theory of Responsibility* (Princeton: Princeton University Press, 1970),

119, 130–37; Michael S. Moore, *Law and Psychiatry: Rethinking the Relationship* (Cambridge: Cambridge University Press, 1984), 49–53; Susan Wolf, "The Legal and Moral Responsibility of Organizations", in *Criminal Justice*, ed. J. Pennock and J. Chapman (New York: New York University Press, 1985), 267, 275–79; Gerald J. Postema, "Risks, Wrongs, and Responsibility: Coleman's Liberal Theory of Commutative Justice, Review of 'Risks and Wrongs' by Jules L. Coleman," *Yale Law Journal* 103 (1993): 879–80; Bailey H. Kuklin, "The Asymmetrical Conditions of Legal Responsibility in the Marketplace," *University of Miami Law Review* 44 (1990): 1008 n. 8.

7. Heidi M. Hurd, "What in the World Is Wrong?" *Journal of Contemporary Legal Issues* (1994): 209.

8. See Sanford H. Kadish, "Foreword: The Criminal Law and the Luck of the Draw," *Journal of Criminal Law and Criminology* 84 (1994): 679–702.

9. See Daniel B. Yeager, "Dangerous Games and the Criminal Law," *Criminal Justice Ethics* 16 (Winter/Spring 1997): 3–12.

10. Daniel Statman, ed., *Moral Luck* (Albany: State University of New York Press, 1993).

11. Stephen G. Giles, "Causation and Responsibility After Coase, Calabresi, and Coleman," *Quinnipiac Law Review* 16 (1997): 255–78; see also Linda Ross Meyer, "Why Me?" *Quinnipiac Law Review* 16 (1997): 299–314 ("Without some sense that the actor's wrong had some moral, rather than merely causal, connection with the harm, it is hard to see why she, rather than someone else in the community, should be required to repair the victim's loss.").

12. *A&C*, 305.

13. William Blackstone, *Of Public Wrongs*, vol. 4 of *Commentaries on the Laws of England* (Chicago: University of Chicago Press, 1979), 21 ("[A]n unwarrantable act without a vicious will is no crime at all.").

14. Terence F. MacCarthy and Kathy Morris Mejia, "The Perjurious Client Question: Putting Criminal Defense Lawyers Between a Rock and a Hard Place," *Journal of Criminal Law and Criminology* 75 (1984): 1197 n. 1 ("[G]uilty and not guilty (not innocent) are for us legal and not moral terms."); Carrie Menkel-Meadow, "Portia Redux: Another Look at Gender, Feminism, and Legal Ethics," *Virginia Journal of Social Policy and Law* 2 (1994): 79 n. 22 (responses to a fable the author has told in law school classes "are often based on legal, not moral principles"); *Jarrett v. Jarrett*, 400 NE 421, 427 (Ill 1979) (courts are equipped to decide legal but not moral issues).

15. See also *HTDTW*, 21 ("Features of this sort would normally come under the heading of 'extenuating circumstances' or of 'factors reducing or abrogating the agent's responsibility', and so on.").

16. Cf. generally Douglas N. Husak, "The Relevance of the Concept of Action to the Criminal Law," *Criminal Law Forum* 6 (1995): 327 (calling Moore's book "the finest and most comprehensive treatment of the connection between the substantive criminal law and that highly specialized branch of philosophy that deals with human action").

17. Sanford H. Kadish and Stephen J. Schulhofer, ed., *Criminal Law and Its Processes: Cases and Materials*, 6th ed. (Boston: Little, Brown, 1995), 893.

18. See *Beyond Causation*, 80.

19. *S&S*, 15 ("One can't abuse ordinary language without paying for it."); ibid., 63 ("Tampering . . . is not so easy as is often supposed, is not justified or needed so

often as is often supposed, and is often thought to be necessary just because what we've got already has been misrepresented.").

20. Ibid., 84–103. (Chapter 9 critiques A. J. Ayer's *The Foundations of Empirical Knowledge*, investigating whether Ayer has identified a "special" sense of the verb "to see," and emphasizing that a special or new sense of a word is quite different from stretching the ordinary sense to cover extraordinary situations. Using the verb "see" in instances of double vision or when someone suffering from the D. T.'s "sees pink rats" are extraordinary circumstances that stretch, but do not create special senses of, an ordinary word.)

21. See note 18 above.

Chapter 1. Mens Rea

1. Ludwig Wittgenstein, preliminary studies for *Philosophical Investigations* (generally known as *The Blue and Brown Books*) (New York: Harper, 1958), 143.

2. Larry Alexander, "Reconsidering the Relationship Among Voluntary Acts, Strict Liability, and Negligence in Criminal Law," *Social Philosophy and Policy* 7 (1990): 100n. 59.

3. *A&C*, 177.

4. Larry Alexander, "Foreword: Coleman and Corrective Justice," *Harvard Journal of Law and Public Policy* 15 (1992): 628.

5. Paul H. Robinson and Jane A. Grall, "Element Analysis in Defining Criminal Liability: The Model Penal Code and Beyond," *Stanford Law Review* 35 (1983): 695–96 n. 60 ("[N]egligent people arguably do not deserve punishment because their defect is not a moral one, but rather one of knowledge or understanding that a particular conduct may cause a particular harmful result. To punish such defendants is to punish them for being stupid" citing Edwin R. Keedy, "Ignorance and Mistake in the Criminal Law," *Harvard Law Review* 22 (1908): 84).

6. See, e.g., Peter Arenella, "Rethinking the Functions of Criminal Procedure: The Warren and Burger Courts' Competing Ideologies," *Georgetown Law Journal* 72 (1983): 197–98 ("Our substantive criminal law requires a moral evaluation of the actor's conduct by including some mental element (e.g., purpose, knowledge, recklessness, or negligence) in its definition of most offenses and by its recognition of affirmative defenses that either justify the defendant's conduct or excuse it.").

7. See Introduction, note 3.

8. See note 4 above.

9. Alexander, "Reconsidering the Relationship," 101 ("Recklessness is the lowest form of actual culpability. . . .").

10. See Introduction, note 5; see also *Scales v. United States*, 367 US 203, 224 (1961); *Korematsu v. United States*, 323 US 214, 243 (1944) (Jackson, J., dissenting); *United States v. Dotterweich*, 320 US 286, 287 (1943) (Murphy, J., dissenting).

11. Alexander, "Reconsidering the Relationship," 101 n. 60 (a defendant's "callousness" is the key to culpability).

12. See Robinson and Grall, "Element Analysis," 695–96 ("[R]ecklessness is considered the norm for criminal culpability, and negligence punished only in the exceptional case."); cf. Richard Singer and Douglas Husak, "Of Innocence and Innocents: The Supreme Court and Mens Rea Since Herbert Packer," *Buffalo Criminal Law Review* 2 (1999): 859, 942 ("'Mens rea is an important requirement, but it is

not a constitutional requirement, except sometimes'" quoting Herbert L. Packer, "Mens Rea and the Supreme Court," *Supreme Court Review* (1962): 107).

13. See Robinson and Grall, "Element Analysis," 691–92, nn. 44–46; Paul Robinson, "A Brief History of Distinctions in Criminal Culpability," *Hastings Law Journal* 31 (1980): 816.

14. Model Penal Code § 2.02 (1962).

15. Ibid.

16. See notes 2 and 4 above.

17. See Larry Alexander, "Negligence, Crime, and Tort: Comments on Hurd and Simons," *Boston University Law Review* 76 (1996): 302; idem, "Crime and Culpability," *Journal of Contemporary Legal Issues* 5 (1994): 2.

18. See *Santillanes v. State*, 115 NM 215, 222 (1993).

19. See Alexander, "Reconsidering the Relationship," 96 ("[T]he voluntary act principle requires fair control, and fair control requires not just choice but a reason to choose the preferred conduct—i.e., a choice between the culpable and the nonculpable"); Michael S. Moore, "Choice, Character, and Excuse," *Social Philosophy and Policy* 7 (1990): 56 ("Responsibility for negligence *is* difficult to square with the choice conception of responsibility for the obvious reason that a negligent actor does not choose to do the complex act (such as killing) that is forbidden . . . because his mind was not adverting to that aspect of his action").

20. See Model Penal Code § 2.02(2)(c) (1962).

21. Ibid.

22. *People v. Watson*, 637 P2d 279 (1981).

23. Ibid., 285–86.

24. Ibid., 289 (Bird, C. J., dissenting).

25. Ibid., 283 ("[A] finding of implied malice depends upon a determination that the defendant *actually appreciated* the risk involved, i.e., a *subjective* standard"); ibid., 285 ("We have said that second degree murder based on implied malice has been committed when a person does 'an act, the natural consequences of which are dangerous to life, which act was deliberately performed by a person who knows that his conduct endangers the life of another and who acts with conscious disregard for life'").

26. Ibid., 283 ("A finding of gross negligence is made by applying an *objective* test: if a *reasonable person* in defendant's position would have been aware of the risk involved, then defendant is presumed to have had such an awareness").

27. Ibid., 285–86 ("He had driven his car to the establishment where he had been drinking, and he must have known that he would have to drive it later. It may also be presumed that defendant was aware of the hazards of driving while intoxicated").

28. Model Penal Code § 3.09 (1962).

29. Ibid., §§ 3.02(2), 3.04(1), 3.09(2). There is an example in a footnote whose content is borrowed from Glanville Williams, who says that "[t]he only common situation in which a person makes an unreasonable mistake in what he believes to be self-defense is when he is drunk or otherwise in an abnormal mental state. For example, a drunken person may misconstrue a gesture as an attempt to kill. . . ." The aptness of Williams's example is neither accepted nor repudiated by the drafters, though the position that Williams takes therein—that *all* beliefs ("reckless," "negligent," or otherwise) are good enough to defeat liability—they expressly reject. Ibid., § 3.09(2) n. 10. Neither does Professor Robinson, who uses the term "unreasonable mistake," offer any specific examples of what could constitute one. See Robinson and Grall, "Element Analysis," 725–32.

30. See *M&S*, 79–80 ("This [passage], I think, tells us what it means to *accept* the world. It is to accept it as a scene of action, of demands, claims, and responses not necessarily mediated by belief, knowledge or certainty").

31. See *People v. Goetz*, 68 NY 2d 96 (1986).

32. See Model Penal Code § 3.09 (1962). The law in Goetz's home state is different. *Goetz*, 68 NY 2d at 109–12.

33. John Updike, "The Widow," in *Flash Fiction*: *Very Short Stories*, ed. James Thomas, Denise Thomas, and Tom Hazuka (New York: W. W. Norton & Co., 1992), 143.

34. George Pitcher, "Austin: A Personal Memoir," in *Essays on J. L. Austin* (Oxford: Clarendon Press, 1973), 20.

35. Model Penal Code § 2.02 (1962).

36. Ibid.

37. Ibid.

38. Ibid.

39. Ibid.

40. Ibid.

41. See Robinson and Grall, "Element Analysis," 696 n. 65 ("The drafters of the Model Penal Code themselves equate the terms").

42. See note 35 above.

43. See Sigmund Freud, *Psychopathology of Everyday Life*, trans. A. A. Brill (New York: New American Library, 1951), 90–124.

44. Or "purposefully," which gets not at a particular type of reason dissociated from the action, but rather, what Austin calls "the style of performance." "EXCUSES," 199–200 (Eating one's soup *with* deliberation is a style matter; eating one's soup *after* deliberation has to do with a process of decision); "INK," 282 ("[A] purposeful air is one of getting the preliminaries, the first stages, each stage *over with*, in order to proceed to the next and get the whole business achieved: it is an air of pressing on").

45. See generally Carlos J. Moya, *The Philosophy of Action: An Introduction* (Oxford: Polity, 1990), 12–13.

46. See "EXCUSES," 179 ("[E]ven the 'simplest' named actions are not so simple—certainly are not the mere makings of physical movements, and to ask what more, then, comes in (intentions? conventions?) and what does not (motives?) . . ."); ibid., 201 ("Should we say . . . that he took her money, or that he robbed her? That he knocked a ball into a hole, or that he sank a putt? That he said 'Done', or that he accepted an offer? How far, that is, are motives, intentions and conventions to be a part of the description of actions?").

47. "PRETENDING," 262 n. 1 ("A pretext may be not a genuine reason or not your real reason; a pretence may be something you are not genuinely doing or not what you are really doing").

48. For a discussion of the United States Supreme Court's struggle with questions that arise when police are said to have searched or seized a suspect "pretextually," see Daniel Yeager, "The Stubbornness of Pretexts," *San Diego Law Review* 40 (spring 2003): 611–44.

49. Jean-Paul Sartre, *The Words*, trans. Bernard Frechtman (New York: Random House, Inc., 1964), 65–66 (emphasis mine).

50. Ibid., 43. Earlier in the text, when Grandfather Schweitzer complains that he does not comprehend a text, his wife explains that his failure is due to the fact that he reads from the middle, not the beginning, of a text.

51. Sartre, *The Words*, 111 (emphasis mine).
52. See "Beyond Causation," 72–73.
53. See *Massachusetts v. Painten*, 389 US 560, 565 (1968) (White, J., dissenting) ("[S]ending state and federal courts on an expedition into the minds of police officers would produce a grave and fruitless misallocation of judicial resources").
54. R. S. Peters, *The Concept of Motivation*, ed. R. F. Holland. (Amherst, N.Y.: Prometheus Books, 1958), 31.
55. Ibid., 28; N. S. Sutherland, "Motives as Explanations," *Mind* 68 (1959): 153.
56. Peters, *Motivation*, 29.
57. Ibid., 32.
58. "Beyond Causation," 73.
59. Ibid.
60. Ibid.
61. See Roy Lawrence, *Motive and Intention* (Evanston, Ill.: Northwestern University Press, 1972), 23.
62. "Beyond Causation," 75.
63. See Kenneth W. Simons, "Rethinking Mental States," *Boston University Law Review* 72 (1992): 465 n. 1 ("The prevailing hierarchy ranks 'purpose' as the most serious mental state. . . .").
64. See note 35 above.
65. Model Penal Code § 2.02(5) (1962).
66. Ibid.
67. See note 35 above.
68. See Sanford H. Kadish, "Codifiers of the Criminal Law: Wechler's Predecessors," *Columbia Law Review* 78 (1978): 1098–1144.
69. Sanford H. Kadish, "Fifty Years of Criminal Law: An Opinionated Review," *California Law Review* 87 (1999): 952–53.
70. See note 35 above; See Robinson and Grall, "Element Analysis," 692–93 nn. 48–49.
71. See note 35 above.
72. See also "INK," 276–77 (similar problem more thoroughly explicated).
73. Model Penal Code § 2.10.6 (1962).
74. Model Penal Code §§ 2.10.2(1)(b), 2.10.6 (1962).
75. Blackstone, *Of Public Wrongs*, 199.
76. Joshua Dressler, *Understanding Criminal Law,* 2d ed. (New York: Matthew Bender/Irwin, 1995), 472.
77. Cf. "INK," 276–77 ("Yet it was not done deliberately: within twenty minutes I may be regretting it"); "MUSIC," 211–12 ("The adolescent, I suppose it is assumed, has strong feelings, and perhaps some of them can be described as feelings of sincerity, which, perhaps, he attaches to the words in his poetry. Does all that make the words, his utterance in the poem, sincere? Will he, for example, *stand by them*, later, when *those* feelings are gone?").
78. Tamar Lewin, "A Cause Worth Killing For?" *New York Times*, July 30, 1994, A1. Hill did not take the stand or put on any evidence at all (or even hire a lawyer). He was convicted of capital murder and sentenced to death after a twenty-minute jury deliberation. Mireya Navarro, "Abortion Clinic Case Reviews a Legal Dilemma," *New York Times*, November 14, 1994, A12.
79. Dressler, *Understanding Criminal Law*, 472 n. 54, 473 n. 60.
80. Kadish and Schulhofer, *Cases and Materials*, 218–19.

81. William Roth, "General vs. Specific Intent: A Time for Terminological Understanding in California," *Pepperdine Law Review* 7 (1979): 67–84.

82. See California Jury Instructions (Criminal) § 3.30 (1988); see also *People v. Matthews*, 70 Cal App 4th 164, 174–75 (1999) ("[I]f the defendant intends to place his penis in the victim's vagina, he has committed the general intent crime of rape, and does not have to have the 'specific intent' to rape"); *People v. Johnson*, 67 Cal App 4th 67, 72 (1998) ("As a general rule, a statute proscribing willful behavior is a general intent crime. A statute which includes 'willfully' language may nevertheless define a specific intent offense. . . ."); *People v. Snyder*, 15 Cal 2d 706, 708 (1940) ("[G]eneral intent is presumed from the doing of an act").

83. See note 35 above.

84. E.g., *Regina v. Cunningham*, 2 QB 396 (1957); *Regina v. Faulkner*, 13 Cox Crim Cas 555, 557 (1877).

85. For Cavell's brief take on the miner's lamp as illustrative of the role of intending (which he recalls from a class he took from Austin as perhaps involving lights on an automobile if not a miner's helmet), see *QUEST*, 117.

86. Ibid.

87. Kadish and Schulhofer, *Cases and Materials*, 216 (citing Robert Goff, "The Mental Element in Murder," *Law Quarterly Review* 104 (1988): 43–44) (quoting *Gollins v. Gollins*, App Cas 644, 664 (UK 1964).

88. Bernard Williams, postscript to *Moral Luck*, ed. Daniel Statman. (Albany: State University of New York Press, 1993), 253; Idem, "Recognising Responsibility," in *Shame and Necessity* (Berkeley: University of California Press, 1993), 67.

89. Bernard Williams, "Moral Luck," in *Moral Luck,* ed. Daniel Statman (Albany: State University of New York Press, 1993), 44–45. Cf. "MWM," 12 ("We are . . . exactly as responsible for the specific implications of our utterances as we are for their explicit factual claims").

90. See, e.g., Barbara Wootten, *Crime and the Criminal Law*: *Reflections of a Magistrate and Social Scientist* (London: Stevens, 1963), 51–53.

91. See Uniform Commercial Code § 2-613 cmt. 1 (1990) (in law, criminal or civil, " '[f]ault' is intended to include negligence and not merely wilful wrong").

92. See Model Penal Code § 2.05; California Jury Instructions (Criminal) § 4.45 (1988).

93. Mark Kelman, "Strict Liability: An Unorthodox View," in *Encyclopedia of Crime and Justice*, ed. Sanford H. Kadish (New York: Free Press, 1983), 4: 1516–57.

94. Ibid., 1516.

95. Ibid., 1517 ("It is difficult to imagine that a strict-liability interpretation ensnares many defendants who have taken extensive steps to avoid mistakes. . . .").

96. See text p. 33.

97. Kelman, "Strict Liability," 1516 ("It is significant to note that only by constructing the underlying material in the strict-liability situations with a very narrow time frame that the distinction between liability predicated on negligence, and strict liability, maintains its practical import in many critical situations").

98. See, e.g., Donald Dripps, "The Exclusivity of the Criminal Law: Toward a 'Regulatory Model' of, or 'Pathological Perspective' on, the Civil-Criminal Distinction," *Journal of Contemporary Legal Issues* 7 (1996): 204 (civil-criminal line expresses that the procedural barriers unique to criminal cases respond to the centrality that criminal accusations maintain in oppressive regimes). Cf. Williams, "Recognising Responsibility," 65–67 ("[A] citizen shall not have the punitive power of the state

fall on him unless he puts himself in jeopardy by what he intentionally does. . . . It is unclear how far that ideal is realised. It is even less clear, when the state makes its responses to those intentional acts, what those responses are supposed to mean. . .").

99. See, e.g., Model Penal Code § 2.02 (1962). (Accident "should not be wholly rejected as a ground of culpability that may suffice for purposes of penal law," but it should nonetheless be seen as "an exceptional basis of liability").

100. See, e.g., Model Penal Code § 2.05 (1962).

101. See Rosanna Cavallaro, "A Big Mistake: Eroding the Defense of Mistake of Fact about Consent in Rape," *Journal of Criminal Law and Criminology* 86 (1996): 840–41 (Mistake functions as a defense in, *inter alia*, cases of rape, larceny, receipt of stolen goods, robbery, burglary, kidnapping, forgery, embezzlement, nonsupport, resisting arrest, and assault).

102. See *Morissette v. United States*, 342 US 246, 250 (1952).

103. See *Staples v. United States*, 511 US 600, 605 (1994).

104. It makes good sense that someone accused of a pre-legal wrong (say, theft) cannot claim to have thought the action was lawful. And it makes just as good sense that we *should* hear the claim that someone accused of something so trivial as, say, shipping paperclips in interstate commerce without a license, had no idea it was unlawful. If a good person would not know of the prohibition, then a mistaken belief in the lawfulness of the act should excuse lest we make action more unbearable than necessary. Dan M. Kahan, "Ignorance of Law *Is* an Excuse—but Only for the Virtuous," *Michigan Law Review* 96 (1997): 127. Still, the law has long been reluctant to see the matter this way, with rare exception. Compare Blackstone, *Of Public Wrongs*, 27 ("For a mistake in point of law, which every person of discretion not only may, but is bound and presumed to know, is in criminal cases no sort of defense"), with *Lambert v. California*, 355 US 225 (1957).

105. *Director of Public Prosecutions v. Morgan*, 1976 App Cas 182, 186 (1976).

106. Ibid., 186, 195.

107. *Regina v. Morgan*, 1 All ER 10 (1975).

108. *Morgan*, 1976 App Cas at 192 (answering 3–2 in the negative "[w]hether in rape a defendant can properly be convicted notwithstanding that he in fact believed the woman consented, if such belief was not based on reasonable grounds"). Parliament changed the law immediately after the decision. See Sexual Offences Act, § 1 (1976). However, it is debatable whether the change was at all significant. Glanville Williams, *Textbook of Criminal Law* (London: Stevens, 1978), 101.

109. See, e.g., Victoria J. Dettmar, "Note, Culpable Mistakes in Rape: Eliminating the Defense of Unreasonable Mistake of Fact as to Victim Consent," *Dickinson Law Review 89* (1985): 473–99.

110. See, e.g., California Jury Instructions (Criminal) § 4.35 (1988).

111. See Wayne R. LaFave and Austin Scott, *Handbook on Criminal Law* (St. Paul: West Publishing Co., 1972), 638 ("One may take the property of another honestly but mistakenly believing . . . that the owner has given him permission to take it as he did. In . . . such event, he lacks the intent to steal required for larceny, even though his mistaken but honest belief was unreasonable").

112. See Model Penal Code § 5.01(1); California Jury Instructions (Criminal) § 6.00 (1988).

113. See California Jury Instructions (Criminal) §§ 8.20–27 (1988) (various modes of first-degree murder).

114. See, e.g., *United States v. Barker and Martinez*, 546 F2d 940, 948 n. 23 (DC Cir 1976).

115. See Paul Robinson, *Criminal Law Defenses* (St. Paul: West Publishing Co., 1984), 374–75; Edwin R. Keedy, "Ignorance and Mistake in the Criminal Law," *Harvard Law Review* 22 (1908–9): 84.

116. Indeed, all five Lords in *Morgan* so concluded by applying section 2(1) of the Criminal Appeal Act of 1968—England's version of the harmless-error rule—in favor of the Crown. *Morgan*, 1 All E.R. at 10.

117. See Model Penal Code § 2.04 (1962) ("There is no justification . . . for requiring that ignorance or mistake be reasonable if the crime or the element of the crime involved requires acting purposely or knowingly for its commission").

118. Kadish and Schulhofer, *Cases and Materials*, 323 (citation omitted).

119. Glanville Williams, *Textbook of Criminal Law*, 2d ed. (London: Stevens and Sons, 1983), 101.

120. Goetz, 68 NY 2d at 101.

121. Ibid., 101–2.

122. New York Penal Law §§ 15.20(1)(a), 35.10, 35.20, 35.25, 125.15, 125.20, 125.25 (1997). But see Richard Singer, "The Resurgence of Mens Rea: II—Honest but Unreasonable Mistake of Fact in Self Defense," *Boston College Law Review* 28 (1987): 493–97 (makes a strong case that *Goetz* establishes that New York law really does recognize "unreasonable mistakes" as a complete excuse).

123. Kadish and Schulhofer, *Cases and Materials*, 812.

124. New York Penal Law §§ 15.20(1)(a); 35.10 (1997).

125. See note 123 above.

126. New York Penal Law § 125.25 (1997).

127. See, e.g., George M. Fredrickson, "Science, Polygenesis, and the Proslavery Argument," in *The Black Image in the White Mind* (New York: Harper and Row, 1972), 71–96.

> The spokesmen for *Herrenvolk* egalitarianism . . . were attracted by the new doctrine precisely because it provided support for the view that Negroes were creatures set apart who did not have to be conceded any social status at all. . . . The difference between a variety and a species meant also . . . the difference between a black man who was inferior to the whites but akin to them, and therefore deserving of affection and a protective social status, and a black man who was more animal than human and could, for most purposes, be treated as such (84).

128. *Morgan*, 1976 App Cas at 186.

129. Ibid., 205.

130. Ibid., 223 (Edmund-Davies, L., dissenting).

131. Ibid., 195.

132. Ibid., 186.

133. Ibid., 207.

134. Ibid.

135. This is how sexual exchanges are characterized in Robin L. West, "Legitimizing the Illegitimate: A Comment on Beyond Rape," *Columbia Law Review* 93 (1993): 1450.

136. Model Penal Code § 3.09 (1962).

137. Ibid.

138. See note 29 and accompanying text above.

139. Douglas Husak, "The Nature and Justifiability of Nonconsummate Offenses," *Arizona Law Review* 37 (1995): 151–83; Douglas N. Husak, "Reasonable Risk Creation and Overinclusive Legislation," *Buffalo Criminal Law Review* 1 (1998): 602.

140. See Steven Shavell, "Deterrence and the Punishment of Attempts," *Journal of Legal Studies* 19 (1990): 451.

141. E.g., *People v. Moran*, 123 NY 254 (Ct App 1890).

142. E.g., *People v. Dlugash*, 41 NY 2d 725 (Ct App 1977); *People v. Thompson*, 15 Cal Rptr 3d 333 (Ct App 1993).

143. E.g., *State v. Mitchell*, 170 Mo 633 (1902).

144. E.g., *State v. Guffey*, 262 SW 2d 152 (Mo Ct App 1953).

145. See Model Penal Code § 5.01 (1962) (calling "the relative appropriateness of means to end" an "important aspect[] of the impossibility problem").

146. Ibid., § 5.01(c).

147. *Guffey*, 262 SW 2d at 153. The statute in question criminalized the unauthorized pursuit, taking, killing, possession, or disposing of all wildlife, not just deer. In fact, the defendants were in search of a wolf they'd seen run across a road they were taking en route to a frog hunting expedition. Ibid., 154. Thus they attempted to take a wolf out of season by shooting at a decoy deer that they took to be a wolf. Ibid.

148. Pitcher, "Austin: A Personal Memoir," 20.

149. *Dlugash*, 41 NY 2d at 729.

150. David Bevington, ed., *Othello* (New York: Bantam Books, 1988), 5.2.18–19.

151. See Model Penal Code § 5.01 (1962) ("The innocuous character of the particular conduct becomes relevant only if the futile endeavor itself indicates a harmless personality, so that immunizing the conduct from liability would not result in exposing society to a dangerous person"). The Code cites "black magic" as an instance in which the means selected are too dilute to bespeak dangerousness. Ibid., 316 n. 88.

152. The Code acknowledges as much when it states that "it is by no means clear that those who make unreasonable mistakes will not be potentially dangerous." Model Penal Code, 316 n. 88 (1962).

153. Plato, *Republic*, trans. Allan Bloom (New York: Basic Books, 1991), 18.

154. 498 US 192 (1991).

155. Ibid., 202.

156. Ibid., 203–4.

157. Ibid., 195–96.

158. U.S. Const., Amend. XVI ("The Congress shall have power to lay and collect taxes on incomes, from whatever source derived. . . .").

159. *Cheek*, 498 US at 194–96.

160. See Larry Alexander, "Inculpatory and Exculpatory Mistakes and the Fact/Law Distinction: An Essay in Memory of Myke Balyes," *Law and Philosophy* 12 (1993): 42 ("[T]here are actual cases interpreting criminal statutes to make awareness of their existence a necessary condition for violation."); Kadish & Schulhofer, *Cases and Materials*, 258, 268–70. Cf. William J. Stuntz, "Substance, Process, and the Civil-Criminal Line," *Journal of Contemporary Legal Issues* 7 (1996): 31–34 (whether mistake of law is a defense is not merely a statutory question).

161. A nearly incomprehensible line of Supreme Court cases so indicates. See, e.g., Yale Kamisar, Wayne R. LaFave and Jerold H. Israel, *Modern Criminal Procedure: Cases, Commentaries and Questions*, 8th ed. (St. Paul: West Publishing Co., 1994), 1687–98 (omitted from the 9th ed.); Robinson, *Criminal Law Defenses*, 265; Alexander, "Fact/Law Distinction," 33–70.

162. See, e.g., *Pullman-Standard v. Swint*, 456 US 273, 288 (1982) (calling the law-fact distinction "vexing").

163. Kahan, "Ignorance of Law," 128 (quoting Oliver Wendell Holmes, *The Common Law* (Cambridge, Mass: Belknap Press, 1963), 41).

164. Ibid., 133–35.
165. 513 NE 2d 1068 (NY 1987).
166. *Marrero*, 513 NE 2d at 1076 n.7.
167. Kahan, "Ignorance of Law," 133.
168. Ibid.
169. Ibid., 136–37.
170. Ibid., 137–41.
171. Ibid., 138.
172. Ibid., 139.
173. Ibid., 139–40.
174. Ibid., 140.
175. Ibid.
176. Ibid., 137–38, 140.
177. Ibid., 141.
178. Ibid.
179. Ibid., 144.
180. Ibid., 140.
181. Ibid., 151.
182. *Benseley v. Bignold*, 106 Eng Rep 1214, 1216 (1822).
183. E.g., *Staples v. United States*, 511 US 600 (1994) (and cases cited therein).
184. Kahan, "Ignorance of Law," 147, 148 n. 83, 149.
185. Ibid., 142, 150–54.
186. See, e.g., Yeager, "Kahan on Mistakes," *Michigan Law Review* 96 (1998): 2113.

In "Ignorance of Law *Is* an Excuse—but Only for the Virtuous," Professor Dan Kahan reconciles what I had thought was an irreconcilable body of law. To be sure, imposing order on whether and when mistakes of law should pass as responsibility-evading accounts of untoward actions is far from light work. Yet Kahan somehow pulls it off in just twenty-seven pages.

187. Kahan, "Ignorance of Law," 147 ("Individuals don't have a moral duty, independent of law," he states, "to turn over a portion of their income to the government").
188. See *People v. Navarro*, 160 Cal Rptr 692 (1979); *United States v. McLeod*, 18 CMR 814 (1955); Mark C. Winings, "Ignorance Is Bliss, Especially for the Tax Evader," *Journal of Criminal Law and Criminology* 84 (1993): 596 (*Cheek*'s acceptance of "honest but mistaken beliefs" in tax prosecutions saddles the government with a heavy burden); Walter C. Morrison IV, "Tax Evasion, Willfullness and the Subjective Standard: The Law Invites a Charlatan," *Mississippi College Law Review* 13 (1992): 218–19.
189. California Jury Instructions (Criminal) § 4.35 (1998).
190. Judith Andre, "Nagel, Williams, and Moral Luck," *Analysis* 43 (1983): 205.
191. Model Penal Code § 210.4 (1962).
192. See note 190 above; "EXCUSES," 181 n. 1.
193. Dripps, 200–01.
194. Wootten, *Crime and the Criminal Law*, 51–53.
195. See Alexander, "Reconsidering the Relationship," 101 n. 60.
196. See Jean Hampton, "Retribution and the Liberal State," *Journal of Contemporary Legal Issues* 5 (1994): 119–20 (quoting Joel Feinberg, *The Moral Limits of the Criminal Law*, vol. 1 (New York: Oxford University Press, 1988), 24).

197. See Williams, "Recognising Responsibility," 63 (cause, not intentionality, is the precondition to responsibility).

198. See, e.g., Thomas W. Hutchinson et al., eds., *Federal Sentencing Law and Practice* (St. Paul: West Publishing Co., 1998), 1095, § 5K2.16 (federal defendants may be eligible at sentencing for a very small reduction if they turn themselves in for the right reasons).

199. Susan Bandes and Jack Beerman, "Lawyering Up," *Green Bag* 2 (1998): 12, n. 25 (citations omitted).

200. Hannah Arendt, *Eichmann in Jerusalem: A Report on the Banality of Evil* (New York: Viking Press, 1963), 244, 254–56.

201. Alan M. Dershowitz, *Reversal of Fortune: Inside the von Bülow Case* (New York: Random House, 1986), 204. Cf. Idem, *The Best Defense* (New York: Vintage Books, 1982), 95 ("One criminal lawyer I know, who charges $50,000 for a criminal trial, says that $45,000 is for advising the client at the close of the prosecution's case whether to take the witness stand").

202. Susan Bandes, "When Victims Seek Closure: Forgiveness, Vengeance, and the Role of Government," *Fordham Urban Law Journal* 27 (June 2000): 1599; Idem, "Reply to Paul Cassell: What We Know about Victim Impact Statements," *Utah Law Review* (1999): 545; Idem, "Victim Standing," *Utah Law Review* (1999): 331.

203. See Williams, "Moral Luck," 44–45; Idem, "Recognising Responsibility," 65–68.

204. Sanford H. Kadish, "Complicity, Cause and Blame: A Study in the Interpretation of Doctrine," *California Law Review* 73 (1985): 381 (citing *Thornton v. Mitchell*, 1 *All ER* 339 (1940)).

205. J. G. Murphy, "Involuntary Acts and Criminal Liability," *Ethics* 51 (1971): 332–42.

206. See Norval Morris, "Somnambulistic Homicide: Ghosts, Spiders, and North Koreans," *Res Judicatae* 5 (1951): 29–30.

207. See Steve Weston, "OK, Now What? Suns Ponder Options with Manning Out," *The Phoenix Gazette*, February 7, 1995, C1; Mike Szostak, "Celtics Journal: New No. 5 Starts on Injured List," *The Providence Journal-Bulletin*, February 9, 1995, 10F.

208. But cf. Robinson, *Criminal Law Defenses*, 70–104, §§ 21–26 (classifying some defenses as neither justifications nor excuses, but rather, as "failure of proof defenses" and "offense modifications").

209. Kent Greenawalt, "The Perplexing Borders of Justification and Excuse," *Columbia Law Review* 84 (1984): 1900. See also Albin Eser, "Justification and Excuse," *American Journal of Comparative Law* 24 (1976): 622–23.

210. Katz, *Bad Acts and Guilty Minds*, 65–66.

211. George P. Fletcher, "Proportionality and the Psychotic Aggressor: A Vignette in Comparative Criminal Law Theory," *Israel Law Review* 8 (1973): 373.

212. Larry Alexander, "Self-Defense, Justification, and Excuse," *Philosophy and Public Affairs* 22 (1993): 53.

213. Lk 10:25–37 NRSV.

214. Terry Teachout, "An American Icon," *The New York Times Book Review*, November 5, 1995, 17.

215. Daniel Yeager, "Does Privacy Really Have a Problem in the Law of Criminal Procedure?" *Rutgers Law Review* 49 (1997): 1289 ("Since the only *desirable* action would be to catch the suspect or talk him into turning himself in, police should try to do so, or at least consider those options, before resorting to shooting the suspect.").

216. See ibid.

217. Robinson, *Criminal Law Defenses*, 83, § 24.

218. Thomas Morawetz, "Reconstructing the Criminal Defenses: The Significance of Justification," *Journal of Criminal Law and Criminology* 77 (1986): 297. For a view endorsing the relevance of utilitarian calculus to distinguishing justified from excused acts, see Michael S. Moore, "Causation and the Excuses," *California Law Review* 73 (1985): 1096–99, and Michael Corrado, "The Place of Legal Formalism in Legal Theory," *North Carolina Law Review* 70 (1992): 1556–61.

219. Kent Greenawalt, "The Perplexing Borders of Justification and Excuse," *Columbia Law Review* 84 (1984): 1908.

220. Fletcher, *Rethinking Criminal Law*, 767, § 10.1.

221. E.g., *A&C*, 182–83; Robinson, *Criminal Law Defenses*, §§ 27(e), 121 (c), 184(c).

222. Paul Robinson, "A Theory of Justification: Societal Harm As a Prerequisite for Criminal Liability," *U. C. L. A. Law Review* 23 (1975): 275–76; see also Dressler, *Understanding Criminal Law*, 195–97 (presenting positions on why justification-excuse distinction matters).

223. See Kent Greenawalt, "Law and Objectivity: How People Are Treated," *Criminal Justice Ethics* 8 (Summer/Fall 1989): 38.

224. Robinson, *Criminal Law Defenses*, 15, § 122(b).

225. Ibid., 14, § 122(b).

226. *A&C*, 180–83.

227. Alexander, "Crime and Culpability," 13; Idem, "A Unified Excuse of Preemptive Self-Protection," *Notre Dame Law Review* 74 (1999): 1485–86; Idem, "Unknowingly Justified Actors and the Attempt/Success Distinction," *University of Tulsa Law Review* 39 (2004): 856–57.

228. See, e.g., Model Penal Code § 3.05 (1962) (justification requires that actor believes act is necessary); Wayne R. LaFave, "Self Defense," in *Handbook on Criminal Law*, 4th ed. (St. Paul: Thomson/West, 2003), 543–44, § 10.4(c) (majority of states follow the Code approach, except they require as well that belief in necessity of intervention be reasonable).

229. See Williams, "Moral Luck," 37–38. Gauguin left his family for Panama and Martinique in 1887 and returned seven months later, only to head off in 1891 for Tahiti, which he left for France in 1893, and then returned to in 1895, staying until 1901, when he left (for good) for Hivoa. The moral and financial abandonment began much earlier, about 1882. See generally David Sweetman, *Paul Gauguin: A Complete Life* (London: Hodder and Stoughton, 1995); Günter Metken, *Gauguin à Tahiti: Le Premier Voyage* (Paris-Munich: Schirmer/Mosel, 1990).

230. Cf. Clement Greenberg, *Arrogant Purpose*, vol. 2 of *The Collected Essays and Criticism*, ed. John O'Brian (Chicago: University of Chicago Press, 1986–93), 76–78 (calling Gauguin "a founding father of modern art," who was nonetheless not "a great artist").

Chapter 2. Inchoate Criminality as Partial Excuse

1. See note 89, chapter 1.

2. Williams, "Moral Luck," 44–45.

3. Joel Feinberg, *Harmless Wrongdoing*, vol. 4 of *The Moral Limits of the Criminal Law* (New York: Oxford University Press, 1988).

4. Douglas Husak, "The Nature and Justifiability of Nonconsummate Offenses," *Arizona Law Review* 37 (1995): 151–83; Idem, "Reasonable Risk Creation and Overinclusive Legislation," *Buffalo Criminal Law Review* 1 (1998): 602.

5. Professor Fletcher's list of risk-based offenses excludes complicity, but includes other offenses as purely risk-based that I leave out. See George Fletcher, "Constructing a Theory of Impossible Attempts," *Criminal Justice Ethics* 5 (winter/spring 1986): 66 (Unlawful possession, even in theft cases, may be viewed as inchoate); Fletcher, *Rethinking Criminal Law*, 124–35 (assault and burglary may be viewed as inchoate). Indeed there are a few other risk-based offenses, such as reckless endangerment, see Model Penal Code § 211.2 (1962), or driving under the influence, see Texas Penal Code § 49.04 (1998).

6. Fletcher, *Rethinking Criminal Law*, § 5.3.3.

7. Judith Jarvis Thomson, "Morality and Bad Luck," *Metaphilosophy* 20 (1989): 213.

8. Ibid., 212.

9. See generally Alexander, "Crime and Culpability"; Joel Feinberg, "Equal Punishments for Failed Attempts: Some Bad but Instructive Arguments Against It," *Arizona Law Review* 37 (1995): 117–33; Steven Sverdlik, "Crime and Moral Luck," *American Philosophical Quarterly* 25 (1988): 79–85.

10. Feinberg, "Equal Punishments," 119.

11. Sverdlik, "Crime and Moral Luck," 79.

12. Because Kant takes a position that morality turns solely on the reasons behind actions, he is considered to be behind the equivalency position. See Thomas Nagel, "Moral Luck," in *Mortal Questions* (New York: Cambridge University Press, 1979), 24 (quoting Immanuel Kant, *Foundations of the Metaphysics of Morals*, ed. Robert P. Wolff (New York: Macmillan, 1969), 12–13; see also Immanuel Kant, *The Metaphysics of Morals*, ed. and trans. Mary Gregor (New York: Cambridge University Press, 1996), 107 (Members "united in a 'plot'"—presumably to murder—as well as accomplices to murder should be put to death). But Kant also "believes that law is supposed to regulate conduct, not intentions, and he famously argued that 'the problem of setting up a state can be solved even by a nation of devils (so long as they possess understanding).'" David Luban, "The Bad Man and the Good Lawyer: A Centennial Essay on Holmes's 'The Path of the Law,'" *New York University Law Review* 72 (1997): 1570; Immanuel Kant, "Perpetual Peace: A Philosophical Sketch," in *Kant's Political Writings*, ed. Hans S. Reiss and trans. H. B. Nisbet (Cambridge: Cambridge University Press, 1970), 93, 112.

13. R. A. Duff, *Criminal Attempts* (Oxford: Clarendon Press, 1996), 335.

14. Feinberg, "Equal Punishments," 119–22.

15. California Penal Code §§ 663–65 (1997).

16. *People v. Orndorff*, 261 Cal App 2d 212 (1968); *People v. Miller*, 2 Cal 2d 527; 42 P2d 308 (1935); California Jury Instructions (Criminal) § 6.00 (1998). But see *People v. Staples*, 6 Cal App 3d 61 (1970).

17. Model Penal Code § 5.01(1)–(3) (1962).

18. California Penal Code § 664(a)–(c) (1997).

19. Model Penal Code § 5.05(1) (1962).

20. *People v. Travis*, 171 Cal App 2d 842, 844 (1959).

21. Model Penal Code §§ 1.07(1)(b), 5.05(3).

22. See ibid., "Introduction to Article 5," 294 (footnote omitted).

23. Model Penal Code §5.05(1) (1962).

24. See Model Penal Code § 223.1(2) (1962) (theft of property worth more than $500 is a third-degree felony); ibid., § 5.05(1) ("Except as otherwise provided in this Section, attempt, solicitation, and conspiracy are crimes of the same grade and degree as the most serious offense that is attempted or solicited or is an object of the conspiracy.").

25. See Model Penal Code § 213.1 (1962) (stranger-rape or rape involving serious bodily injury is a first-degree felony); ibid., § 5.05(1) ("An attempt, solicitation or conspiracy to commit a capital crime or a felony of the first degree is a felony of the second degree.").

26. See Model Penal Code § 5.05 cmt. 2 (1962).

27. See Joshua Dressler, "Reassessing the Theoretical Underpinnings of Accomplice Liability: New Solutions to an Old Problem," *Hastings Law Journal* 37 (1985): 111–12.

28. Katz, *Bad Acts and Guilty Minds*, 261 ("Psychological evidence" backs up that "two heads are better than one" is more likely true than the competing folk-saying about too many cooks spoiling the broth).

29. Ibid., 252.

30. Seven states take, at least up to a point, an equivalency position on solicitation. See Illinois Compiled Statutes Annotated ch. 720, 5/8-1 (1993); Montana Code Annotated § 45-4-101 (1997); New Hampshire Revised Statutes Annotated § 629:2 (1996); Pennsylvania Consolidated Statutes Annotated § 905 (1998); Rhode Island General Laws § 11-1-9 (1994); Wisconsin Statutes Annotated § 939.30(2) (1996); Wyoming Statutes Annotated § 6–1-304 (1997).

31. Twenty-three states take, at least up to a point, an equivalency position on conspiracy. See California Penal Code § 182 (1998); Connecticut General Statutes § 53a-51 (1997); D.C. Code Annotated § 22-105(a) (1996); Idaho Code § 18-1701 (1997); Illinois Compiled Statutes Annotated ch. 720, sec. 5/8-2 (1993); Indiana Code Annotated § 35-41-5-2 (1994); Iowa Compiled Statutes Annotated § 706.3 (1996); Maryland Annotated Code art. 27, § 38 (1996); Michigan Compiled Laws Annotated § 750.157 (1991); Mississippi Code Annotated § 91-1-1 (1994); Montana Code Annotated § 45-4-102 (1997); Nebraska Revised Statutes § 28-202 (1995); New Hampshire Revised Statutes Annotated § 629:3 (1996); New Jersey Statutes Annotated § 2C:5-4(a) (1995); North Dakota Century Code § 12.1-06-04 (1997); Ohio Revised Code Annotated § 2923.03 (1996); Oregon Revised Statutes § 161.450(c) (1990); Pennsylvania Consolidated Statutes Annotated § 905 (1998); Rhode Island General Laws § 11-1-6 (1994); South Dakota Codified Laws § 22-3-8(2) (1998); Virginia Code Annotated § 18.2-22 (1996); Vermont Statutes Annotated § 1409 (1997); Wisconsin Statutes Annotated § 939.31 (1991).

32. See, e.g., *United States v. Church*, 29 Military Justice Reporter 679 (1989) *aff'd*, 32 Military Justice Reporter 70 (Court of Military Review 1991).

33. Phillip Johnson, "The Unnecessary Crime of Conspiracy," *California Law Review* 61 (1973): 1137–88.

34. See ibid., 1164–67.

35. Model Penal Code § 5.01(2)(a) (1962).

36. Ibid., § 5.01(2)(c).

37. Ibid., § 5.01(2)(f).

38. Jimmy Carter, "*Playboy* Interview: Jimmy Carter—A Candid Conversation with the Democratic Candidate for the Presidency," interview by Robert Scheer, *Playboy* 23, no. 11 (1976): 86.

39. Peter Winch, "Trying," in *Ethics and Action*, ed. D. Z. Phillips (London: Routledge and Kegan Paul, 1972), 141.

40. Ibid., 144.

41. Louis Menand, "Jerry Don't Surf," *New York Review of Books* 45 (Sept. 24, 1998): 7–8.

42. Fourteen states take, up to a point, an equivalency approach to attempts. See Connecticut General Statutes Annotated § 53a-51 (1997); Delaware Code Annotated § 531 (1995); Hawaii Revised Statutes Annotated (Michie 1994), sec. 705-502; Indiana Code Annotated (Michie 1994), sec. 35-41-5-1(a); Maryland Annotated Code § 644A (1996); Mississippi Code Annotated § 91-1-7 (1994); Montana Code Annotated § 45-4-103 (1997); New Hampshire Revised Statutes Annotated § 629:1 (1996); New Jersey Statutes Annotated § 2C:5-4(a) (1995); New York Penal Code § 110.05 (1997); North Dakota Century Code § 12.1-06-01 (1997); Virginia Code Annotated § 18.2-28 (1996); Wisconsin Statutes Annotated § 939.32(c) (1996); Wyoming Statutes Annotated § 6-1-304 (1997).

43. E.g., Model Penal Code § 2.06(1)-(5) (1962); California Penal Code § 971 (1998).

44. E.g., Model Penal Code § 2.06(3); California Jury Instructions (Criminal) § 3.01 (1998). The intentions of the principal are part of what it means for him to "act" criminally or "commit" a crime. Likewise, the intentions of the helper are part of what it means for him to "act" criminally, "help," or "try to help" the principal offender. Cf. generally Jennifer Hornsby, "Action and Aberration," *University of Pennsylvania Law Review* 142 (1994): 1727 ("There is an action if and only if there is an event of a person's intentionally doing something").

45. Daniel Yeager, "Helping, Doing, and the Grammar of Complicity," *Criminal Justice Ethics* 15 (winter/spring 1996): 29.

46. "[F]irstly, the distinction between doing and trying to do is already there in the illocutionary verb [e.g., argue] as well as in the perlocutionary verb [e.g., convince]; we distinguish arguing from trying to argue as well as convincing from trying to convince. Further, many illocutionary acts are not cases of trying to do any perlocutionary act; for example, to promise is not to try to do anything" *HTDTW*, 126.

47. American criminal law has "abrogated" the distinction between helpers and doers. See, e.g., Model Penal Code § 2.06, cmt. 1 (1962) ("As in the states that have abolished the common law distinctions between principals and accessories, it would suffice under this draft to charge commission of the substantive crime. It seems unnecessary, however, in framing an entire system to declare that the offender is a 'principal'; such language has meaning only because of the special background of the common law and it has been abandoned in most recent legislative reforms").

48. See William Prosser et al., *Prosser and Keeton on the Law of Torts*, 5th ed., 265–69, § 41; LaFave, "Causation" in *Handbook on Criminal Law*, 4th ed. (St. Paul: Thomson/West, 2003), 331–59, § 6.4.

49. K. J. M. Smith, *A Modern Treatise on the Law of Criminal Complicity* (Oxford: Clarendon Press, 1991), 55–93; Francis Sayre, "Criminal Responsibility for the Acts of Another," *Harvard Law Review* 43 (1930): 702–8; Grace Mueller, "The Mens Rea of Accomplice Liability," *Southern California Law Review* 61 (1988): 2170–72.

50. Rollin M. Perkins, "Parties to Crime," *University of Pennsylvania Law Review* 89 (1941): 600.

51. Kadish, "Complicity," 359.

52. Fletcher, *Rethinking Criminal Law*, 680–81, § 8.82.

53. See note 51 above.

54. See Smith, *Treatise*, 19, 87–88; Dressler, "Accomplice Liability," 132, 139–40; Paul H. Robinson, "Imputed Criminal Liability," *Yale Law Journal* 93 (1984): 657–58.

55. See note 52 above.

56. See RGst 8, 267.

57. *State ex rel Attorney General v. Tally*, 102 Ala 25 (1894).

58. But see note 51 above.

59. See Kadish, "Complicity," 361 ("[I]f I provide the crowbar that the principal uses to gain illegal entry, my assistance was a but-for condition of the entry. To be sure, he might have entered anyway—with his crowbar or by other means. But he did not. My aid was necessary for what actually happened"); Glanville Williams, *Criminal Law: The General Part*, 2d ed. (London: Sweet and Maxwell, 1961), 359, § 121 ("[I]t is enough that the accused has facilitated the crime, even though it would probably have been committed without his assistance.").

60. Smith, *Treatise*, 84.

61. Kadish, "Complicity," 360.

62. Ibid., 336 (citing H. L. A. Hart and Antony Honoré, *Causation in the Law*, 69).

63. John Searle, *Intentionality* (New York: Cambridge University Press, 1983), 110.

64. See, e.g., Model Penal Code § 5.01(3) (1962).

65. *United States v. Peoni*, 100 F2d 401, 402 (2d Cir 1938).

66. See *Hicks v. United States*, 150 US 442 (1893).

67. E.g., *Commonwealth v. Atencio*, 189 NE 2d 627, 630 (Mass 1963); *Jacobs v. State*, 184 So 2d 711, 716 (Fla Dist Ct App 1966); *People v. Abbot and Moon*, 84 AD 2d 11 (NY App Div 1981).

68. See *Standefer v. United States*, 447 US 10, 15–20 (1980) (reviewing legislative history here and in England); LaFave, "Parties to Crime," in *Criminal Law*, 4th ed. (St. Paul: Thomson/West, 2003), 663–70 (discussing procedural problems that led to legislative changes and the changes themselves).

69. Fletcher, *Rethinking Criminal Law*, 654–73, §§ 8.6.2-7.4.

70. Katz, *Bad Acts and Guilty Minds*, 258.

71. Ibid. (quoting Fritz Hartung, "Der Badewannenunfall," *Juristenzeitung* (1954): 430–31).

72. Without suggesting that the helper be treated more leniently than the doer, the following acknowledge that complicity may have an inchoate basis: Model Penal Code § 2.06(3)(a)(ii) (1962); ibid., 297 (explanatory note), 314 (cmt.); ibid., § 5.01(3); Fletcher, *Rethinking Criminal Law*, 679–81, § 8.82; Smith, *Treatise*, 93; Williams, *Criminal Law*, 382, § 126; Richard Buxton, "Complicity in the Criminal Code," *Law Quarterly Review* 85 (1969): 268; Richard Buxton, "Complicity and the Law Commission," *Criminal Law Review* (1973): 223–30; Kadish, "Complicity," 356; J. R. Spencer, "Trying To Help Another Person Commit a Crime," in *Criminal Essays in Honour of JC Smith*, ed. Peter Smith (London: Butterworths, 1987), 148; Great Britain Law Commission, *Assisting and Encouraging Crime: A Consultation Paper* (London: H. M. S. O., 1993), 90–91, § 4.24-.26.

73. Peter Heath, "Trying and Attempting," *Proceedings of the Aristotelian Society*, Supplementary Volume 45 (1971).

74. Sir William David Ross, *Foundations of Ethics; The Gifford Lectures delivered in the University of Aberdeen, 1935–6* (Oxford: Clarendon Press, 1960), 108.

75. Judith Jarvis Thomson, "The Decline of Cause," *Georgetown Law Journal* 76 (1987): 140.
76. Nagel, "Moral Luck," 37.
77. Winch, "Trying," 140.

Chapter 3. Is Criminal Law (Especially) Moral?

1. See *Statistical Abstract of the U.S. Tab. No. 312,* 1996, 202 (nine murders per 100,000 population make larceny 350 times as likely to occur than murder); U.S. Department of Justice, Federal Bureau of Investigation, *Uniform Crime Reporting Press Release*, October 1996, 2 (property crimes occurred 551 times more frequently than murder in 1995).
2. E.g., Steven F. Shatz and Nina Rivkind, "The California Death Penalty Scheme: Requiem for *Furman?*" *New York University Law Review* 72 (1997): 1327, 1339 (less than one out of eight of the 346 persons convicted yearly of first-degree murder in California are sentenced to death).
3. See generally Bandes, "Victim Standing," 339, n. 35 ("The state's police power and the judicial power enforcing it are deployed for society, not for any individual").
4. Jeffrie G. Murphy, "Legal Moralism and Liberalism, "Unpublished Manuscript," quoted in Jean Hampton, "Retribution," 119–20.
5. Hampton, "Retribution," 120 ("[I]n this society stigmatization cannot be taken to track the moral seriousness of harm in our legal system, and thus cannot be interpreted as a device used simply to enhance the deterrent consequences of performing what are called 'criminal' behaviors").
6. Ibid., 119.
7. E.g., "Symposium: The Intersection of Tort and Criminal Law," *Boston University Law Review* 76 (1996): 1–370; "Symposium: The Civil-Criminal Distinction," *Journal of Contemporary Legal Issues* 7 (1996): 1–398; "Symposium: Punishment," *Yale Law Journal* 101 (1992): 1681–1908.
8. E.g., "Trials," vol. 44 of *American Jurisprudence*, § 27.
9. See Feinberg, *Harm to Others*, 24; George P. Fletcher, "What Is Punishment Imposed For?" *Journal of Contemporary Legal Issues* 5 (1994): 110. Criminal punishment is the only remedy by which the defendant can be subjected to incarceration, or constant "surveillance" of the body. Michel Foucault, *Discipline and Punish: The Birth of the Prison*, trans. Alan Sheridan, 2d ed. (New York: Vintage Books, 1995), 199–200.
10. Cf. Donald Dripps, "Exclusivity," 204 ("I think hardship—the idea that unjust criminal conviction is too much like having a safe fall on you—is only part of the answer").
11. See, e.g., Stewart Macaulay, "The Use and Non-Use of Contracts in the Manufacturing Industry," *The Practical Lawyer* (1963): 13–40; Stewart Macaulay, "Non-Contractual Relations in Business: A Preliminary Study," *American Sociological Review* 28 (1963): 55 (cited in "Contract Theory," 793–95).
12. See Kahan, "Ignorance," 144.
13. See ibid., 147, 148 n. 83 (discussing the plight of Justice Breyer, who failed to pay taxes on the wages of his weekly maid). In addition to the technical side of tax

law, other examples of *malum-prohibitum* offenses that Kahan mentions are banking law, broadcasting law, and election law. Ibid., 149.

14. Ronald Dworkin, *Taking Rights Seriously* (Cambridge, Mass.: Harvard University Press, 1977), 191.

15. Kahan, "Ignorance," 144.

16. Richard A. Posner, *Economic Analysis of the Law*, 4th ed. (Boston: Little, Brown, 1992), 261–62.

17. Richard A. Posner, *The Economics of Justice* (Cambridge, Mass.: Harvard University Press, 1981), 110–11, n. 47.

18. Posner, *Economic Analysis*, 218; Idem, "An Economic Theory of the Criminal Law," *Columbia Law Review* 85 (1985): 1199.

19. See Luban, "Bad Man," 1566–71.

20. "Certainly there must be a difference between taking moral positions and moralizing, just as there must be a difference between exercising judgment and expressing one's preferences." Yeager, "Kahan on Mistakes," 2122. I suspect that this distinction is one with which Professor Kadish would not concur. See Sanford H. Kadish, "Moral Excess in the Law," *McGeorge Law Review* 32 (2000): 71–72.

21. See Yeager, "Kahan on Mistakes," 2122.

22. This is a term of which Michael Moore is especially fond. E.g., *A&C*, 183, 338, 339, 342, 345, 361, 362.

23. Restatement (First) of Contracts § 475 (1932).

24. See, e.g., John P. Dawson, "Economic Duress—An Essay in Perspective," *Michigan Law Review* 45 (1947): 253–90.

25. See Uniform Commercial Code § 2-302 (1990). Indeed, even the "excuse" of impracticability hardly seems to be an excuse since it makes no reference whatsoever to the intentions of the breaching party. See ibid., § 2–615; *B's Co v. BP Barber and Assoc*, 391 F2d 130 (4th Cir 1968) ("[S]ubjective impossibility, that is, impossibility which is personal to the promisor and does not inhere in the nature of the act to be performed, does not excuse nonperformance").

26. See "Contract Theory," 788–91 (discussing *Foley v. Interactive Data Corp*, 765 P2d 373 (Cal 1988)); ibid., 777–84 (discussing *Pugh v. See's Candies, Inc*, 171 Cal Rptr 917 (Cal Ct App 1981)).

27. See *Contract Theory*, 789.

28. See, e.g., Bandes, "When Victims Seek Closure," 1599–1606.

29. Emile Zola, *Au Bonheur des Dames* (Paris: Bookking Int'l., 1994), 8.

30. G. E. M. Anscombe, *Intention*, 2d ed. (Ithaca: Cornell University Press, 1976), 44–45.

31. For an involving treatment of Michael Fried's notion of theatricality, see *M&S*.

32. See Alan C. Michaels, "Acceptance: The Missing Mental State," *Southern California Law Review* 71 (1998): 953–1035; Kenneth W. Simons, "Rethinking Mental States," *Boston University Law Review* 72 (1992): 463–554.

33. E.g., LaFave, *Criminal Law*, 2d ed., 242–67, §§ 3.8-.11.

34. E.g., Model Penal Code § 2.01 (1962).

35. Cf. "MEANING IT," 233–34 (Cavell asks us to suppose that a man who is said to have frightened a child "had known about the child but had forgotten. Reminded, he is stunned, and quickly acknowledges his forgetfulness. Without that, or some similar, acknowledgment, the excuse/apology would not be acceptable—would not *be* an excuse or apology").

36. "Beyond Causation," 84.

37. Ibid., 85 (footnotes omitted) (emphasis mine).

38. Cf. *PI*, para. 628 ("[V]oluntary movement is marked by the absence of surprise").

39. Aristotle, *Nichomachean Ethics*, trans. Martin Oswald (Indianapolis, Ind.: Bobbs-Merrill, 1962), § III.1, 1110a3 ff. (cited in Martha Nussbaum, "The Use and Abuse of Philosophy in Legal Education," *Stanford Law Review* 45 (1993): 1632–33, n. 25.

40. John R. Searle, *Speech Acts: An Essay in the Philosophy of Language* (Cambridge: Cambridge University Press, 1969), 141 ("[T]he reason it would be odd to say such things is that they are too *obvious* to be worth saying.").

41. See *S&S*, 11–15, 70–71; "MINDS," 86–89. Compare "INK," 284 ("What would be wholly untrue is to suggest that 'unintentionally' is the word that 'wears the trousers'—that is, that until we have grasped certain specific ways of doing things unintentionally, and except as a way of ruling these out, 'intentionally' has no positive meaning. There are words of this description: 'real', for example, is one. But in the present case, to mention nothing more, there is the verb 'intend' to take into account, and it must obviously have a highly 'positive' sense; it cannot just be used to rule out 'don't (or didn't) intend.'"), with "EXCUSES," 180 ("While it has been the tradition to present [Freedom] as the 'positive' term requiring elucidation, there is little doubt that to say we acted 'freely' (in the philosopher's use, which is only faintly related to the everyday use) is to say only that we acted *not* un-freely, in one or another of the many heterogeneous ways of so acting (under duress, or what not). Like 'real', 'free' is only used to rule out the suggestion of some or all of its recognized antitheses").

42. See H. L. A. Hart, "Ascription of Responsibility and Rights," *Proceedings of the Aristotelian Society* 49 (1949): 179–80.

43. See "EXCUSES," 190 n. 2 ("For we are sometimes not so good at observing what we *can't* say as what we can, yet the first is pretty regularly the more revealing").

44. See "PRETENDING," 271 (justifying "the long-term project of classifying and clarifying all possible ways and varieties of not-exactly doing things, which has to be carried through if we are ever to understand properly what doing things is").

45. See *HTDTW*, v–vi ("The views which underlie these lectures were formed in 1939").

46. E.g., Model Penal Code § 2.01 (1962); Restatement (Second) of Torts, § 2 (1965). Michael Corrado, "Automatism and the Theory of Action," *Emory Law Journal* 39 (1990): 1195–96, nn. 11–23 (citing other leading authorities who subscribe to such a theory of human action).

47. Kadish and Schulhofer, *Cases and Materials*, 179.

48. Aristotle, *Nichomachean Ethics*, 52.

49. J. G. Murphy, "Involuntary Acts and Criminal Liability," *Ethics* 51 (1971): 332–42 (quoted in Kadish and Schulhofer, *Cases and Materials*, 179).

50. See note 205, chapter 1 and accompanying text above.

51. Kadish and Schulhofer, *Cases and Materials*, 179.

52. Ibid., 210–13.

53. Ibid., 204, 257.

54. Ibid., 205.

Chapter 4. The Ghost in the Machine

1. See *A&C*, 91 ("That my arm muscles move is one type of event; that my entire arm moves is another").

2. Timothy Gould, "The Names of Action," in *Stanley Cavell*, ed. Richard Eldridge (Cambridge: Cambridge University Press, 2003), 55 (term Tim Gould uses to describe the view of human action Austin sought to debunk).

3. Katz, *Bad Acts and Guilty Minds*, 164 ("We have been preoccupied in this chapter with the physical half of the criminal offense, the 'bad act.' We concentrate next on the mental part, the 'guilty mind.' A crime can be perpetrated in a variety of mental states: intentionally, knowingly, recklessly, negligently, to name only the most important ones").

4. As examples of the staying power of ordinary-language philosophy, Moore cites: Antony Duff, "Intention," *Agency and Criminal Liability* 130 (1990); Fletcher, *Rethinking Criminal Law*, 436; Jerome Hall, *General Principles of Criminal Law*, 2d ed. (Indianapolis: Bobbs-Merrill, 1960), 227. See also *A&C*, 92, 172 n. 6.

5. Quoting Hart, *Punishment and Responsibility*, 101.

6. Compare "EXCUSES," 180–83, with "K&A," 238, "CRITICISM," 111, and *M&S*, 39–41.

7. *PI*, para. 599 ("Philosophy only states what everyone admits"). See Ludwig Wittgenstein, *Philosophical Remarks*, ed. Rush Rhees, trans. Raymond Hargreaves and Roger White (New York: Barnes and Noble Books, 1975), 65, para. 24 ("In philosophy we are always in danger of giving a mythology of the symbolism, or of psychology: instead of simply saying what everyone knows and must admit").

8. In addition to Austin and Berlin, regularly present at the Thursday evening discussions were Freddie Ayer, Stuart Hampshire, Donald MacKinnon, Donald Macnabb, and Anthony Woozley. Berlin, "Austin and the Early Beginnings," 9; *Isaiah Berlin, Letters 1928–46,* ed. Henry Hardy (Cambridge: Cambridge University Press, 2004), 233–34.

9. Berlin, "Austin and the Early Beginnings," 1–16.

10. Warnock, "Saturday Mornings," 36.

11. Ibid., 45.

12. For a discussion of Cavell's claim that the knowledge that ordinary-language procedures can produce is of the self, see Stephen Mulhall, *Stanley Cavell: Philosophy's Recounting of the Ordinary* (Oxford: Clarendon Press, 1994), 4–11.

13. Ordinary-language procedures are what Espen Hammer has described as a defense against positivism's obsession with scientific proof and its denial of the ordinary (that is, human) world:

> While excluding most of what mathematics and science, using constructed languages, refer to, the world of the ordinary includes all the objects, people, events, values, and ideals we encounter in our ordinary lives. Such a philosophy will have little or nothing to say about "quantum leaps" or "mass society," though it presents us with a procedure with which to clarify the nature of cultural phenomena such as morality, knowledge, love, art, religion, thinking, and so forth—as well as material ones such as trees or chairs. It should thus be able to relate to all aspects and corners of ordinary human concern; accordingly, it demands to be taken seriously as a "new philosophy", capable of challenging other schools of contemporary thought.

Espen Hammer, *Stanley Cavell: Skepticism, Subjectivity, and the Ordinary* (Cambridge: Polity Press, 2002), 7.

14. Mulhall, *Recounting of the Ordinary*, 9.

15. As for why we would ask what *we* should say rather than what *I* should say, that is, on the extent to which we can speak for (not just to) others, see "LATER WITTGENSTEIN," 67–68.

16. Mulhall, *Recounting of the Ordinary*, 11.

17. Ibid.

18. Ibid.

19. See Stuart Hampshire, "J. L. Austin, 1911–1960," in *Symposium on J. L. Austin*, ed. K. T. Fann (London: Routledge, 1969), 37. Evidently their cotaught class was not an isolated event. See "EXCUSES," 195 n. 1 (*Regina v. Finney* is "[a] somewhat distressing favourite in the class that Hart used to conduct with me in the years soon after the war"). Both Hart and Austin are reputed to have profited from the exchange. See J. O. Urmson, W. V. O. Quine, and Stuart Hampshire, "A Symposium on Austin's Method," in *Symposium on J. L. Austin*, ed. K. T. Fann (London: Routledge, 1969), 83 (J. O. Urmson wagers that "Hart would not object" to his stating that Austin influenced Hart's jurisprudence). Equally, George Pitcher observes that "Hart must also have strongly influenced Austin's views about the meaning of many excuse-terms." See Pitcher, "Austin: A Personal Memoir," 20 n. 2.

20. Timothy Gould, "The Names of Action," in *Stanley Cavell*, ed. Richard Eldridge (Cambridge: Cambridge University Press, 2003), 57.

21. Ibid., 73.

22. See ibid., 61–62 (in a criticism leveled more generally at "action theory" that could easily apply to Moore, Tim Gould has said that "such investigations tend to rely on a kind of one-to-one correspondence between the idea of agency and the idea of that which produces actions. . . . [T]hat puts all the weight on 'action,' and 'agency' becomes a dummy word for 'that which produces actions. . . .' ").

23. P. F. Strawson, "Intention and Convention in Speech Acts," in *Symposium on J. L. Austin*, ed. K. T. Fann (London: Routledge, 1969), 390.

24. In his commentary on Derrida's reading of Austin—*Signature Event Context*—the Cavell of the past decade or so has begun to work out a position on the differences between how physical action and speech can misfire. These differences, Cavell states, can be seen by comparing Austin's "Excuses" (the realm where the scope of responsibility for action is determined) with his "Pretending" (the realm where the scope of responsibility for speech is determined). See *A PITCH*, 91 ("[W]hat the doctrine of excuses does for cases of extenuation, Austin's work represented in his paper 'Pretending' . . . in part does for, and is meant eventually to do more for, cases of etiolation, parasitism, and in general the realm of the 'non-serious'; it is the place in which pretending is linked with, and initially defined so as to be distinguishable from, feigning or posing as, affecting or shamming, mimicking or merely imitating, rehearsing or acting. . . ."); Stanley Cavell, "What Did Derrida Want of Austin," in *Philosophical Passages: Wittgenstein, Emerson, Austin, Derrida* (Oxford: Blackwell Publishers, 1995), 63 ("[T]he saying of words is not excusable the way the performance of actions is, or in a word, that saying something is, after all, or before all, on Austinian grounds not exactly or merely or just or quite or transparently doing something").

25. Frank I. Michelman, "Conceptions of Democracy: The Case of Voting Rights," Dunwody Lecture at Holland Law Center, March 10, 1989.

26. J. O. Urmson and G. J. Warnock, "Comments on Hampshire," in *Symposium on J. L. Austin*, ed. K. T. Fann (London: Routledge, 1969), 47.

27. Hart, *Punishment and Responsibility*, 103.
28. Mulhall, *Recounting of the Ordinary*, 15–16.
29. Ibid., 15.
30. Hart, *Punishment and Responsibility*, 197.
31. Ibid., 109–10 (emphasis mine).
32. Here is a small sample of criminal-law texts that devote early chapters to the "separate" subjects of "actus reus" and "mens rea": John M. Brumbaugh, *Cases and Materials on Criminal Law and Approaches to the Study of Law*, 2d ed. (Westbury, N.Y.: Foundation Press, 1991); George E. Dix and M. Michael Sharlott, *Criminal Law: Cases and Materials*, 4th ed. (St. Paul: West Publishing Co., 1996); Dressler, *Understanding Criminal Law*, 69–124; Phillip E. Johnson, *Criminal Law: Cases, Materials, and Text*, 4th ed. (St. Paul: West Publishing Co., 1994); John Kaplan, Robert Weisberg, and Guyora Binder, *Criminal Law: Cases and Materials*, 3d ed. (Boston: Little, Brown, 1996); Andre A. Moenssens, Fred E. Inbau, and Ronald Bacigal, *Cases and Comments on Criminal Law*, 5th ed. (Mineola, N.Y.: Foundation Press,, 1991); Myron Moskovitz, *Cases and Problems in Criminal Law*, 3d ed. (Cincinnati, Oh.: Anderson Publishing Co., 1996); Paul H. Robinson, *Fundamentals of Criminal Law* (Boston: Little, Brown, 1988); Russell L. Weaver, John M. Burkhoff, Catherine Hancock, Alan Reed, and Peter J. Seago, *Readings in Criminal Law* (Cincinnati, Oh.: Anderson Publishing Co., 1998).
33. *United States Postal Serv Bd of Governors v. Aikens*, 460 US 711, 716–17 (1983) (quoting *Edington v. Fitzmaurice*, 29 Ch Div 459, 483 (1885)).
34. E.g., California Penal Code § 20 (1998) ("In every crime or public offense there must exist a union, or joint operation of act and intent, or criminal negligence"); Model Penal Code § 2.01 (1962) ("The term 'voluntary' involves inquiry into the mental state of the actor, and, indeed, the demand that an act or omission be voluntary can be viewed as a preliminary requirement of culpability").
35. Michael S. Moore, "Reply, More on 'Act and Crime,'" *University of Pennsylvania Law Review* 142 (1994): 1767 n. 70.
36. See, e.g., Deborah W. Denno, "Crime and Consciousness: Science and Involuntary Acts," *Minnesota Law Review* 87 (December, 2002): 269 (a sort of philosophy-of-mind tract that cites Moore and the 18th century Austin who influenced Moore, but nowhere cites J. L. Austin or even refers to principles or methods of ordinary language). Limited use of "A Plea for Excuses" can be found in Douglas N. Husak, "Partial Defenses," *Canadian Journal of Law & Jurisprudence* 11 (1998): 167–92.
37. See *M&S*, 39 ("[T]he goal of [Socratic dialectic] . . . is not refutation, which is the province of rhetoric and which is accomplished when one's opponent can say nothing more, but reconciliation, in both the intellectual and erotic senses of the term, which is accomplished only when one's opponent no longer wants to say anything, when he is not merely silenced, but satisfied").
38. See "CRITICISM," 102 ("His repeated disclaimer that ordinary language is certainly not the last word, only it *is* the *first* word . . . is reassuring only during polemical enthusiasm. For the issue is why the first, or *any*, word can have the kind of power Austin attributes to it"). For another take on the "first word," see G. J. Warnock, *J. L. Austin*, 5–6.
39. In actuality, it is difficult to determine the extent that in this passage Moore is attacking Abraham Melden or ordinary-language philosophy at large.
40. *M&S*, 39 (treating "the problem of skepticism not only as a problem *within* epistemology, but as a problem *of* epistemology, or the problem posed by epistemology").

41. See notes 18–21, Introduction, and accompanying text above.

42. See "Beyond Causation," 90 (citing Abraham I. Melden, *Free Action* [London: Routledge and Kegan Paul Ltd., 1961], 75).

43. See generally Kenneth Burke, *A Grammar of Motives* (Berkeley: University of California Press, 1969), 324 ("If you don't select [an anecdote] that is representative in a good sense, it will function as representative in a bad sense").

44. See *A&C*, 104 ("Suppose a pregnant woman who wishes to abort her fetus wills (and thus causes) the constriction of the blood-vessels leading to her uterus, thereby cutting off the blood supply to her fetus, causing it to die. Is not such a constricting part of an action of constricting (which is also, given its further effect, also an action of killing)?").

45. Peters, *Motivation*, 13.

46. Citing Donald Davidson, *Essays on Actions and Events* (Oxford: Clarendon Press, 1980), 110–11. Moore says that the doctor has "removed the appendix" if "the doctor's old Lincoln has sharp edges that cut out the appendix with the deftness of a surgeon's scalpel" (*A&C*, 231). He reaches this conclusion despite the obvious constraints of the grammar of the verb "remove."

47. See *A&C*, 236, citing Jonathan F. Bennett, *Events and Their Names* (Indianapolis: Hackett Publishing Co., 1989), 222 ("For example, 'if I start up a machine that a minute later thrusts my booted foot into your midriff, it need not ever be the case that I have kicked you'").

48. *Journal of Contemporary Legal Issues* 5 (1994): 217.

49. See Thomas Morawetz, "Review Essay, Crime and Moral Conundrums," *Criminal Justice Ethics* 8 (winter/spring 1989): 36. Reviewing Katz's first book, *Bad Acts and Guilty Minds*, Morawetz said that "much more often than not Katz unpacks the legal issue with examples that are only remotely connected to it or that are, to understate the matter, unlikely to occur in the world of experience." Ibid. "The reader," Morawetz adds, "amused as she is by the tales, will struggle to see their relevance." Ibid., 39.

50. Katz, "Crime, Consent, and Insider Trading," 221.

51. Leo Katz, "Proximate Cause in Michael Moore's *Act and Crime*," *University of Pennsylvania Law Review* 142 (1994): 1527.

52. Ibid., 1525.

53. Leo Katz, "Incommensurable Choices and the Problem of Moral Ignorance," *University of Pennsylvania Law Review* 146 (1998): 1482.

54. Katz, "Proximate Cause," 1521–22. Beyond reproach? How could anyone who rigs his life to make possible his performing surgery while drunk be beyond reproach and not a monster?

55. Ibid., 1519. That this is the law is not at all clear. See, e.g., Keeton et al., *Prosser and Keeton on the Law of Torts*, § 56.

56. Leo Katz, "The Limits of Libertarianism," University of San Diego School of Law, April 24, 1997.

57. I don't mean to single out Moore and Katz for having a corner on the deployment of unrepresentative examples. Larry Alexander and Judith Thomson write about so-called trolley or lesser-evil problems, which include meditations on whether you are "justified" or "excused" when "[a] fat man accidentally falls from a cliff above you. If you shift the position of your awning, he will be deflected away from you and be killed. If you do not do this, he will fall on you and kill you, though he will not be killed." See Larry Alexander, "Self-Defense, Justification, and Excuse,"

Philosophy and Public Affairs 22 (1993): 53–66; Judith Jarvis Thomson, "Self-Defense," *Philosophy and Public Affairs* 20 (1991): 287.

58. Gilbert Ryle, *The Concept of Mind* (New York: Barnes and Noble, 1959), 65.

59. P. J. Fitzgerald, "Voluntary and Involuntary Acts," in *Oxford Essays in Jurisprudence, A Collaborative Work,* ed. A. G. Guest (London: Oxford University Press, 1961), 1, 8.

60. "Beyond Causation," 89. If Moore's position were correct—that the relation between an intention and its intended action is causal (contingent) not logical, then "my intention to go to the Bus Station could be fulfilled by my taking a bath. Yet this is manifestly absurd." Ibid., 90–91 (quoting T. F. Devaney, "Intentions and Causes," *Analysis* 27 (1966): 24).

61. Cf. "MWM," 32–33 ("Since saying something is never *merely* saying something, but is saying something with a certain tune and at a proper cue and while executing the appropriate business, the sounded utterance is only a salience of what is going on when we talk. . . ."). But cf. *A&C*, 129 ("[T]o learn to speak English is, among other things, to learn how to move one's tongue"). This is true to a point, but it only highlights that learning to do an activity is not really doing the activity. Anyone who thinks about their tongue while speaking (or their fingers, for that matter, while playing the piano) is in trouble.

62. I disagree. Lip-touching is not necessarily a kiss-making property. I can touch you with my lips but not kiss you. Perhaps I am just touching you with my lips as when I *fake* a kiss of some relative I really dislike.

63. P. F. Strawson, "On Referring," in *The Theory of Meaning,* ed. G. H. R. Parkinson (London: Oxford University Press, 1968), 77.

64. I first encountered this colorful word in K. J. M. Smith, *A Modern Treatise on the Law of Criminal Complicity* (London: Clarendon Press, 1991), 167.

65. See Richard A. Posner, "So What *Has* Pragmatism to Offer Law?" in *Overcoming Law* (Cambridge, Mass.: Harvard University Press, 1995), 397 ("Judges and juries do not, as a precondition to finding that a killing was intentional, peek into the defendant's mind in search of the required intent. They look at the evidence of what the defendant did and *try to infer* from it whether there was advance planning or some other indication of a high probability of success, whether there was concealment of evidence or other indicia of likely escape, and whether the circumstances of the crime argue a likelihood of repetition. . . .") (emphasis added); *Richmond v. Lewis,* 506 U.S. 40, 50 (1992) ("The statutory concepts of heinous and depraved involve a killer's vile state of mind at the time of the murder, as evidenced by the killer's actions").

66. For a reconciliation of Wittgenstein's notion of the private and Cavell's attempt to accommodate Wittgenstein and the insights of skepticism, see *M&S*, 47 (Close analysis of the problem of "other minds" reveals that skepticism "results in the denial of the *otherness of others* . . . [o]r let us just say it results in the denial of others").

67. See *A&C*, 8.

68. See California Penal Code §§ 203–5 (1962) (mayhem); ibid., § 261 (rape); ibid., § 451 (arson).

69. California Jury Instructions (Criminal) §§ 9.30-.32 (1998) (mayhem); ibid., §§ 1.23.1, 10.00 (rape); ibid., §§ 14.80-.84 (arson).

70. *Stanford Law Review 33* (1981): 591–673.

71. *Martin v. State,* 17 So 2d 427 (Ala Ct App 1944).

72. Kelman, "Interpretive Construction in the Substantive Criminal Law," 604–5, n. 32.

73. See, e.g., *People v. Watson,* 637 P2d 279 (Cal Ct App 1981).

74. See, e.g., *People v. Whitfield,* 868 P2d 272 (Cal Ct App 1994); Larry Alexander, "The Supreme Court, Dr. Jekyll, and the Due Process of Proof," *Supreme Court Review* (1996): 191–217.

75. See, e.g., Blackstone, *Of Public Wrongs*, 25–26; California Penal Code §§ 191.5, 192, 193 (1997) (gross vehicular manslaughter while intoxicated carries much stiffer sentence than same action performed while sober).

76. See, e.g., *Palsgraf v. Long Island Railroad Co.*, 162 NE 99, 103 (NY 1928) (Andrews, J., dissenting); William L. Prosser, *Handbook on the Law of Torts*, 4th ed. (St. Paul: West Publishing Co., 1971), 244; Keeton et al., *Law of Torts*, 272–73; Richard W. Wright, "Causation in Tort Law," *California Law Review* 73 (1985): 1742 (The proximate cause inquiry asks: "[i]s there an applicable policy or principle which absolves the defendant from liability, even though his tortious conduct was a cause of the injury?").

77. E.g., Mark Kelman, *A Guide to Critical Legal Studies* (Cambridge, Mass.: Harvard Univesity Press, 1987), 316 n. 30 (dubious assertion that attempt law's presupposing that people will do what they intend to do is an example of determinism).

Conclusion

1. Joseph Conrad, *The Secret Agent*, Modern Library ed. (New York: Knopf, 1998).

2. Ibid., 245.

3. Ibid., 247.

4. Ibid., 253.

5. Ibid.

6. Ibid., 253–56.

7. Ibid., 255.

8. Ibid., 251.

Bibliography

Alexander, Larry. "Crime and Culpability." *Journal of Contemporary Legal Issues* 5 (1994): 1–30.

———. "Foreword: Coleman and Corrective Justice." *Harvard Journal of Law and Public Policy* 15 (1992): 621–36.

———. "Inculpatory and Exculpatory Mistakes and the Fact/Law Distinction: An Essay in Memory of Myke Balyes." *Law and Philosophy* 12 (1993): 33–70.

———. "Negligence, Crime, and Tort: Comments on Hurd and Simons." *Boston University Law Review* 76 (1996): 301–5.

———. "Reconsidering the Relationship Among Voluntary Acts, Strict Liability, and Negligence in Criminal Law." *Social Philosophy and Policy* 7 (1990): 84–104.

———. "Self-Defense, Justification, and Excuse." *Philosophy and Public Affairs* 22 (1993): 53–66.

———. "The Supreme Court, Dr. Jekyll, and the Due Process of Proof." *Supreme Court Review* (1996): 191–217.

———. "A Unified Excuse of Preemptive Self-Protection." *Notre Dame Law Review* 74 (1999): 1475–1505.

———. "Unknowingly Justified Actors and the Attempt/Success Distinction." *University of Tulsa Law Review* 39 (2004): 851–59.

American Law Institute. *Model Penal Code*. Philadelphia: American Law Institute, 1985.

Andre, Judith. "Nagel, Williams, and Moral Luck." *Analysis* 43 (1983): 202–7.

Anscombe, G. E. M. *Intention*, 2d ed. Ithaca: Cornell University Press, 1976.

Arendt, Hannah. *Eichmann in Jerusalem: A Report on the Banality of Evil*. New York: Viking Press, 1963.

Arenella, Peter. "Convicting the Morally Blameless: Reassessing the Relationship Between Legal and Moral Accountability." *U.C.L.A. Law Review* 39 (1992): 1511–1622.

———. "Rethinking the Functions of Criminal Procedure: The Warren and Burger Courts' Competing Ideologies." *Georgetown Law Journal* 72 (1983): 185–248.

Aristotle, *Nichomachean Ethics*. Trans. Martin Oswald. Indianapolis: Bobbs-Merrill, 1962.

Austin, J. L. *How to Do Things With Words*, 2nd ed. Ed. J. O. Urmson and M. Sbisa. Oxford: Clarendon Press, 1975.

———. *Philosophical Papers*, 3rd ed. Ed. J. O. Urmson and G. J. Warnock. Oxford: Oxford University Press, 1979.

———. *Sense and Sensibilia*. Ed. G. J. Warnock. Oxford: Clarendon Press, 1962.

Bandes, Susan. "Reply to Paul Cassell: What We Know about Victim Impact Statements." *Utah Law Review* (1999): 545–52.

———. "Victim Standing." *Utah Law Review* (1999): 331–47.

———. "When Victims Seek Closure: Forgiveness, Vengeance, and the Role of Government." *Fordham Urban Law Journal* 27 (June 2000): 1599–1606.

Bandes, Susan and Jack Beerman. "Lawyering Up." *The Green Bag* 2 (1998): 5–14.

Bennett, Jonathan F. *Events and Their Names*. Indianapolis: Hackett Publishing Co., 1989.

Berlin, Sir Isaiah. "Austin and the Early Beginnings of Oxford Philosophy." In *Essays on J. L. Austin*. Oxford: Clarendon Press, 1973.

Bevington, David, ed. *Othello*. New York: Bantam Books, 1988.

Blackstone, William. *Of Public Wrongs*, vol. 4 of *Commentaries on the Laws of England*. Chicago: University of Chicago Press, 1979.

Brumbaugh, John M. *Cases and Materials on Criminal Law and Approaches to the Study of Law*, 2d ed. Westbury, N.Y.: Foundation Press, 1991.

Burke, Kenneth. *A Grammar of Motives*. Berkeley: University of California Press, 1969.

Buxton, Richard. "Complicity in the Criminal Code." *Law Quarterly Review* 85 (1969): 252–74.

———. "Complicity and the Law Commission." *Criminal Law Review* (1973): 223–30.

Carter, Jimmy. "*Playboy* Interview: Jimmy Carter—A Candid Conversation with the Democratic Candidate for the Presidency." By Robert Scheer. *Playboy* 23, no. 11 (1976): 63–86.

Cavallaro, Rosanna. "A Big Mistake: Eroding the Defense of Mistake of Fact about Consent in Rape." *Journal of Criminal Law and Criminology* 86 (1996): 815–60.

Cavell, Stanley. *Cities of Words*. Cambridge, Mass.: Harvard University Press, 2004.

———. *The Claim of Reason: Wittgenstein, Skepticism, Morality, and Tragedy*. Oxford: Oxford University Press, 1979.

———. *Must We Mean What We Say? A Book of Essays*. 2nd ed. Cambridge: Cambridge University Press, 2002.

———. *A Pitch of Philosophy: Autobiographical Exercises*. Cambridge, Mass.: Harvard University Press, 1994.

———. "What Did Derrida Want of Austin?" In *Philosophical Passages: Wittgenstein, Emerson, Austin, Derrida*. Oxford: Blackwell Publishers, 1995.

Cohen, Ted, Paul Guyer, and Hilary Putnam, eds. *Pursuits of Reason: Essays in Honor of Stanley Cavell*. Lubbock: Texas Tech University Press, 1993.

Conrad, Joseph. *The Secret Agent*, Modern Library ed. New York: Knopf, 1998.

Corrado, Michael. "Automatism and the Theory of Action." *Emory Law Journal* 39 (1990): 1191–1228.

———. "The Place of Legal Formalism in Legal Theory." *North Carolina Law Review* 70 (1992): 1545–61.

Davidson, Donald. *Essays on Actions and Events*. Oxford: Clarendon Press, 1980.

Dawson, John P. "Economic Duress—An Essay in Perspective." *Michigan Law Review* 45 (1947): 253–90.

Denno, Deborah W. "Crime and Consciousness: Science and Involuntary Acts." *Minnesota Law Review* 87 (December 2002): 269–389.

Dershowitz, Alan M. *The Best Defense*. New York: Vintage Books, 1982.

———. *Reversal of Fortune: Inside the von Bülow Case*. New York: Random House, 1986.

Dettmar, Victoria J. "Note, Culpable Mistakes in Rape: Eliminating the Defense of Unreasonable Mistake of Fact as to Victim Consent." *Dickinson Law Review* 89 (1985): 473–99.

Devaney, T. F. "Intentions and Causes." *Analysis* 27 (1966): 23–28.

DiGiovanna, Joseph J. *Linguistic Phenomenology: Philosophical Method in J. L. Austin*. New York: Peter Lang Publishing, Inc., 1989.

Dix, George E. and M. Michael Sharlott. *Criminal Law: Cases and Materials*, 4th ed. St. Paul: West Publishing Co., 1996.

Dressler, Joshua. "Reassessing the Theoretical Underpinnings of Accomplice Liability: New Solutions to an Old Problem." *Hastings Law Journal* 37 (1985): 91–140.

———. *Understanding Criminal Law*, 2d ed. New York: Matthew Bender/Irwin, 1995.

Dripps, Donald. "The Exclusivity of the Criminal Law: Toward a 'Regulatory Model' of, or 'Pathological Perspective' on, the Civil-Criminal Distinction." *Journal of Contemporary Legal Issues* 7 (1996): 199–221.

Duff, R. A. *Criminal Attempts*. Oxford: Clarendon Press, 1996.

———. *Intention, Agency and Criminal Liability*. Oxford: Blackwell Publishing, 1990.

Dworkin, Ronald. *Taking Rights Seriously*. Cambridge, Mass.: Harvard University Press, 1997.

Eldridge, Richard. *Leading a Human Life: Wittgenstein, Intentionality, and Romanticism*. Chicago: University of Chicago Press, 1997.

———. *Stanley Cavell*. Cambridge: Cambridge University Press, 2003.

———. *The Persistence of Romanticism: Selected Essays in Philosophy and Literature*. Cambridge: Cambridge University Press, 2001.

Eser, Albin. "Justification and Excuse." *American Journal of Comparative Law* 24 (1976): 621–31.

Fann, K. T., ed. *Symposium on J. L. Austin*. London: Routledge: 1969.

Feinberg, Joel. "Action and Responsibility." In *Doing and Deserving: Essays in the Theory of Responsibility*. Princeton: Princeton University Press, 1970.

———. "Equal Punishments for Failed Attempts: Some Bad but Instructive Arguments Against It." *Arizona Law Review* 37 (1995): 117–33.

———. *Harm to Others*. Vol. 1 of *Moral Limits of the Criminal Law*. New York: Oxford University Press, 1984.

———. *Harmless Wrongdoing*. Vol. 4 of *Moral Limits of the Criminal Law*. New York: Oxford University Press, 1988.

Fischer, Michael. *Stanley Cavell and Literary Skepticism*. Chicago: University of Chicago Press, 1989.

Fitzgerald, P. J. "Voluntary and Involuntary Acts." In *Oxford Essays in Jurisprudence, A Collaborative Work*, ed. A. G. Guest. London: Oxford University Press, 1961.

Fleming, Richard. *First Word Philosophy: Wittgenstein-Austin-Cavell: Writings on Ordinary Language Philosophy*. Lewisburg: Bucknell University Press, 2004.

———. *The State of Philosophy: An Invitation to a Reading in Three Parts of Stanley Cavell's "The Claim of Reason."* Lewisburg: Bucknell University Press, 1993.

Fleming, Richard and Michael Payne, eds. *The Senses of Stanley Cavell.* Lewisburg: Bucknell University Press, 1989.

Fletcher, George P. "Constructing a Theory of Impossible Attempts." *Criminal Justice Ethics* 5 (Winter/Spring 1986): 53–66.

———. "Proportionality and the Psychotic Aggressor: A Vignette in Comparative Criminal Law Theory." *Israel Law Review* 8 (1973): 367–90.

———. *Rethinking Criminal Law*. Boston: Little, Brown, 1978.

———. "What Is Punishment Imposed For?" *Journal of Contemporary Legal Issues* 5 (1994): 101–11.

Foucault, Michel. *Discipline and Punish: The Birth of the Prison*. Trans. Alan Sheridan, 2d ed. New York: Vintage Books, 1995.

Fredrickson, George M. *The Black Image in the White Mind*. New York: Harper and Row, 1972.

Freud, Sigmund. *Psychopathology of Everyday Life*. Trans. A. A. Brill. New York: New American Library, 1951.

Giles, Stephen G. "Causation and Responsibility After Coase, Calabresi, and Coleman." *Quinnipiac Law Review* 16 (1997): 255–78.

Gladwell, Malcolm. "The Art of Failure." *The New Yorker* (August 21 and 28, 2000): 84.

Gould, Timothy. "The Names of Action." In *Stanley Cavell*. Ed. Richard Eldridge. Cambridge: Cambridge University Press, 2003.

———. "Stanley Cavell." In *A Companion to Aesthetics*. Oxford: Basil Blackwell, 1992.

Great Britain Law Commission. *Assisting and Encouraging Crime: A Consultation Paper*. London: H. M. S. O., 1993.

Greenawalt, Kent. "Law and Objectivity: How People Are Treated." *Criminal Justice Ethics* 8 (Summer/Fall 1989): 31–55.

———. "The Perplexing Borders of Justification and Excuse." *Columbia Law Review* 84 (1984): 1897–1927.

Greenberg, Clement. *Arrogant Purpose*. Vol. 2 of *The Collected Essays and Criticism*. Ed. John O'Brian. Chicago: University of Chicago Press, 1993.

Gudel, Paul J. "Beyond Causation: The Interpretation of Action and the Mixed Motives Problem in Employment Discrimination Law." *Texas Law Review* 70 (1991): 17–107.

———. *Modernism and Skepticism: Terms of Criticism in Clement Greenberg, Michael Fried, and Stanley Cavell.* California Western School of Law, 1998.

———. "Relational Contract Theory and the Concept of Exchange." *Buffalo Law Review* 46 (1998): 763–96.

Hall, Jerome. *General Principles of Criminal Law*, 2d ed. Indianapolis, Ind.: Bobbs-Merrill, 1960.

Hall, Ronald L. *The Human Embrace: The Love of Philosophy and the Philosophy of*

Love: Kierkegaard, Cavell, Nussbaum. University Park: Pennsylvania State University Press, 1999.

Hammer, Espen. *Stanley Cavell: Skepticism, Subjectivity, and the Ordinary*. Cambridge, Mass.: Polity Press, 2002.

Hampton, Jean. "Retribution and the Liberal State." *Journal of Contemporary Legal Issues* 5 (1994): 117–44.

Hardy, Henry, ed. *Isaiah Berlin, Letters 1928–46*. Cambridge: Cambridge University Press, 2004.

Hart, H. L. A. "Ascription of Responsibility and Rights." *Proceedings of the Aristotelian Society* 49, 1949.

———. *Punishment and Responsibility: Essays in the Philosophy of Law*. Oxford: Clarendon Press, 1968.

Heath, Peter. "Trying and Attempting." *Proceedings of the Aristotelian Society*, Supplementary Volume 45, 1971.

Holdcroft, David. *Words and Deeds*. Oxford: Clarendon Press, 1978.

Hornsby, Jennifer. "Action and Aberration." *University of Pennsylvania Law Review* 142 (1994): 1719–46.

Hurd, Heidi M. "What in the World is Wrong?" *Journal of Contemporary Legal Issues* 5 (1994): 157–216.

Husak, Douglas N. "Justifications and the Criminal Liability of Accessories." *Journal of Criminal Law and Criminology* 80 (1989): 201–30.

———. "The Nature and Justifiability of Nonconsummate Offenses." *Arizona Law Review* 37 (1995): 151–83.

———. "Partial Defenses." *Canadian Journal of Law & Jurisprudence* 11(1998):167–92.

———. *Philosophy of the Criminal Law*. Lanham: Rowman & Littlefield, 1989.

———. "Reasonable Risk Creation and Overinclusive Legislation." *Buffalo Criminal Law Review* 1 (1998): 599–626.

———. "The Relevance of the Concept of Action to the Criminal Law." *Criminal Law Forum* 6 (1995): 327–44.

Hutchinson, Thomas W. et al., eds. *Federal Sentencing Law and Practice*. St. Paul: West Publishing Co., 1998.

Johnson, Phillip E. *Criminal Law: Cases, Materials, and Text*, 4th ed. St. Paul: West Publishing Co., 1994.

———. "The Unnecessary Crime of Conspiracy." *California Law Review* 61 (1973): 1137–88.

Kadish, Sanford H. "Codifiers of the Criminal Law: Wechler's Predecessors." *Columbia Law Review* 78 (1978): 1098–1144.

———. "Complicity, Cause and Blame: A Study in the Interpretation of Doctrine." *California Law Review* 73 (1985): 323–410.

———. "Fifty Years of Criminal Law: An Opinionated Review." *California Law Review* 87 (1999): 943–82.

———. "Foreword: The Criminal Law and the Luck of the Draw." *Journal of Criminal Law and Criminology* 84 (1994): 679–702.

———. "Moral Excess in the Law." *McGeorge Law Review* 32 (2000): 63–76.

Kadish, Sanford H. and Stephen J. Schulhofer. *Criminal Law and Its Processes: Cases and Materials*, 6th ed. Boston: Little, Brown, 1995.

Kahan, Dan M. "Ignorance of Law *Is* an Excuse—but Only for the Virtuous." *Michigan Law Review* 96 (1997): 127–54.

Kamisar, Yale, Wayne R. LaFave and Jerold H. Israel. *Modern Criminal Procedure: Cases, Commentaries and Questions*, 8th ed. St. Paul: West Publishing Co., 1994.

Kant, Immanuel. *Foundations of the Metaphysics of Morals*. Ed. Robert P. Wolff. New York: Macmillan, 1969.

———. *The Metaphysics of Morals*. Ed. and trans. Mary Gregor. New York: Cambridge University Press, 1996.

———. "Perpetual Peace: A Philosophical Sketch." In *Kant's Political Writings*. Ed. Hans S. Reiss and trans. H. B. Nisbet. Cambridge: Cambridge University Press, 1970.

Kaplan, John, Robert Weisberg, and Guyora Binder. *Criminal Law: Cases and Materials*, 3d ed. Boston: Little, Brown, 1996.

Katz, Leo. *Bad Acts and Guilty Minds: Conundrums of the Criminal Law*. Chicago: University of Chicago Press, 1987.

———. "Crime, Consent, and Insider Trading." *Journal of Contemporary Legal Issues* 5 (1994): 217–35.

———. "Incommensurable Choices and the Problem of Moral Ignorance." *University of Pennsylvania Law Review* 146 (1998): 1465–85.

———. "The Limits of Libertarianism." (lecture, University of San Diego School of Law, April 24, 1997).

———. "Proximate Cause in Michael Moore's *Act and Crime*." *University of Pennsylvania Law Review* 142 (1994): 1513–28.

Keedy, Edwin R. "Ignorance and Mistake in the Criminal Law." *Harvard Law Review* 22 (1908–9): 75–96.

Kelman, Mark. *A Guide to Critical Legal Studies*. Cambridge, Mass.: Harvard University Press, 1987.

———. "Interpretive Construction in the Substantive Criminal Law." *Stanford Law Review* 33 (1981): 591–673.

———. "Strict Liability: An Unorthodox View." In vol. 4 of *Encyclopedia of Crime and Justice*. Ed. Sanford H. Kadish. New York: Free Press, 1983.

Kuklin, Bailey H. "The Asymmetrical Conditions of Legal Responsibility in the Marketplace." *University of Miami Law Review* 44 (1990): 893–1008.

LaFave, Wayne R. & Austin Scott. *Handbook on Criminal Law*. St. Paul: West Publishing Co., 1972.

———. *Handbook on Criminal Law*, 2d ed. St. Paul: West Publishing Co., 1986.

———. *Handbook on Criminal Law*, 3d ed. St. Paul: West Publishing Co., 2000.

———. *Handbook on Criminal Law*, 4th ed. St. Paul: Thomson/West, 2003.

Lawrence, Roy. *Motive and Intention*. Evanston, Ill.: Northwestern University Press, 1972.

Lewin, Tamar. "A Cause Worth Killing For?" *New York Times*, July 30, 1994, A1.

Luban, David. "The Bad Man and the Good Lawyer: A Centennial Essay on Holmes's 'The Path of the Law.'" *N.Y.U. Law Review* 72 (1997): 1547–83.

Macaulay, Stewart. "Non-Contractual Relations in Business: A Preliminary Study." *American Sociological Review* 28 (1963): 55–67.

———. "The Use and Non-Use of Contracts in the Manufacturing Industry." *The Practical Lawyer* (1963): 13–40.

MacCarthy, Terrence F. and Kathy Morris Mejia. "The Perjurious Client Question: Putting Criminal Defense Lawyers Between a Rock and a Hard Place." *Journal of Criminal Law and Criminology* 75 (1984): 1197–1221.

Melden, Abraham I. *Free Action*. London: Routledge and Kegan Paul Ltd., 1961.

Menand, Louis. "Jerry Don't Surf." *New York Review of Books* 45 (Sept. 24, 1998): 7–8.

Menkel-Meadow, Carrie. "Portia Redux: Another Look at Gender, Feminism, and Legal Ethics." *Virginia Journal of Social Policy and Law* 2 (1994): 75–114.

Metken, Günter. *Gauguin à Tahiti: Le Premier Voyage*. Paris-Munich: Schirmer/Mosel, 1990.

Meyer, Linda Ross. "Why Me?" *Quinnipiac Law Review* 16 (1997): 299–314.

Michaels, Alan C. "Acceptance: The Missing Mental State." *Southern California Law Review* 71 (1998): 953–1035.

Michelman, Frank I. "Conceptions of Democracy: The Case of Voting Rights" (lecture, Holland Law Center, Gainesville, Florida, March 10, 1989).

Moenssens, Andre A., Fred E. Inbau, and Ronald Bacigal. *Cases and Comments on Criminal Law*, 5th ed. Mineola, N.Y.: Foundation Press, 1991.

Moore, Michael S. *Act and Crime: The Philosophy of Action and Its Implications for Criminal Law*. Oxford: Oxford University Press, 1993.

———. "Causation and the Excuses." *California Law Review* 73 (1985): 1091–1149.

———. "Choice, Character, and Excuse." *Social Philosophy and Policy* 7 (1990): 29–58.

———. "The Independent Moral Significance of Wrongdoing." *Journal of Contemporary Legal Issues* 5 (1994): 239–81.

———. *Law and Psychiatry: Rethinking the Relationship*. Cambridge: Cambridge University Press, 1984.

———. "Reply, More on 'Act and Crime.'" *University of Pennsylvania Law Review* 142 (1994): 1749–1840.

Morawetz, Thomas. "Reconstructing the Criminal Defenses: The Significance of Justification." *Journal of Criminal Law and Criminology* 77 (1986): 277–307.

———. "Review Essay, Crime and Moral Conundrums." *Criminal Justice Ethics* 8 (Winter/Spring 1989): 35–45.

Morris, Norval. "Somnambulistic Homicide: Ghosts, Spiders, and North Koreans." *Res Judicatae* 5 (1951): 29–33.

Morrison IV, Walter C. "Tax Evasion, Willfullness and the Subjective Standard: The Law Invites a Charlatan." *Mississippi College Law Review* 13 (1992): 195–219.

Moskovitz, Myron. *Cases and Problems in Criminal Law*, 3d ed. Cincinnati, Oh.: Anderson Publishing Co., 1996.

Moya, Carlos J. *The Philosophy of Action: An Introduction*. Oxford: Polity in association with Blackwell, 1990.

Mueller, Grace. "The Mens Rea of Accomplice Liability." *Southern California Law Review* 61 (1988): 2169–91.

Mulhall, Stephen. *On Being in the World: Wittgenstein and Heidegger on Seeing Aspects*. London: Routledge, 1990.

———. *Stanley Cavell: Philosophy's Recounting of the Ordinary*. Oxford: Clarendon Press, 1994.

Murphy, J. G. "Involuntary Acts and Criminal Liability." *Ethics* 51 (1971): 332–42.

Nagel, Thomas. "Moral Luck." In *Mortal Questions*. New York: Cambridge University Press, 1979.

Navarro, Mireya. "Abortion Clinic Case Reviews a Legal Dilemma." *New York Times*, November 14, 1994, A12.

Nussbaum, Martha. "The Use and Abuse of Philosophy in Legal Education." *Stanford Law Review* 45 (1993): 1627–45.

Packer, Herbert L. "Mens Rea and the Supreme Court." *Supreme Court Review* (1962).

Perkins, Rollin M. "Parties to Crime." *University of Pennsylvania Law Review* 89 (1941): 581–623.

Peters, R. S. *The Concept of Motivation*. Ed. R. F. Holland. Amherst, N.Y.: Prometheus Books, 1958.

Pitcher, G. W., ed. *Truth*. Englewood Cliffs, N.J.: Prentice Hall, 1964.

Pitcher, George. "Austin: A Personal Memoir." In *Essays on J. L. Austin*. Oxford: Clarendon Press, 1973.

———. *The Philosophy of Wittgenstein*. Englewood Cliffs, N.J.: Prentice Hall, 1964.

Plato. *Republic*. Trans. Allan Bloom. New York: Basic Books, 1991.

Posner, Richard A. *Economic Analysis of the Law*, 4th ed. Boston: Little, Brown, 1992.

———. "An Economic Theory of the Criminal Law." *Columbia Law Review* 85 (1985): 1193–1231.

———. *The Economics of Justice*. Cambridge, Mass.: Harvard University Press, 1981.

———. "So What *Has* Pragmatism to Offer Law?" In *Overcoming Law*. Cambridge: Harvard University Press, 1995.

Postema, Gerald J. "Risks, Wrongs, and Responsibility: Coleman's Liberal Theory of Commutative Justice, Review of 'Risks and Wrongs' by Jules L. Coleman." *Yale Law Journal* 103 (1993): 861–97.

Prosser, William L. *Handbook on the Law of Torts*, 4th ed. St. Paul: West Publishing Co., 1971.

Prosser, William, et al. *Prosser and Keeton on the Law of Torts*, 5th ed. St. Paul: West Publishing Co., 1984.

Robinson, Paul H. "A Brief History of Distinctions in Criminal Culpability." *Hastings Law Journal* 31 (1980): 815–53.

———. *Criminal Law Defenses*. St. Paul: West Publishing Co., 1984.

———. *Fundamentals of Criminal Law*. Boston: Little, Brown, 1988.

———. "Imputed Criminal Liability." *Yale Law Journal* 93 (1984): 609–76.

———. "A Theory of Justification: Societal Harm As a Prerequisite for Criminal Liability." *U. C. L. A. Law Review* 23 (1975): 266–92.

Robinson, Paul H. and Jane A. Grall. "Element Analysis in Defining Criminal Liability: The Model Penal Code and Beyond." *Stanford Law Review* 35 (1983): 681–762.

Ross, Sir William David. *Foundations of Ethics; The Gifford Lectures delivered in the University of Aberdeen, 1935–36*. Oxford: Clarendon Press, 1960.

Roth, William. "General vs. Specific Intent: A Time for Terminological Understanding in California." *Pepperdine Law Review* 7 (1979): 67–84.

Rothman, William and Marian Keane. *Reading Cavell's "The World Viewed": A Philosophical Perspective on Film*. Detroit: Wayne State University Press, 2000.

Ryle, Gilbert. *The Concept of Mind*. New York: Barnes and Noble, 1959.

Sartre, Jean-Paul. *The Words*. Trans. Bernard Frechtman. New York: Random House, 1964.

Sayre, Francis. "Criminal Responsibility for the Acts of Another." *Harvard Law Review* 43 (1930): 702–8.

Schiffer, S. R. *Meaning*. Oxford: Clarendon Press, 1972.

Searle, John R. *Intentionality*. New York: Cambridge University Press, 1983.

———. *Speech Acts: An Essay in the Philosophy of Language*. London: Cambridge University Press, 1969.

Shatz, Steven F. and Nina Rivkind. "The California Death Penalty Scheme: Requiem for *Furman*?" *N. Y. U. Law Review* 72, (1997): 1283–1343.

Shavell, Steven. "Deterrence and the Punishment of Attempts." *Journal of Legal Studies* 19 (1990): 435–66.

Simons, Kenneth. "Rethinking Mental States." *Boston University Law Review* 72 (1992): 463–554.

Singer, Richard. "The Resurgence of Mens Rea: II—Honest but Unreasonable Mistake of Fact in Self Defense." *Boston College Law Review* 28 (1987): 459–519.

Singer, Richard and Douglas Husak. "Of Innocence and Innocents: The Supreme Court and Mens Rea Since Herbert Packer." *Buffalo Criminal Law Review* 2 (1999): 861–945.

Smith, K. J. M. *A Modern Treatise on the Law of Criminal Complicity*. London: Clarendon Press, 1991.

Spencer, J. R. "Trying To Help Another Person Commit a Crime." In *Criminal Essays in Honour of JC Smith*. Ed. Peter Smith. London: Butterworths, 1987.

Statistical Abstract of the U.S. Tab. No. 312, 1996.

Statman, Daniel, ed., *Moral Luck*. Albany: State University of New York Press, 1993.

Strawson, P. F. "On Referring." In *The Theory of Meaning*. Ed. G. H. R. Parkinson. London: Oxford University Press, 1968.

Stuntz, William J. "Substance, Process, and the Civil-Criminal Line." *Journal of Contemporary Legal Issues* 7 (1996): 1–41.

Sutherland, N.S. "Motives as Explanations." *Mind* 68 (1959): 145–59.

Sverdlik, Steven. "Crime and Moral Luck." *American Philosophical Quarterly* 25 (1988): 79–85.

Sweetman, David. *Paul Gauguin: A Complete Life*. London: Hodder and Stoughton, 1995.

"Symposium: The Civil Criminal Distinction." *Journal of Contemporary Legal Issues* 7 (1996): 1–398.

"Symposium: The Intersection of Tort and Criminal Law." *Boston University Law Review* 76 (1996): 1–370.

"Symposium: Punishment." *Yale Law Journal* 101 (1992): 1681–1908.

Szostak, Mike. "Celtics Journal: New No. 5 Starts on Injured List." *The Providence Journal-Bulletin*, February 9, 1995, 10F.

Teachout, Terry. "An American Icon." *New York Times Book Review* (November 5, 1995): 15–18.

Thomson, Judith Jarvis. "The Decline of Cause." *Georgetown Law Journal* 76 (1987): 137–50.

———. "Morality and Bad Luck." *Metaphilosophy* 20 (1989): 203–21.

———. "Self-Defense." *Philosophy and Public Affairs* 20 (1991): 283–310.

Updike, John. "The Widow." In *Flash Fiction: Very Short Stories* 72. Eds. James Thomas, Denise Thomas, and Tom Hazuka. New York: W. W. Norton & Co., 1992.

van den Haag, Ernest. "The Ultimate Punishment: A Defense." *Harvard Law Review* 99 (1986): 1662–69.

Warnock, G. J. *J. L. Austin: The Arguments of the Philosophers*. Ed. Ted Honderich. London: Routledge, 1989.

———. "Saturday Mornings." In *Essays on J. L. Austin*. Oxford: Clarendon Press, 1973.

Weaver, Russell L., et al. *Readings in Criminal Law*. Cincinnati, Oh.: Anderson Publishing Co., 1998.

West, Robin L. "Legitimizing the Illegitimate: A Comment on 'Beyond Rape.'" *Columbia Law Review* 93 (1993): 1442–59.

Weston, Steve. "OK, Now What? Suns Ponder Options with Manning Out." *The Phoenix Gazette*, February 7, 1995, C1.

Wiley, Jr., John S. "Not Guilty by Reason of Blamelessness: Culpability in Federal Criminal Interpretation." *Virginia Law Review* 85 (1999): 1021–1162.

Williams, Bernard. "Moral Luck." In *Moral Luck*. Ed. Daniel Statman. Albany: State University of New York Press, 1993.

———. "Recognising Responsibility." In *Shame and Necessity*. Berkeley: University of California Press, 1993.

Williams, Glanville. *Criminal Law: The General Part*, 2d ed. London: Sweet and Maxwell, 1961.

———. *Textbook of Criminal Law*. 2d ed. London: Stevens and Sons, 1983.

Winch, Peter. "Trying." In *Ethics and Action*. Ed. D. Z. Phillips. London: Routledge and Kegan Paul, 1972.

Winings, Mark C. "Ignorance Is Bliss, Especially for the Tax Evader." *Journal of Criminal Law and Criminology* 84 (1993): 575–603.

Wittgenstein, Ludwig. *The Blue and Brown Books*. New York: Harper, 1958.

———. *Philosophical Investigations*. Trans. G. E. M. Anscombe. Oxford: Blackwell, 1953.

———. *Philosophical Remarks*. Ed. Rush Rhees, trans. Raymond Hargreaves and Roger White. New York: Barnes and Noble Books, 1975.

Wolf, Susan. "The Legal and Moral Responsibility of Organizations." In *Criminal*

Justice. Eds. J. Pennock and J. Chapman. New York: New York University Press, 1985.

———. *Freedom Within Reason*. New York: Oxford University Press, 1990.

Wootten, Barbara. *Crime and the Criminal Law: Reflections of a Magistrate and Social Scientist*. London: Stevens, 1963.

Wright, Richard W. "Causation in Tort Law." *California Law Review* 73 (1985): 1735–1828.

Yeager, Daniel B. "Dangerous Games and the Criminal Law." *Criminal Justice Ethics* 16 (winter/spring 1997): 3–12.

———. "Does Privacy Really Have a Problem in the Law of Criminal Procedure?" *Rutgers Law Review* 49 (1997): 1283–1315.

———. "Helping, Doing, and the Grammar of Complicity." *Criminal Justice Ethics* 15 (winter/spring 1996): 25–35.

———. "Kahan on Mistakes." *Michigan Law Review* 96 (1998): 2113–22.

———. "The Stubbornness of Pretexts." *San Diego Law Review* 40 (spring 2003): 611–44.

Zola, Emile. *Au Bonheur des Dames*. Paris: Bookking International, 1994.

Index

aberration, 116, 158, 184 n. 44
abortion, 57, 174 n. 78, 192 n. 44
accessory, 101, 104, 108, 184 n. 47
accidents, 10, 12, 25–37, 40, 42, 45, 52, 59–64, 82–88, 120, 122, 127, 176 n. 99; "accidentally on purpose," 12; excusing, 29–63, 35, 40, 60–61, 84; inexcusable, 40, 84
accomplice, 65, 86, 101, 182 n. 12; liability, 183 n. 27, 184 n. 49, 185 n. 54
accuse, 51, 64, 111–17, 120–22, 159–62, 166–67, 175; accuser, 24–29, 33, 81, 92, 115, 117, 167; accused, 24–29, 33, 50–51, 54–55, 60, 64–65, 81, 84, 96, 115, 120, 136, 140, 157, 176 n. 104, 185 n. 59; versus excuse, 24, 26, 120, 122
acknowledgment, 36, 64, 94, 137–38, 161–62
act: excusable, 94, 190 n. 24; "illocutionary," 138–39, 184 n. 46; "locutionary," 138; mental, 122; moral, 111; "perlocutionary," 138–39, 184 n. 46; requirement, 122, 125, 134–35, 152–53, 157, 162–63, 165; speech-act, 75, 99; "univocal act requirement," 124, 134, 163
actions: burden of, 39, 59, 62, 94, 155–56; doing, 124–60; human, 24, 26, 31, 36, 38, 41, 58, 61, 90–91, 95, 117–18, 124–27, 132–35, 151, 156–67, 170 n. 16, 188 n. 46, 189 n. 2; causal theory of, 162; role of alternatives, 31–45; speaking, 127–28; inaction, 38; infelicitous, 29, 60, 121; interpretation of, 24–25, 119, 122, 151, 161; judging an, 160–65; misfired, 27, 45, 64, 69, 74–75, 91, 97, 138, 190 n. 24; physical, 122–23, 138, 190 n. 24; pretextual, 45–50, 173 nn. 47 and 48; and their reasons, 45–55; skepticism about. *See* action, judging an; theory, 22
African-American, 40, 67, 79
agent, 30, 33, 43, 78–79, 82, 87, 95–96, 103, 139, 149, 155, 166, 194 nn. 1–8; provocateur, 104; regret, 87, 89–92; responsible, 31, 71, 86, 135
aggravate. *See* inculpatory
agreement, 24, 29, 63, 97–98, 112, 125, 129–30, 137–38, 142, 150, 156
aid, 89, 102–5, 185 n. 59; and abet, 25, 101
Alexander, Larry, 12, 30–31, 82, 89–92, 171 nn. 2, 4, and 9, 172 nn. 17 and 19, 178 nn. 160 and 161, 179 n. 195, 180 n. 212, 181 n. 227, 182 n. 9, 192 n. 57, 194 n. 74
Amendment, Sixteenth, 75, 178 n. 158
Andre, Judith, 82–83, 179 n. 190, 191 n. 32
Anscombe, Elizabeth, 115, 187 n. 30
answerable, 24–25, 55, 84, 98, 108, 112–13, 124, 151, 160
Arendt, Hanna, 85, 180 n. 200
Arenella, Peter, 23, 110, 169 n. 1, 171 n. 6
Aristotle, 118, 122, 126, 139, 188 nn. 39 and 48
arson, 56, 79, 92–93, 152, 163, 193 nn. 68 and 69; attempted, 92
assassinate, 154–56
assault, 103–5, 150, 176 n. 101, 182 n. 5
assertion, ordinary, 125, 153
attempt, 25, 40, 65–66, 70–73, 77, 92–101, 137–41, 157, 172 n. 29, 178 nn. 140, 147, and 181 n. 227, 182 n. 13, 183 nn. 24 and 25, 184 n. 42, 185 n. 73, 194 n. 77; arson. *See* arson, attempted; California law, 97–98; failure, 70, 182 n. 9; impossible, 70–74, 178 nn. 145 and 146, 182 n. 5, 187 n. 25; mur-

der. *See* homicide, attempted; solicitation. *See* solicitation, attempted; theft. *See* theft, attempted
attitude, 11, 41, 44
Austin, John, 125
automatically, 106, 116, 130–33, 144, 149, 188n. 46
autonomy, 99
Ayer, A.J., 126, 171n. 20
awareness, 30–31, 35–38, 41, 50, 59, 76, 111, 127, 144, 163, 165, 172n. 26, 178n. 160

B's Co. v. BP Barber and Association, 187n. 29
Bandes, Susan, 180nn. 199 and 202, 186n. 3, 187n. 28
battery, 30, 102, 137
behavior, 23, 33, 79, 90, 92, 97, 154, 175, 186n. 5
belief, 30, 38–40, 61, 65–67, 69–70, 72, 76–77, 80–81, 104, 127, 136, 169, 172–73, 176, 179, 181; wrong. *See* wrong belief
Belli, Melvin, 86
Benseley v. Bignold, 179n. 182
Berlin, Isaiah, 11, 126, 169n. 4, 189nn. 8 and 9
Blackstone, William, 170n. 13, 174n. 75, 176n. 104, 194n. 194
blame, 23–32, 36–37, 40, 53, 63, 82–100, 109, 115, 167, 180n. 204; moral. *See* moral blame; versus hold responsible, 82–86; blameworthy, 24, 31, 51, 79, 82, 98
body, 26, 46, 128, 137, 144–46, 149, 153–57, 160–61, 167, 186n. 9; *see* also: mind-body, 132
Breyer, Stephen G., Justice, 79, 80, 186–87n. 13
Britain: House of Lords,65; Oxford. *See* Oxford; Parliament, 107
burden: of action, 39, 59, 62, 94, 155–56; of proof, 39, 59, 62, 94, 155–56
burglar, 102–4, 157, 160; burglary, 58, 102, 160, 176n. 101, 182n. 5

California: Jury Instructions, 81, 175nn. 82 and 92, 176nn. 110, 112, and 113, 179n. 189, 182n. 16, 184n. 44, 193n. 69; Penal Code, 163, 182nn. 15 and 18, 183n. 31, 184n. 43, 191n. 34, 193n. 68, 194n. 75; Supreme Court, 36
capacity, 70, 129, 161; incapacity, 103
cause, 24, 33, 35, 42, 48, 67, 85–88, 94–95, 97–98, 101–6, 124–25, 131–38, 144, 147–49, 152–55, 157–61, 170nn. 11 and 18, 171n. 5, 174n. 52, 58–60, 62, 180nn. 197 and 204, 184n. 48, 185n. 62, 186n. 75, 188n. 36, 192nn. 42 and 44, 193 n. 60, 194n. 76; mind-body orientation, 132; moral, 24; proximate, 155, 164–65, 192n. 51–52, 54–55, 194n. 76
Cavell, Stanley, 10–19, 38–39, 62, 67, 114, 119–22, 125–31, 148, 159, 162, 175n. 85, 187n. 35, 189nn. 2 and 12, 189–90n. 13, 190nn. 20 and 24, 193n. 66
certainty, 35, 161, 173n. 30
Cheek v. United States, 76, 79–80, 81, 178n. 159, 179n. 188
choice, 31–33, 59
choke, 145–46
civil, 30, 84, 110–13, 175n. 91, 175–76n. 98, 178n. 160, 186n. 7; law, 110–13; rights, 65; War, 67
Code. *See* Model Penal Code
Cohen, Ted, 10
commitment, 43–44, 64, 74–75, 80–82, 124, 160
Commonwealth v. Atencio, 185n. 67
community, 12, 23, 84–85, 92, 112, 116, 120, 129–31, 160, 162, 167, 170n. 11
complicity, 94, 96, 101–8, 180n. 204, 182n. 5, 184nn. 45, 49, and 51, 185n. 59, 61, 72, 193n. 64; broad view of, 104
concurrence of act and intent, 123, 151
confession, 84–85
Congress, 76, 107, 178n. 158
Conrad, Joseph, 166, 194n. 1
conscious, 36, 42, 59, 144, 191n. 36; disregard, 37, 40, 60, 63, 172n. 25
consequence, 24, 26–27, 31–39, 43, 48, 51, 58–60, 63, 82, 86, 94, 147, 150, 155, 167, 172n. 25, 186n. 5
conspiracy, 94, 96–101, 137, 139–41, 183nn. 24, 25, 31, 33, and 34; unilateral, 138

constitutional, 10, 140, 171–72 n. 12; law, 134
contract, 23, 111, 113–14, 124, 153, 155, 186 n. 11, 187 n. 23, 26, 27
conventions, 129, 142, 147, 158, 162, 173 n. 46; linguistic, 158
convulsion, 87, 122
corrupt, 11, 55, 142
cost-justified, 30, 60
creditor, 33–35, 52–53
crime, 23, 25, 31, 36–38, 40, 51, 54–55, 58, 61, 64–65, 70–71, 73, 78, 81, 85, 87, 93, 96–99, 101–6, 110–11, 114, 131–41, 147, 154, 160, 162–64, 169 n. 3, 170 n. 13, 172 n. 17, 175 nn. 82, 90, and 93, 177 n. 117, 179 n. 194, 181 n. 227, 182 nn. 9 and 11, 183 nn. 24–25, and 33, 184 nn. 44, 47, and 50, 185 nn. 59, 68, and 72, 186 nn. 1 and 3, 191 nn. 34, 35, and 36, 192 n. 49, 50, and 51, 193 n. 65; choosing, 31–41; thought, 134
criminal: association, 98–99, 104–5; choice, 31–41; justice, 14, 23, 169–70 nn. 6 and 9, 181 n. 223, 182 n. 5, 184 n. 45, 192 n. 49; law, 11–12, 23–31, 37, 46, 52–64, 70, 78, 82, 90–97, 101, 104, 110–25, 132–35, 139, 142, 151–52, 155, 160–67, 170 nn. 8 and 9, 16–17, 171 nn. 2, 5, and 6, 174 nn. 68 and 69, 76, 79, 175 nn. 90 and 98, 176 nn. 108 and 111, 177 nn. 115 and 119, 178 n. 161, 179 nn. 194 and 196, 180 nn. 208 and 211, 181 nn. 217–18, 220–22, 224, and 228, 3 (chap. 2), 182 nn. 5 and 6, 184 nn. 47–48, and 52, 185 nn. 59, 68–69, and 72, 186 n. 7, 187 nn. 18 and 33, 189 n. 4, 191 n. 32, 194 n. 72; liability, 23, 29–31, 135, 151, 163, 171 n. 5, 180 n. 205, 181 n. 222, 185 n. 54, 188 n. 49; trial, 37, 65, 76, 85–86, 106, 163
culpable, 23, 24, 31, 40–42, 50–51, 54, 57, 92, 95–96, 122–23, 169 n. 4, 171 nn. 9, 11, and 12, 172 nn. 13, 17, and 19, 176 nn. 99 and 109, 191 n. 227, 182 n. 9, 191 n. 34; morally. *See* morally culpable

damages, 86; punitive, 113
dangerous, 37–38, 62, 73, 105–6, 170 n. 9, 172 n. 25, 178 nn. 151 and 152; non-dangerous, 73
death, 23, 36–37, 40, 67, 80, 84, 87, 106, 133–36, 147–61, 166, 174 n. 78, 182 n. 12; causing, 105, 134–36, 159; penalty, 110, 186 n. 2
debtor, 33–35, 52–53
deception, 10, 49, 131
decision, 37–40, 52, 56–63, 79, 90–91, 139, 148, 160, 163, 165, 173 n. 44, 176 n. 108
decoy deer, 71–72, 178 n. 147
deliberate, 9, 24, 29, 33–36, 40–45, 52–57, 63, 77–78, 112–18, 131, 142, 146, 172 n. 25, 174 n. 77
delusion, 67–68, 71–73, 79–81
drag racing, 105–6
Dripps, Donald, 12, 175 n. 98, 179 n. 193, 186 n. 10
drunk. *See* intoxicated
die, 133–35, 147, 192 n. 44
Duff, R.A., 13, 95–96, 182 n. 13, 189 n. 4
due process, 134, 194 n. 74
Duke and Duchess of Kent, 146
Dworkin, Ronald, 111, 187 n. 14

Edington v. Fitzmaurice, 191 n. 33
Eichmann, Adolf, 85–86, 180 n. 200
encourage, 87, 99, 103, 105, 108
epistemology, 151, 191 n. 40
equivalency, 106; position 95–101, 106, 109, 182 n. 12, 183 nn. 30 and 31, 184 n. 42; thesis, 95, 135–37
error, 27, 145, 177 n. 116
Escape from Alcatraz, 71–72
exculpatory, 88, 98, 104, 115, 120
excuse, 24–43, 54–56, 60–70, 73–97, 100–101, 104, 112–23, 160–62, 165–67, 171 n. 6, 172 n. 19, 176 n. 104, 177 n. 122, 179 n. 186, 180 nn. 208 and 09, 212, 181 nn. 218 and 19, 222, 227, 187 nn. 25 and 35, 190 n. 24, 192–93 n. 57; accidents, 29–63; consent, 63, 65–66, 77, 80, 84, 154, 176 n. 101, 176 nn. 108–9, 192 n. 50; duress, 87, 113, 122, 187 n. 24, 188 n. 41; function of in moral discourse, 114–123; “ignorance of the law,” 76–78; inchoate criminality as, 94–109; inexcusable, 40, 84,

167; insanity, 73, 166; mistakes, 63–82; non-excuse, 73; partial, 26, 29, 38, 40, 56, 69–70, 73, 94–96, 106–9
extenuate, 24, 29, 88, 122, 170 n. 15, 190 n. 24
extreme emotional disturbance, 56

fallibility, 61, 88, 92
false imprisonment, 137
fantasy, 67, 71–75, 81, 153, 169 n. 2; paranoid, 99
fault, 26, 30, 34, 58, 60–61, 87, 116; no-fault, 78
Feinberg, Joel, 97, 169 n. 6, 179 n. 196, 181 n. 3, 182 n. 10, 182 n. 14, 186 n. 9
felony, 56, 183 nn. 24 and 25
fishy. *See* voluntary means fishy
Fletcher, George, 89–90, 94, 180 n. 211, 181 n. 220, 182 nn. 5 and 6, 184 n. 52, 185 nn. 69, 72, 186 n. 9, 189 n. 4
Foley v. Interactive Data Corporation, 187 n. 26
force, 38, 60, 105, 136, 146, 166; deadly, 38, 40, 66–67, 70, 90
Ford, Gerald, President, 154
foreseen, 34–36, 164
Forguson, L. W., 45–46
fraud, 113, 121
Freud, Sigmund 11, 173 n. 43
Fromme, Squeaky, 154

Gauguin, Paul, 93
German, 46; Reichsgericht, 107
Gladwell, Malcom, 145–46
Gollins v. Gollins, 175 n. 87
Good Samaritan, 89
Gould, Timothy, 132–35, 185 n. 2, 190 nn. 20 and 22
Graf, Steffi, 145–46
grammar, 33, 45, 71–72, 81, 86, 105–6, 125, 128, 134, 156, 184, 192 nn. 43 and 46
Greenawalt, Kent, 88, 90, 180 n. 209, 181 nn. 219 and 223
Gudel, Paul, 10–13, 19, 117, 157
guilt, 81, 165; guilty, 30, 81, 84–86, 108, 160, 169 n. 4, 170 n. 14; guilty minds, 123–24, 167, 180 n. 210, 183 nn. 28 and 29, 185 nn. 70–71, 189 n. 3, 192 n. 49; personal, 23, 30

Hammer, Espen, 189–90 n. 13
Hampton, Jean, 110–11, 179 n. 196, 186 nn. 4 and 5
Hand, Learned, Judge, 104
harm, 24, 29–36, 51, 61–63, 70, 82–90, 94–105, 110, 114, 124, 131, 134, 137, 160, 163, 167, 170 n. 11, 181 n. 222, 186 nn. 5 and 9; causing, 33, 35, 40, 85, 88, 94–98, 101, 131, 134, 137; moral harm, 94, 97; orientation, 97–98, 104; harmful, 24–29, 36, 83, 88, 94, 97, 104, 164, 171 n. 5; -, versus wrongful, 86–88; -, wrong, 24, 90; wrongless, 24, 94
Harvard, 11, 41, 72
Hart, H. L. A., 121, 132, 143, 149–50, 169 n. 6, 185 n. 62, 188 n. 42, 189 n. 5, 190 n. 19, 191 nn. 27 and 30
Hicks v. United States, 185 n. 66
Hill, Paul, 57, 174 n. 78
Holmes, Oliver Wendell, justice, 112, 124, 178 n. 163, 182 n. 12
Holocaust, 86
help, 25, 49, 89–90, 94–98, 101–9, 184 nn. 44 and 45, 185 n. 72; merely helping, 101–09
homicide, 36, 40, 56–57, 67, 70–72, 79, 85, 88, 97, 99, 102, 108–11, 135–38, 155, 159–60, 172 n. 25, 174 n. 78, 175 n. 87, 176 n. 113, 180 n. 206, 182 n. 12, 186 n. 1, 193 n. 65; attempted, 66, 72, 97; negligent, 69, 88
Husak, Douglas N., 170 n. 16, 171 n. 12, 177 n. 139, 182 n. 4, 191 n. 36

impulse, 12, 36, 56, 156
imputed, 33, 37, 118, 185 n. 54
inaction. *See* action, inaction
idiomatic, 139, 150
illusion, 67–68
inadvertently, 12, 29–31, 51, 60, 69, 87, 103, 120, 130–31, 161–62, 166
inattentive, 24, 51, 60, 79, 111
inchoate criminality, 25–26, 94–101, 108–9, 137, 141, 182 n. 5, 185 n. 72; as a partial excuse, 94–109; offenders,

100; attempt. *See* attempt; conspiracy. *See* conspiracy; solicitation. *See* solicitation
incidental, 34–36, 48, 52–54, 59–60, 83
inconsiderateness, 27, 51, 112
inculpatory, 9, 24, 51–54, 121–23; inappropriate, 62; thoughtless, 62; self-defeating, 62
indifferent, 36–37, 51, 92, 99, 159
infallible, 75; quasi-infallible, 62–64, 167
Infelicities doctrine, 44, 75, 121
infelicitous, 29, 60, 121
infer, 37, 120, 148, 151–52, 161–62, 193n. 65
insider trading, 135, 154, 192n. 50
intent, 9–10, 25–26, 30–37, 41–50, 52–59, 64–67, 70, 77, 81, 93, 95, 98–104, 108–9, 112, 114–18, 120–21, 136, 138, 140–46, 151–54, 161–67, 169n. 3, 173n. 46, 174n. 61, 175–76n. 98, 176n. 111, 180n. 197, 182n. 12, 184n. 44, 185n. 63, 187nn. 25 and 30, 188n. 41, 189nn. 3 and 4, 190n. 23, 191n. 34, 193nn. 60 and 65; general, 41, 54, 57–59, 64, 81, 175nn. 81–82; manifested, 98, 104, 109; not-intentional, 33–36, 52, 180n. 197; questioning intentions, no modification without aberration, 116–23; questioning intentions to limit responsibility, 114–16; presumed, 41, 54; specific, 57–59, 64–65, 81, 175nn. 81 and 82; unintentional, 33–36, 42, 52–54, 120–21, 188n. 41
Internal Revenue Code, 76, 111
interpret, 24–25, 32, 57, 63, 119, 134, 151, 158–65, 169n. 4, 175n. 95, 178n. 160, 180n. 204, 194n. 72; interpretive construction, 163–64, 194n. 72; interpretive strategy, 160, 180n. 204
intervening, 164
intoxicated, 104, 155, 163–65, 172n. 29, 192n. 54; driver, 36–37, 60–62, 83–84, 165, 172n. 27, 194n. 75; publicly, 164
involuntary, 118–19, 130, 134, 150, 164, 180n. 205, 188n. 49, 191n. 36, 193n. 59

Jacobs v. State, 185n. 67
Jarrett v. Jarrett, 170n. 14
Johnson, Phillip, 99, 183n. 33
jurisprudence, 190n. 19; moral. *See* moral jurisprudence
jury instructions, 65–66, 72, 81, 163, 174n. 78
justification, 24, 34, 38, 52, 86–92, 112, 123, 134, 140–41, 148, 177n. 117, 180nn. 208, 209, and 212, 181nn. 181, 219, 222, and 228, 192n. 57

Kadish, Sanford H., 54–55, 59, 86–88, 103, 122–24, 151, 170nn. 8 and 17, 174nn. 68–69, 80, 175n. 87, 93, 177nn. 118 and 123, 178n. 160, 180n. 204, 184n. 51, 185nn. 59, 61, and 72, 187n. 20, 188nn. 47 and 49, 51–54
Kahan, Dan, 77–80, 111, 176n. 104, 178n. 163, 179nn. 167–81, 184, and 186–87, 186nn. 12–13, 187nn. 15, 20, and 21
Kant, Immanuel, 95, 139, 182n. 12
Katz, Leo, 13, 89, 90, 107–8, 154–56, 180n. 210, 183n. 28, 185n. 70, 189n. 3, 192nn. 49–56, and 57
Keane, Marian, 11, 169n. 3
Kelman, Mark, 60–61, 163–65, 175nn. 93 and 97, 194nn. 72 and 77
kill, 35–43, 50, 56–57, 67, 69, 71, 73, 82–87, 90, 99–101, 106, 108, 125, 133–37, 142–44, 147, 150, 153–61, 166, 172nn. 19 and 29, 174n. 78, 178n. 147, 192nn. 44 and 57, 193n. 65; mercy killer, 56–57
King, Cleora, 78–79
King v. Cogden, 87
knowledge, 27, 35, 37–41, 51–52, 58–63, 67, 71, 74–77, 81, 107–8, 119, 123, 127, 140, 151–52, 161–62, 167, 171nn. 20, 5 and 6 (chap. 1), 173n. 30, 189nn. 12 and 13; constructive, 106, 140
know-how, 74–75
Korematsu v. United States, 171n. 10

LaFave, Wayne R., 176n. 111, 178n. 161, 181n. 228, 184n. 48, 185n. 68, 187n. 33
Lambert v. California, 176n. 104
larceny, 65, 70, 79, 95–98, 104–5, 110–11,

137, 176 n. 101, 182 n. 5, 183 n. 24, 186 n. 1
learning, 76–78, 140–48, 193 n. 61
Lewis, C.I., 11
liability, 30–31, 58, 61, 65, 86, 97, 102–5, 134, 155, 172 n. 29, 176 n. 99, 178 n. 151, 183 n. 27, 184 n. 49, 185 n. 54, 194 n. 76; derivative, 101–5; criminal, 23, 29–31, 135, 151, 163, 171 n. 5, 180 n. 205, 181 n. 222, 185 n. 54, 188 n. 49, 189 n. 4; legal, 124, 139–42; prima facie, 164; strict, 30, 60–61, 78, 171 n. 2, 175 nn. 93, 94, and 95, 97; vicarious, 101–2
libertarian, 155, 192 n. 56
lie, 64–66, 70, 76, 82
linguistic, 26, 127, 143, 148, 158; phenomenology, 149
legislation, 24, 50, 94, 135, 140, 151, 167, 177 n. 139, 182 n. 4, 184 n. 47, 185 n. 68
luck, 24, 85, 95–96, 109, 170 n. 8; moral, 24, 170 n. 10, 175 nn. 88 and 89, 179 n. 190, 180 n. 203, 181 n. 229, 2 (chap. 2), 182 nn. 7, 8, and 9, 11–12, 186 n. 76; outcome, 95–96

Macaulay, Stewart, 111, 186 n. 11
Macbeth, 50, 150
"mala in se". *See* "malum in se"
malice, 36, 41, 54–55, 58; implied, 172 n. 25
"malum in se," 23, 64, 79, 111
"malum prohibitum," 78–79, 111, 186–87 n. 13
Manchurian Candidate, 159
manslaughter, 37–40, 66, 69, 83, 105–6, 135; vehicular, 165, 194 n. 75
Martin v. State, 163–65, 193 n. 71
Massachusetts v. Painten, 174 n. 53
mayhem, 137, 152, 163, 193 nn. 68 and 69
meaning, 156–63
Melden, A. I., 143, 191 n. 39, 192 n. 42
"mens rea," 23–25, 29–93 passim, 37, 41, 54–63, 123–24, 157, 164, 191–92; accident. *See* accident; calculation, 36–37, 41, 74–75, 91; skepticism of, 37–41
mental: act. *See* act, mental; element, 55, 171 n. 6, 175 n. 87; event, 117; state. *See* "mens rea;" willings, 136
metaphor, 129, 150
Michelman, Frank, 140, 190 n. 25
mind, 26, 52, 56, 68, 125–27, 151, 161, 167, 172 n. 19, 189 n. 3, 193 n. 65; frame of, 41; state of, 41; mind-body orientation, 132; philosophy of, 135, 191 n. 36
miner's lamp, 58–59, 175 n. 85
misfired, 27, 40, 45, 96, 132, 138, 190 n. 24; action. *See* action, misfired
mistake, 25–29, 45, 63–82, 87, 120–23, 127, 160, 171 n. 5, 178 n. 160, 179 n. 186, 187 nn. 20–21; distraction, 60, 75; exculpatory, 65–70; excusing, 63–65, 73, 77, 80–82, 175 n. 95, 176 nn. 101 and 104, 109, 177 nn. 115, 117, and 122; inculpatory, 70–75; of fact, 65–76, 81, 176 n. 109, 177 n. 122; of law, 76–80, 178 n. 160; reasonable, 30, 61, 64–69, 76–78, 80, 176 n. 108, 177 n. 117; unreasonable, 38, 64–70, 80, 172 n. 29, 176 nn. 101, 109, and 111, 177 n. 122, 178 n. 152
misunderstanding, 10, 26, 76, 80, 131
mitigate. *See* exculpatory
Model Penal Code, 31, 38–45, 50–60, 65, 69, 73, 94, 97–99, 140–41, 163, 171–75, 176 nn. 99 and 100, 112, 177 nn. 136 and 37, 178–81, 182 nn. 17, 19, 21, 183, nn. 24, 25, and 26, 35, 36, and 37, 184 nn. 43, 44, and 47, 185 nn. 64 and 72, 187 n. 34, 188 n. 46, 191 n. 34, 193 n. 68, 194 n. 75
Moore, Michael, 26, 31, 92, 124–28, 124–65 passim, 131, 169 n. 6, 170 n. 16, 172 n. 19, 181 n. 218, 187 n. 22, 189 n. 4, 190 n. 22, 191 nn. 35 and 36, 39, 192 nn. 46, 51, and 57, 193 n. 60
moral: 23–27, 49, 56–57, 66, 69, 79–81, 88, 93–97, 100, 109–24, 141, 154, 156, 166, 169–70 n. 6, 170 nn. 11 and 14, 171 n. 5, 179 n. 187, 181 nn. 229 and 3 (chap. 2), 182 n. 12, 186 n. 5, 187 n. 20, 189 n. 13, 192 n. 53; accountability, 23, 169 n. 1; activity, 27, 122; blame, 23, 79, 169 n. 1; character, 30–31; condemnation, 31, 95, 110; discourse, 26, 49, 112–14; encounter, 81, 151, 189, 193 n. 64; evaluation, 27, 168, 171 n. 6;

function, 26, 110; interesting, 95, 112; judgment, 110, 134, 162; jurisprudence, 54; justice, 23; legal moralism, 78–79, 186n. 4; luck. *See* luck, moral; morality and criminal law, 110–23, 192n. 49; morally culpable, 23–24; morally responsible, 23, 124, 134, 141, 169–70n. 6; norms, 23, 112
Morawetz, Thomas, 15, 90–91, 181n. 218, 192n. 49
Morissette v. United States, 169n. 3, 176n. 102
motive, 42–50, 85, 121, 143, 173n. 46, 174nn. 55 and 61, 192n. 43,
movement: "bodily movement caused by a volition," 152–60; finger, 136, 142; muscular, 124, 142; physical, 122–23, 138, 157, 160, 173n. 46, 190n. 24; willed bodily, 124, 135–36, 142, 152, 159
Mulhall, Stephen, 12, 130, 189n. 12, 190nn. 14, 16–18, 191n. 28
murder. *See* homicide
murderer, 36, 40, 56, 70–71, 157
Murphy, J. G., 87, 110–11, 122, 171n. 10, 180n. 205, 186n. 4, 188n. 49
Murphy, Jeffrie, 110, 186n. 4

natural, 59, 116, 121, 127–32, 149, 172n. 25
necessary, 44, 53–54, 62, 93, 101, 105–6, 112, 127, 137, 140, 161, 170–71n. 19, 176n. 104, 178n. 160, 185n. 59; unnecessary, 88, 105, 118, 184n. 47
necessity, 30, 38, 89, 181n. 228
negligence, 30, 38, 41, 51, 57–58, 61, 77–79, 83, 112, 123, 171nn. 6 and 12, 172nn. 19, 26, 175nn. 91 and 97, 191n. 34; gross, 172n. 26
New Yorker, 145
Nicomachean Ethics, 126
Novotna, Jana, 146

obligation, 24, 62, 76, 81–82, 109–13, 122; civil, 112; contractual, 113; legal, 111; moral, 24, 79, 111–12
omission, 84, 134, 163, 191n. 34
ordinary-language, 26–27, 124–32, 139–42, 146–55, 170n. 19, 191nn. 36 and 38; methodology, 124–53; procedure, 10, 26, 46, 129, 138–39, 149, 151, 153, 189nn. 12 and 13; philosophy, 4, 12, 27, 119, 125–28, 131, 148–53, 163, 189n. 4, 191n. 39; "what we should say when," 11, 125–32, 140, 152, 163, 190n. 15
Ossipon, Alexander "Tom," 166–67
Othello, 35, 67, 178n. 150
otherness, 161, 193n. 66
outcome, 31–33, 58–60, 74, 80, 90–92, 95–98, 100–01, 104, 107, 109, 124; unhappy, 60, 74, 92, 124
Oxford, 126, 132; All Souls College, 126; analysis, 126; philosophy, 126, 169n. 4

palliation, 24, 29
Palsgraf v. Long Island Railroad Co., 194n. 76
panic, 146
paranoid, 40, 66, 99
pardon, 91
partial excuse. *See* excuse, partial
payoff, 9, 42–43, 49, 54, 77–78, 119, 128, 133
People v. Abbot and Moon, 185n. 67
People v. Dlugash, 178nn. 142, 149
People v. Goetz, 39–40, 66–69, 74, 76, 80–81, 173nn. 31 and 32, 177nn. 120 and 122
People v. Johnson, 175n. 82
People v. Marrero, 77–79, 179n. 166
People v. Matthews, 175n. 82
People v. Miller, 182n. 16
People v. Moran, 178n. 141
People v. Navarro, 179n. 188
People v. Orndorff, 182n. 16
People v. Snyder, 175n. 82
People v. Staples, 182n. 16
People v. Thompson, 178 n. 182
People v. Travis, 182n. 20
People v. Watson, 36–37, 40, 60, 172n. 22, 174n. 73
People v. Whitfield, 194n. 74
perpetrator, 107–8, 189n. 3
philosophical: language, 125; practice, 142; statements, 152–53, 159
philosophy, 11, 125–28, 132, 138–39, 148, 169nn. 4, 6, 189nn. 7, 13; ana-

lytic, 151; legal, 11, 132, 135, 151, 188 n. 39; of action, 153, 170 n. 16; of mind, 135; ordinary-language. *See* ordinary-language, philosophy; use of terms, 152
Pitcher, George, 41, 72, 173 n. 34, 178 n. 148, 190 n. 19
plan, 33–35, 44–48, 52–59, 73, 96, 98, 103, 137–39, 145
Plato, 139, 178 n. 153
plea, 34–35, 40, 53, 60, 65, 69, 80–85, 92–93, 96, 116, 167; guilty, 84–85
police, 46, 68, 79, 85, 90, 113, 138, 163–65, 173 n. 48, 174 n. 53, 180 n. 215, 186 n. 3
polygenesis, 67, 80, 177 n. 27
Posner, Richard A., Judge, 111, 187 nn. 16, 17, 193 n. 65
possession, 67, 79, 99, 126, 131, 140, 178 n. 147, 182 n. 5, 182 n. 12; constructive, 140
pragmatic, 147–48, 193 n. 65
precaution, 30, 33, 60–62, 151, 167
premeditated, 46, 56–57, 156
pretext. *See* action, pretext
principal, 65, 96, 101–8, 184 nn. 44, 47, 185 n. 59; "constructive," 106; "joint principality," 105–6
prison, 64, 72, 77, 133, 186 n. 9; prisoners, 72, 137, 153, 156
privacy, 10–11, 162, 165, 180 n . 215
private, 110, 129–31, 161–62, 193 n. 66
probable, 59
procedures, 26, 68, 76, 79, 127–29, 148; ordinary-language, 10, 46, 129, 138–39, 149–53, 175 n. 98, 189 nn. 12 and 13
promise, 24, 43–44, 109, 112–13, 154, 184 n. 46
pros and cons, 35–36, 56–57
provoke, 70, 104
proximate cause. *See* causation, proximate
psychology, 10, 49, 66, 125, 183 n. 28, 189 n. 7
psychosis, 73
"public, observable world," 34, 44, 118, 120, 162
Public Prosecutions, Director of v. Morgan, 176 nn. 105–6
Pullmain-Standard v. Swint, 178 n. 162
Pugh v. See's Candies, Inc., 187 n. 26
punish, 23–25, 51, 56, 59, 64, 70, 73, 78, 85, 96–99, 101, 105–11, 114, 134–35, 163, 169 nn. 5 and 6, 171 nn. 5 and 12, 178 n. 140, 186 n. 9
purpose, 9, 12, 24, 30–34, 38, 41–58, 70, 103–04, 116, 120–23, 171 n. 6, 173 n. 44, 174 n. 63, 176 n. 99, 177 nn. 117 and 27

racism, 67
rape, 56, 65–66, 70–73, 79–80, 98, 112, 125, 136–37, 152, 163, 175 n. 82, 176 nn. 101, 108–9, 177 n. 135, 183 n. 25, 193 nn. 68–69; principal rapist, 65; statutory, 61
reality, 67, 72, 126, 142
reckless, 30–41, 51–55, 59, 69–70, 154, 172 n. 29, 182 n. 5, 189 n. 3; recklessness, 32–41, 51, 58–59, 83, 123, 171 nn. 6 and 9, 172 n. 29
reconciliation, 26–27, 84–86, 114–17, 168, 191 n. 37, 193 n. 66
Regina v. Cunningham, 175 n. 84
Regina v. Faulkner, 175 n. 84
Regina v. Finney, 190 n. 19
Regina v. Morgan, 65–69, 76, 80–81, 176 nn. 107 and 108, 177 n. 116, 128–34
remedy, 78, 83, 86, 113, 186 n. 9; civil, 111; noncompensatory, 83; criminal, 111, 186 n. 9
representation, 140; constructive, 140
representativeness, 153–56
response, 27, 38–39, 54–55, 59, 68, 73, 95–96, 109, 112–20, 129, 137, 141–43, 151–53, 159–62, 167–68, 170 n. 14, 173 n. 30, 175–76 n. 98; non-response, 43
responsible, 25, 33, 53, 59–60, 65, 71, 86–88, 92, 94, 103, 109, 115, 18, 124, 134, 138, 140, 149, 161, 167, 175 n. 89; hold, 25–26, 29, 63, 82–85, 92, 115, 124, 167; be, 25, 29, 94; localizing, 167; morally. *See* morally responsible
result, 37, 41–42, 45, 54, 58–62, 70, 79, 91, 109–10, 137, 148, 171 n. 5, 178 n. 151; natural and probable, 59

Richmond v. Lewis, 193 n. 65
risk, 30–40, 53, 60, 62–63, 84, 90, 94, 97–98, 104–6,108, 159–60, 164, 172 nn. 25 and 26, 182 n. 5; risk taking, 25, 101, 106; orientation, 97; unjustifiable, 32–33, 60, 63
robbery, 105–6, 176 n. 101
Robinson, Paul H., 90, 92, 171 nn. 5, 12, 172 nn. 13, 29, 173 n. 41, 174 n. 70, 177 n. 115, 178 n. 161, 180 n. 208, 181 nn. 217, 221 and 222, 224 and 225, 185 n. 54, 191 n. 32
Ross, Sir William David, 109
Russian Roulette, 105
Rothman, William, 11, 169 n. 3
Ryle, Gilbert, 157, 193 n. 58

Santillanes v. State, 172 n. 18
Sartre, Jean-Paul, 46–48, 173 n. 49, 50, 174 n. 51
Saving Private Ryan, 101
Scales v. United States, 171 n. 10
scapegoating, 60, 83
scholastic, 127, 167
Schulhofer, Stephen, 59, 122–24, 151, 170 n. 17, 174 n. 80, 175 n. 87, 177 nn. 118 and 123, 178 n. 160, 188 nn. 47, 49, 51–54
Schweitzer, Charles, 46–47, 173 n. 50
Secret Agent, The, 166, 194 nn. 1–7, and 8
secret selves, 162, 167
seizure, 87, 122, 149–50
self-defense, 30, 38, 40, 66–67; imperfect, 66–67
semantics, 147–48
Sense and Sensibilia, 9, 157
sentencing, 64, 86, 97, 174 n. 78, 180 n. 198, 186 n. 2, 194 n. 75; indeterminate, 107
separateness, 10, 83, 161
Sinatra, Frank, 89, 93
Sirius, 157–58
slavery, 112
sleepwalking. *See* unconscious states, sleepwalking
slip, 27, 52, 83, 117
Smith, Keith, 14, 102–3, 184 n. 49, 185 n. 54, 185 n. 60, 185 n. 72, 193 n. 64
skepticism, 24–26, 29, 34, 37–39, 61, 151–52, 160–61, 167, 191 n. 40, 193 n. 66
Socrates, 74
solicitation, 25, 94–101, 137–41, 183 nn. 24 and 25, 30; attempted, 141
speech, 27, 31, 49, 74–76, 99, 121, 138, 145–49, 152, 190 n. 24; act, 75, 99, 121, 138, 152, 188 n. 40, 190 n. 23; ordinary, 27, 49, 64, 75–76, 129, 159; situations, 27, 47, 75, 121, 128–29, 142, 145–46, 152
spontaneous, 12, 36, 56, 99, 103
standards, 60, 68–69, 80–81, 172 n. 25, 179 n. 188
Standefer v. United States, 185 n. 68
Staples v. United States, 169 n. 4, 176 n. 103, 179 n. 183
state, 69, 107, 132, 136–38, 145, 149–50, 153–56, 164; internal, 69, 87; mental. *See* "mens rea"
State v. Dotterweich, 171 n. 10
State v. Guffey, 178 nn. 144 and 147
State v. Mitchell, 178 n. 143
State ex rel. Attorney General v. Tally, 187 n. 57
steal. *See* theft
Strawson, P.F., 10, 158, 190 n. 23, 193 n. 63
strict liability. *See* liability, strict
subjective, 131
Supreme Court, 23, 36, 76–77, 105, 171 n. 12, 171–72 n. 12, 178 n. 161, 194 n. 74; Reports, 151

Teachout, Terry, 89
tennis, 146, 152; "American Twist," 152
theft, 70, 79, 95–98, 104, 110–13, 137, 176 n. 104, 182 n. 5, 183 n. 24; attempted, 70, 137
theory, 25–26, 61, 67, 79–80, 98, 113, 125–26, 132–35, 137, 142, 147, 150, 162, 167, 169 n. 6, 180 n. 211, 181 nn. 205, 218, 182 n. 5, 187 n. 18, 187 nn. 26 and 27, 188 n. 46, 190 n. 22, 193 n. 63; action. *See* action theory; sense-datum, 126
Thomson, Judith, 95, 182 nn. 7 and 8, 186 n. 75, 192–93 n. 57
Thornton v. Mitchell, 180 n. 204

thought-experiments, 155
Thrasymachus, 74
"ticky-tack," 79, 81, 111
time-framing, 163–65
tort, 23, 30, 36, 57, 82, 102, 110–13, 172n. 17, 184n. 48, 186n. 7, 188n. 46, 194n. 76
try, 43–44, 70–74, 78–81, 92, 96–103, 109, 137, 154–59, 184nn. 39, 44, and 46, 185nn. 72 and 73, 186n. 77

unconscionability, 113
unconscious states, 149–50; automatism, 149–50, 188n. 46; epilepsy, 149; hypnosis, 122, 149; posthypnotic, 159; reflex, 87, 122, 149; seizure, 87, 122, 149–50; sleepwalking, 87, 122, 149–50, 159; St. Vitus Dance, 149
unforeseen, 34–36
United States v. Barker and Martinez, 176n. 114
United States v. Church, 183n. 32
United States v. McLeod, 179n. 188
United States v. Peoni, 185n. 65
United States Postal Service v. Aikens, 191n. 33
University of Pennsylvania, 154; Law Review, 151, 184nn. 44 and 50, 191n. 35, 192nn. 51 and 53
University of Virginia, 145
unrepresentative, 153–56
Updike, John, 41, 173n. 33
usage, 41, 139, 147; ordinary, 128, 141–43, 150
utterance, 11, 43–44, 75, 110, 115, 121–28, 141, 147–49, 152, 157–58, 174n. 77, 175n. 89, 193n. 61; incorrigible, 160; ordinary, 125, 152, 159

verb, 45, 116–17, 135, 139–42, 147–52, 171n. 20, 184n. 46, 188n. 41, 192n. 46; action, 149–52
Verloc, Winnie, 166
volition, 24, 136, 142, 144–45, 152–53, 157, 160
voluntary, 10, 59, 90, 94, 116–25, 130–31, 134, 150–52, 163–64, 171n. 2, 172n. 19, 180n. 205, 188n. 49, 191nn. 34 and 36, 193n. 59; act requirement, 125; means fishy, 10, 69, 89–91, 103, 116, 119–21, 130, 188n. 41; muscular contraction, 124

Warnock, G.J., 169nn. 1 and 2, 189nn. 10 and 11, 190n. 26, 191n. 38
willful, 41, 54–57, 175n. 91
Williams, Bernard, 59, 93, 94, 175nn. 88, 89, and 98, 180nn. 197 and 203, 181nn. 229 and 2 (chap. 2), 185n. 72
Williams, Glanville, 172n. 29, 176n. 108, 177n. 119, 185n. 59
willing, 136, 152, 157
Winch, Peter, 100, 184n. 39, 186n. 77
Wisdom, John Henry, 126
Wittgenstein, Ludwig, 11, 29–31, 41, 115, 125–26, 131, 143, 171n. 1, 189n. 7, 190nn. 15 and 24, 193n. 66
wrong, 24–27, 30, 36, 84, 87, 90–91, 111–14, 167, 169–70n. 6, 170nn. 7, 11, and 13, 174n. 75, 194n. 75; belief, 81; harmful, 24, 94; harmless, 94, 181n. 3; justified, 90–92; moral, 113, 124; not-intentional, 36; pre-legal, 64, 78–79, 111–13, 176n. 104; unintentional, 36
wrongdoer, 23, 30, 82, 104, 111, 114, 169n. 6, 181n. 3
wrongful death, 84

Zola, Emile, 115, 187n. 29

www.ingramcontent.com/pod-product-compliance
Ingram Content Group UK Ltd.
Pitfield, Milton Keynes, MK11 3LW, UK
UKHW041637031026
15587UKWH00001B/348